FANTASY
—THE—
100
BEST BOOKS

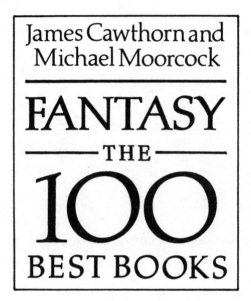

James Cawthorn and
Michael Moorcock

FANTASY
THE
100
BEST BOOKS

CARROLL & GRAF

DEDICATION
To my mother – J.C.

First published in Great Britain by
Xanadu Publications Ltd 1988
First published in the United States of America by
Carroll & Graf Publishers, Inc. 1988

Carroll & Graf Publishers, Inc.
260 Fifth Avenue
New York, NY 10001

Library of Congress Cataloging-in-Publication Data
Cawthorn, James
    Fantasy : the 100 best books / James Cawthorn and Michael
Moorcock. — 1st Carroll & Graf ed.
        p. cm.
    Includes index.
    ISBN 0-88184-335-0 : $15.95
    1. Fantastic fiction—Bibliography. 2. Bibliography—Best books—
Fantastic fiction. I. Moorcock, Michael, 1939– . II. Title.
Z5917.F3C38 1988
[PN3435]
016.80883'876—dc19

Manufactured in Great Britain

Contents

Introduction

All fiction is fantasy. In all of its forms, including the historically recent 'realistic' novel, it springs from the human urge to fantasize. For a while, as popular fiction burgeoned under the demands of a newly literate public, the term was restricted to a sub-category of stories which dealt with atavistic fears and allegedly discredited beliefs. A public which happily accepted private eyes who solved fiendishly complicated mysteries despite repeated blows to the head and stupefying doses of alcohol, cowboys who never had to count the cost of ammunition, and lovers whose most intimate problems concerned their cheque-books, baulked at the implausibilities of space-travel and the supernatural. The current contents of bookshop shelves suggest that these prejudices are fading.

If all fiction is fantasy, how can it be possible to select the one hundred best? It isn't. The reader will not find *Little Dorrit, Blood on the Moon,* or *The High Window* among these choices, nor expect to. Fantasy has been narrowed down to 'Fantasy'. The only quibble, apart from the merits of the chosen books, is likely to be over whether some might more properly belong to another sub-category, sf. The answer, to misquote an American critic, is that 'Fantasy' is what I point to when I say it.

Greater public acceptance has stimulated publishers and authors to step up production. To keep abreast of the torrent of dragons, unicorns, mages and moody swords sluicing through the bookstores is impossible; the spate of the late '80s is represented here by a single title, *Expecting Someone Taller*. Most of the choices are considerably older, from less prolific years. An immensely helpful side-effect of the boom has been the resurrection of such rarities as Lindsay's *A Voyage to Arcturus, The Haunted Woman,* and the novels of William Hope Hodgson. Reading the encylopedic *The Gothic Quest* by Montague Summers, however, almost makes me grateful that much of the literature of the past two centuries is no longer available. There are limits.

In an earlier volume in the '100 Best' series, H.R.F. Keating says that he excluded certain titles because they are now almost unobtainable. The contrary view is taken here, in the hope that it might help to revive interest in neglected works and encourage their reprinting. An example is *Caravan for China* by the late Frank Stuart. Published at the outbreak of World War Two, it was obliterated by subsequent events, like so many of the books of that time. My own copy, discovered after the war, is the only one I have ever seen, as was my copy (now lost) of his *Elephant in Jet*.

It is a depressing fact that the quality of a book does not guarantee it against neglect. Maurice Richardson's *The Exploits of Engelbrecht,* last seen in 1977 in a limited paperback edition, is surely due for revival in a more ambitious format. The massive and unique fantasies of Wm. Hope Hodgson virtually disappeared from his native Britain for decades, kept in print only by the superb Arkham House edition from America, until fairly recently. Jack Vance's *The Dying Earth* became a much-sought item by those who had missed its original appearance in 1950, but they had to wait twelve years for a second chance.

The many references to films are the result of growing up in a time and place where radio and the cinema were the chief sources of mass family entertainment. There was less concern then about the effects of films upon the infant psyche; consequently, I was three years old when I saw *King Kong*, which proved to be the first item in a steady diet of mummies, werewolves, vampires, zombies and other future cult figures. Later, having learned that they mostly originated in books, I became intrigued and puzzled by the discrepancies between literary and cinematic horrors. Later still, I became familiar with the bizarre philosophies of film-makers, and some of the discrepancies were explained.

Looking back, the fiction and films of those days seem wholesome by comparison with current offerings, however resolutely they set out to titillate and scare us. Still influenced by nineteenth-century traditions and constrained by the morality of their times, authors and directors used indirection to heighten the impact of whatever crawled, leaped, lurched or flapped through the shadowed chambers of their fancies. It has been left to today's exponents to stake all upon explicitness, inducing nausea rather than the shivery thrill, and replacing the haunted room with the abattoir. Overkill has become the norm; Spielberg's *Indiana Jones* series, supposedly his homage to the Saturday matinées of his childhood, are actually banana-fingered and costly exercises in gratuitous, sadistic violence. The widespread feedback between book and screen is part of a growing preference for clubbing the audience into acceptance, rather than prodding it into awareness.

The selections in this book naturally reflect this background and these views, but offer, I think, an interesting cross-section of the genre. In the end, all such lists are highly personal—and, as it turned out, the choices are mainly of one person rather than two . . .

—JAMES CAWTHORN

I was originally commissioned to write this book by Xanadu, but when other commitments made it clear that I would not be able to deliver it for a long while, the publishers and I agreed that James Cawthorn was the person to take it over. We could think of no one better qualified or better read, and I think that his text—by far the greater portion, including the parts about a certain albino—bears out our judgement: his range, expertise and the witty, affectionate judgement he displays are, as always, impressive.

I should not be so impressed. I have now worked with Jim for over thirty years, first on fanzines like BURROUGHSIANA, later on TARZAN ADVENTURES and then on NEW WORLDS, where his reviews were regularly published, together with his fine illustrations. We were also co-authors of a Sexton Blake story, *Caribbean Crisis*, wrote *The Distant Suns* together for THE ILLUSTRATED WEEKLY OF INDIA and co-scripted the film version of Burrough's *The Land That Time Forgot*. My only disappointment is that *Mythago Wood* and/or *Lavondyss* by Robert Holdstock did not find a place here, though I have written about *Mythago Wood* in a companion to the present volume, *Horror: 100 Best Books*. But overall, I am rather glad of the circumstances which lead to Jim, rather than myself, doing the main work on the book: I believe that he has done a far better job than I could have done alone, and am convinced that thanks to him this will remain a standard work when most other guides to fantastic fiction are forgotten.

—MICHAEL MOORCOCK

NOTES AND ACKNOWLEDGEMENTS

The books chosen are presented in broadly chronological sequence: 'broadly' because it is sometimes difficult to know exactly where a particular piece belongs. The 'Zothique' stories of Clark Ashton Smith, for instance, were not collected together until 1970, but were mostly written in the 1930s. More important, they are very much *of* the 1930s, and so that is where they appear in this book. In quite a few other cases too, stories appeared in magazines some time before attaining book form, so the sharp-eyed reader will occasionally notice a discrepancy between the date at the top of an essay and the one in the bibliographical details at the end, which list first *book* editions only (the true first edition comes first, followed by the first transatlantic edition if there is one). This information was kindly supplied by John Clute.

Thanks are also due to Dave Britton, Charles Partington and the publisher for advice and copies of hard-to-find titles, to our families and the staff of Gateshead Central Library, and to others who offered encouragement. The piece on *Expecting Someone Taller* first appeared in THE LOS ANGELES TIMES, 1988.

All errors, particularly of fact and taste, are our own.

1
JONATHAN SWIFT
Gulliver's Travels

When William (*Rural Rides*) Cobbett was eleven years old, he set out to walk from Windsor to Kew, a crow's-flight of fifteen miles. He was seeking work as a gardener, demonstrating that mobility of labour is not an exclusively modern preserve. In a Richmond shop, a book-title caught his fancy. The book cost three pence, exactly as much as stood between himself and a supperless night. He bought it. Luckily, he got the job he sought. The title was *A Tale of a Tub*. The author, by then thirty years dead, was Jonathan Swift.

Two centuries later, Swift is still persuading people to part with their money. A Dublin-born Protestant, he was ordained a minister in 1694. In an age which did not subscribe to our curious notion that religion should exist in a vacuum, he plunged deeply into English politics. Inevitably, this involved the unhappy relationship between England and Ireland, a problem already old. The death of Queen Anne and the crowning of George the First precipitated a political witch-hunt which obliged him to retreat to Dublin. There, while serving as Dean of St Patrick's Cathedral, he transformed his experiences into the stuff of fiction, in the adventures of a ship's surgeon from London, Lemuel Gulliver.

Terra, diminishingly *incognita*, was already being processed by travel-writers for the benefit of a readership hungry for wonders. These forerunners of coffee-table books and endless television series were a mixture of accurate observation, pardonable ignorance and perhaps less pardonable misinterpretation. In this latter aspect, they were more akin to those specious works telling us how interstellar visitors taught us to tie up our shoelaces. Swift, with malice aforethought, adapted the form to satirical uses. Published under a pseudonym, after undercover negotiations carried out during a return visit to England, the book sold out within a week.

Plainly, a satire which is still bought and read after 250 years does owe its continuing popularity to the reader's interest in the Whigs and Tories. For anyone desiring specific political references, there are numerous scholarly commentaries available. Those who are content to find universal applications for Swift's lampooning of the ways of statesmen and princes will appreciate that depressingly little has changed, in that respect, since the eighteenth century. Dramatizations tend to be confined to the Lilliputian episodes, skipping lightly over the more pungent details; suitably bowdlerized, the unfailing doll's-house appeal of the miniature kingdoms has made it a children's classic.

The savagery of Swift's view of humanity grows as Gulliver, for whom the perilous seas seem preferable to any extended contact with his wife and family, takes ever more improbable voyages. Imaginary islands in profusion dot the world's oceans, a vast peninsula is grafted on to North America, while ships whizz from Africa to the Pacific at speeds which suggest supersonic winds. Throughout, the good doctor protests his honesty and unwillingness to exploit the reader's credulity. He is the most impressionable of travellers, for ever taking on the characteristics of the peoples he encounters, only to be discomfited by his return to European ways. The generally humane attitudes of the sea-captains who rescue him, and their patience with one whom they not surprisingly consider to be deranged, never seem to dent his soured opinion of his kind. Only once, after recruiting a crew of obvious malcontents, is he ill-treated, and even then his life is spared.

A giant in Lilliput, Gulliver becomes a midget in monstrous Brobdingnag. His friend and guardian is a girl of nine, Glumdalclitch, who stands a mere forty feet tall. Older girls submit him to titillatory indignities and he is exploited as a physical freak. Carried off by an eagle and rescued by British seamen, he is soon outward bound again, fated to land anywhere but at his intended destination.

His third voyage presents the literature with its first fully fashioned flying saucer, Laputa. Clashing head-on with the scientific New Men of the Royal Society, Swift populates his airborne island with purblind introverts bent on devising implausible means for achieving the impossible. Ironically, his Laputians anticipated the real world's discovery of the twin satellites of Mars, then unsuspected by stargazers. A passage in which Laputa was clearly meant to represent the British Government was judged to be too subversive to print, but Swift, back in Ireland, knew nothing of the deletion until after publication.

Encounters with magicians and immortals precede Gulliver's final and most controversial adventure, in the country of the Houyhnhnms. These graceful and intelligent horse-like beings employ as labourers the squalid, man-like Yahoos. Gulliver, in common with many of Swift's critics, shrinks from being equated with the latter; in particular, from being embraced by a female Yahoo on heat. Upon returning to England, he transfers this antipathy to his long-suffering family. Had Swift fallen among the Houyhnhnms, it seems probable that he would soon have found their nobility as unbearable as the hypocrisy and shallowness of his fellow men. Whatever Jesus took him for, it can't have been a sunbeam.

As *Travels into Several Remote Nations of the World . . . by Lemuel Gulliver*   London: Benjamin Motte, 1726
First US edition, as *The Adventures of Gulliver*   Philadelphia: Young and M'Culloch, 1787
As *Gulliver's Travels*   London: Walker, 1808

2

HORACE WALPOLE
The Castle of Otranto

There are novels so fundamental to the development of a particular genre that the question of their literary merit is of secondary importance. Horace Walpole did not invent the basic constituents of the Gothic novel, but in *The Castle of Otranto* he combined them in a manner which became a standard formula for the next two centuries. It was the publisher's equivalent of sliced bread. Their readers took to its clammy horrors with delight, and in growing numbers as the 'penny dreadfuls' set out to wring the last drop of ichor from its lurid lexicon.

By then, the Gothic had travelled far from its original sources of inspiration. The prevalence of castles in the literature was no accident, nor was the frequency with which they were built on the iceberg principle, with nine-tenths of their structure consisting of subterranean vaults. These spectre-infested spaces were rooted in the fantasies of an architect, Giovanni Piranesi. A revised edition of his *Carceri d'Invenzione* appeared in 1761, featuring a series of drawings of prison interiors conceived on a titanic and overpowering scale.

Walpole, who had already converted his Twickenham home into a mock-Gothic castle, took from Piranesi the central image of his novel, a black-plumed helmet of monstrous size. Around it he gathered the now familiar cast of wronged and lovesick maidens, unhinged and tyrannical nobles, younger sons of ancient families travelling incognito. Among the male and female writers who followed in Walpole's wake, some, apparently unwilling to commit themselves to the supernatural, rationalized their apparitions and so destroyed their credibility. Walpole went to the other extreme, decking his narrative lavishly with examples of the inexplicable.

Otranto stands squarely in that Continental never-never land later to be staked out by Universal Studios and Hammer Films. Within its walls, the situation is ripe for calamity. Piranesi's helmet merely serves to bring matters to a head. The castle's lord, Prince Manfred, whose grandfather was granted tenure by the last of the original heirs, Alfonso the Good, is haunted by an enigmatic prophecy. When the 'real owner' of the castle grows too large to inhabit it, runs the message, Manfred's family will be dispossessed. As he presses forward with the wedding of his sickly son, Conrad, and the daughter of the Marquis of Vicenza, Isabella, disaster strikes. Conrad is crushed beneath the suddenly materialized helmet, a gigantic replica of that worn by an effigy of Alfonso. At the same moment, the original vanishes.

Hippolita, Manfred's wife, is unable to bear him another child. He resolves to marry Isabella himself. Meanwhile, he imprisons an impetuous young peasant on a charge of using sorcery to kill Conrad. As Isabella retreats from his abrupt advances,the towering black plumes on the helmet rustle and sway, violently. Manfred is halted in his pursuit of her by the spectacle of the figure of his grandfather stepping from a portrait on the wall. Temporarily distracted by this novel phenomenon, he is too late to prevent Isabella from taking refuge in the vaults.

Undeterred, he follows her. Traffic is already heavy down below. To his astonishment, he meets the young peasant, escaped from his prison, who in turn has met Isabella. He is diverted from this baffling underground episode by two knockabout comics, nominally household servants, who claim to have seen a colossal armoured leg in one of the castle galleries. Though he is cast in the role of oppressor, it is impossible not to have a sneaking admiration for Manfred as he charges off to greet this new manifestation. Scarcely has he done so before a troop of horsemen arrive, bearing an enormous sword, the property of a being straightfacedly referred to as The Knight of the Gigantic Sabre.

False identities are endemic to the Gothic novel and *Otranto* is no exception. Stalwart youths in peasant garb cannot be taken at face value and anything may be concealed by a monkish cowl, from displaced aristocracy to death's-heads. *Otranto* has both. Characters show a marked inability to recognize their next of kin in subdued lighting, usually with fatal or near-fatal results. As revelations and visitations multiply, Manfred ploughs on, tenaciously hugging his resolve to perpetuate his line. Like Ted Hughes's *Iron Man*, the spectral giant gathers to himself appendages, here a leg, there a hand, finally arising in majestic totality to provide a literally shattering climax.

Walpole's headlong dialogue, punctuated by hyphens, aptly suggests the terror and panic of the castle's inhabitants but can be confusing in places. Occasionally a note of genuine horror is struck amid the creaking of the Gothic mechanisms. Though some of the finest flowerings of the genre were yet to come, including *Melmoth* and *Dracula*, Jane Austen and Thomas Peacock had skilfully parodied it with *Northanger Abbey* and *Headlong Hall* by 1818. There is enough evidence in *Otranto* to suggest that Walpole might have taken the joke more lightly than some of his doom-laden successors.

First edition   London: T. Lownds, 1765
First US edition   New York: Shakespeare Gallery, 1801

3
WILLIAM BECKFORD
Vathek

In the beginning, the Gothic was not so much a literary movement as a way of life. Under the influence of the visionary architect Piranesi, its more affluent disciples surrounded themselves with mock-medieval trappings. Among that fraction of the population which could afford to live vicariously in the past instead of scrabbling for survival in the present, William Beckford was pre-eminent. Inheritor of a huge income derived from the labour of slaves on his father's West Indian sugar plantations, he was said to be the richest man in England. He was also extravagant upon an heroic scale.

The project which eventually sapped even his resources formed a fitting setting for 'The Caliph', as he was dubbed. Artistic talent combined with vast wealth produced Fonthill Abbey, a dream-palace which anticipated Coleridge's 'Kubla Khan' by a year. Twelve miles of wall enclosed a park ornamented with woods and lakes, surrounding a building in which forty-foot doors gave admission to halls crammed with beautiful and costly objects. *Vathek,* published a decade earlier, reads like a prospectus for the life which Beckford was to lead within his Xanadu.

Unlike the standard Gothic romance, the novel draws heavily upon the *Arabian Nights* for inspiration. Vathek, a grandson of Haroun al Raschid, is outwardly a generous and affable Caliph, devoted to wordly pleasures. Only rarely does he manifest his anger, and then his baleful glance terrifies those upon whom it falls. In the service of his pleasure he builds five palaces, each designed to gratify one of the senses. A sixth structure, a tower ascended by means of 1,500 steps, offends Mahomet. Regarding it from Paradise, he prophesies disaster for such overweening ambition. Beckford crowned Fonthill with a tower almost 300 feet high. Being built chiefly of wood, it fell without benefit of prophecy.

Vathek's tower is an instrument of his fatal curiosity, bringing him closer to the stars and portents of the heavens. They do not forewarn him of the arrival of his Fate, in the guise of a nameless and superlatively ugly Indian purveying strange merchandise. So singular are this traveller's powers that Vathek pursues him, after many misadventures, to the brink of a great black chasm. There he is revealed as an agent of Eblis, the Devil, and proposes a bargain.

Unable to resist the promised revelations of Infernal secrets, Vathek agrees to supply the Indian with the blood of fifty of his realm's fairest boys, the sons of his viziers and grandees. Tricking them into approaching the chasm's brink, he hurls them into the depths. Or so he thinks. Whereupon the shadowy gulf closes, shutting him out.

Pursued by his infuriated subjects and vassals, he retreats to the sanctuary of his tower. Carathis, his mother, a fearsome Greek matron, takes the situation in her stride. As a keen student of the black arts, she decides that further sacrifices are the answer. Soon a bonfire of disinterred mummies and freshly strangled citizens is blazing merrily. The offering is accepted and Vathek regains the favour of Eblis. Contented, he returns to his favourite form of recreation, eating.

So far, the parallels between author and character are plain enough. Both were deprived of their fathers at an early age; both inherited vast fortunes, which they used to translate their visions into reality; both, if Beckford's envious critics can be believed, had perverse tastes. Vathek now moves into regions denied to the merely rich, where only Beckford's fancy, steeped in Oriental imagery, could follow. Obeying Eblis, the Caliph organizes a magnificent caravanserai with which to approach the gates of the underworld. He has been warned not to turn aside along the way, but is diverted by the hospitality of the Emir Fakreddin and his lissom daughter, Nouronihar. Carathis, finding her son entangled with his new love, berates him for endangering his good standing with Eblis. Vathek defies her, and so seals Nouronihar's doom. Together, they ride to Hell.

Among modern masters of the ironic and macabre, Clark Ashton Smith comes readily to mind as a literary heir of Beckford. Lovecraft might have devised horrors to match those which inhabit the domain of Eblis, but only Smith could equal Beckford's dark humour. As Nouronihar and the Caliph, hand in hand, enter the endless subterranean Fonthill, they gaze appalled upon throngs of the lamenting dead, whose hearts are literally and visibly burning.

The promised knowledge is theirs, but only fleetingly. Deciding that his upbringing by Carathis is the cause of his plight, Vathek uses his brief authority to summon her below. She arrives by Afrit and plunges enthusiastically into the Infernal afterlife, discounting her son's recriminations. Soon, however, her heart is burning as agonizingly as any of them.

Beckford was cast down from his custom-built Paradise by nothing more fiendish than bad management and the ending of the slave trade. He built himself a lesser palace near Bath, where he died at eighty-four and so added longevity to his ill-gotten gains.

First edition London: J. Johnson, 1786 as *An Arabian Tale*
First US edition Philadelphia: P. Carey, 1816 as *Vathek*

4
MATTHEW GREGORY LEWIS
The Monk

To have written, and had published, a sensational first novel crammed with sex, violence and diabolism, and then to be condemned for combining this achievement with being a Member of Parliament, is the stuff of which tabloid headlines are made. Add to it the fact that the perpetrator of these offences was twenty-one years old and you have Gregory 'Monk' Lewis, a man for all frissons.

Twenty years before his birth, the Great Lisbon Earthquake of 1755 had shaken the foundations of orthodox Christianity in Western Europe. Was it an Act of God which brought down the city around the ears of the faithful on a day of worship or a device of Satan? Or, more frightful still, the chance blow of a blind, uncaring Universe? The question of which would be the greater impiety was only one of many troubling the philosophers of that revolutionary era. The shock, however, had not unseated Hypocrisy. Only when Lewis became a member of the legislature did his novel draw serious criticism.

That the youthful author, bored with his minor diplomatic post in Holland, revelled in this outlet for his fantasies cannot be doubted. A gleeful mockery of the narrow monastic life surfaces time and again amid the welter of sadism, necrophilia, rape and incest. Those who profess celibacy exercise an unfailing fascination for the public imagination, inflamed by the high walls which make it impossible to watch them not At It. Lewis exploits this voyeuristic element to the full. Religious observance in the Convent of St Clare appears to consist largely of the browbeating of errant nuns, followed by their incarceration in those indispensable architectural adjuncts of Gothic fiction, the cellars.

The ramifications of the cellars are matched by those of the narrative. Ambrosio, the Monk, spends long stretches in the wings, gnawing his beads, while supporting players take centre-stage. Eventually, however, all the strands of Lewis's complex web of subplots are drawn together. Though Ambrosio tries to play the spider, he is in reality the most thoroughly entrapped of flies. Parted from his parents in early infancy, he has passed his formative years within the confines of the Church, knowing little of the world. His faith has the fragile inflexibility of a stained-glass window and the pressure which will reveal its flaws is already being applied.

Satan obviously rates Ambrosio's influence upon the people of Madrid very highly, for his scheme to overthrow the Monk is long laid and subtle. A painting of the Madonna, the only female image permitted by his religion, hangs in Ambrosio's cell. Often in his cell too is the youthful novice Rosario, who professes admiration for him bordering on worship. This being a Gothic novel, beautiful young boys are not what they seem. Rosario confesses 'himself' to be Matilda and the model for the Madonna. Ambrosio, already conditioned by the painted image, is soon being introduced to his submerged sexual self by a suspiciously proficient Matilda. The versatile novice has a third aspect, yet to be revealed. She is a demon, an agent of Satan.

The Monk is now firmly on the downward path. Having exhausted the charms of Matilda, or having been allowed to think that he has, he discovers a new inamorata. Antonia, a fair and impressionable virgin, admires him from her place in the cathedral. His compliant demon-mistress turns procuress to obtain her favours. The dashing Don Lorenzo also admires Antonia, but his path, as with all of the novel's lovers, is destined to be rocky. Lorenzo's sister, Agnes, is loved by his friend, Raymond, who is travelling incognito at the time. In a disastrous attempt at elopement, Raymond finds himself sharing a coach with the spectral Bleeding Nun. Not surprisingly, the coach crashes. The subsequent complications are resolved in an encounter with the Wandering Jew, but Raymond recomplicates the relationship by pursuing Agnes to the Convent of St Clare. Agnes becomes pregnant. The Lady Prioress, feeling that convent discipline has become lax, resolves to make an example of her.

From here on, though it may not seem possible, the plot thickens. Duels, illnesses—every one of the principals, save for Ambrosio and Matilda, suffers a nervous breakdown at some point—murders, apparitions, graveyard worms, the full Gothic armoury is deployed with amazing deftness and vivacity by the nineteen-year-old author. More impressive than the charnel-house apparatus is the way in which the Monk and his supporting cast emerge as characters who engage the reader's sympathies. At the terrific climax, Ambrosio, driven by fear of the Inquisition into making a pact with the Devil, finds himself betrayed by God and Satan. In an involuntary aping of his infernal master's fall from grace, he is hurled to his death upon eagle-haunted crags.

As if providing an ironical coda to the Monk's damnation, Lewis compromised with his critics by bowdlerizing later editions. Ambrosio would have appreciated that.

First edition   London: J. Bell, 1796
First US edition   Philadelphia: W. Cobbett, 1798

5
MARY SHELLEY
Frankenstein

'An uncouth tale,' said the *Monthly Review* in 1818, 'setting probability at defiance'.

'Hubris clobbered by Nemesis' is the succinct definition of SF devised by Brian Aldiss. Yet the phrase applies equally well to Fantasy, and aptly describes *Frankenstein*. Science is the ostensible generative force behind Victor Frankenstein's creation of an artificial man, but the Monster's true origin lies in the alchemical texts which he was taught to despise. The odour of a Gothic charnel-house hangs about his labours from the beginning. His achievement is the reanimation of the dead rather than an electrochemical immaculate conception.

Dramatizations of the story usually make no bones about this. No grave-yard is left unturned in the vicinity of Frankenstein's laboratory. In the series of films illuminated by Boris Karloff's powerful, if inaccurate, portrayal of the Monster, the visual aspects rise to grandiose heights. The original ill-lit, fetid chamber cluttered with chemical apparatus and unspeakable components gives way to reeling Expressionist towers thunderous with Promethean light-nings. Only when Hammer Films injected new vigour into the flagging genre, incidentally setting it on a slippery slope to bloody mindlessness, did something of the huddled, pathological furtiveness of Frankenstein's activi-ties reach the screen.

Where Hammer fell short was in the choice of an actor for the title-role. Peter Cushing was a convincing figure as a ruthless scientist driven beyond society's limits of toleration by an unacceptable obsession. What he was not was the Romantic hero, young and idealistic, graceful of physique and spirit, yet fatally flawed. At one point, Mary Shelley has Frankenstein compare his plight to that of a fallen angel. Such comparisons, spoken or implied, echo throughout the text. He has usurped the Divine prerogative and must suffer accordingly.

Frankenstein and the Monster would seem to be cast in the roles of pseudo-God and pseudo-Adam respectively. Yet it is the Monster which possesses inhuman strength and endurance, and the power to determine the fate of his creator. Man, as in Percy Bysshe Shelley's later 'Prometheus Unbound', has made God in his own image. When Frankenstein first confronts his living handiwork, he flees from it in revulsion, no longer sustained by the frenzy of the creative act. The Monster, understandably enraged, resolves to wreak des-truction upon him and his kin. Rejected by Man, it has become a God of Vengeance, all capacity for good destroyed by the withdrawal of love and recognition.

When Mary began work upon *Frankenstein* in 1816, she was barely nineteen and had been Shelley's lover for two years. He was in many ways the personification of the Romantic spirit: highly gifted, headstrong, iconoclastic, physically attractive. Like the young Victor, he had studied chemistry and mathematics, in his case in the teeth of academic disapproval. Latin and Greek were considered fitter subjects for a gentleman. Shelley, in fact, had mastered both of these subjects and in addition could out-quote his critics in the matter of Biblical studies. Given the intimacy of their relationship, signs of his influence upon Mary are to be expected, but her work after his death in 1822 refutes assertions that his was the dominant hand. The story of the agreement between Mary, Shelley, Byron and Byron's physician, Dr Polidori, to write a tale of the supernatural is now almost as well known as her novel. Oddly, the enduring products of the agreement were written by the lesser-known participants. Polidori's *The Vampyre* is still obtainable and is no longer seriously attributed to Byron.

Whatever elements of Shelley there may be in Victor Frankenstein, they do not include the poet's tangled marital relationships. When he leaves Geneva for the University at Ingolstadt, Victor's consuming passion is for knowledge; he has devoured the writings of such ancients as Paracelsus, Agrippa and Albertus Magnus. He is astounded to learn that their theories are obsolete and discredited, but this setback is only temporary. Soon he is outstripping his tutors in the sciences and applying their teachings to a search for the generating principle of Life, his private obsession. Mary Shelley's account of the construction of the Monster is necessarily impressionistic rather than precise. Electricity—the miracle-worker of the age—chemistry, live animals and human cadavers figure in it, rather as writers of the 1930s invoked radium and cosmic rays to back up their flights of evolutionary fancy.

Deserted by his creator, the Monster learns how to fend for himself. He acquires clothing, literacy and a fluent command of language, through a series of happenstances made somewhat less implausible by being related in his own words. None of these attributes softens the terrifying effect of his size (he is eight feet tall, a fact which filmmakers seem reluctant to face) and overpowering hideousness, which makes all sighted mankind his enemy. Goblin-like, his deformities do not prevent him from moving with superhuman speed and agility as he pursues his vendetta against Frankenstein's hapless family. As the climax approaches, Monster and Maker flee across the icebound *terra incognita* of the Arctic in an epic pursuit, each given purpose only by the presence of the other.

In an age in which monsters have become acceptable industrial by-products, even the illusion of effective individual action has a nostalgic charm.

As *Frankenstein; or, the Modern Prometheus*
First edition   London: Lackington, Hughes, Harding, Mavor & Jones, 1818
First US edition   Philadelphia: Carey, 1833

6
CHARLES ROBERT MATURIN
Melmoth the Wanderer

'Call me Melmoth,' Oscar Wilde told the world as he sailed for France, bereft of fortune and reputation. In the manner of devotees of Fantasy the world over, he had adopted the identity of a fictitious personality in whom he saw aspects of himself reflected. Strangely, the personality was not a product of his own imagination, but that of another Irishman, Charles Maturin. Maturin's Satanic reaver of souls came into being seventy-seven years before Wilde went into exile, yet his baleful influence lingered.

It had long preceded Wilde into France. Poe, Maturin and others of the Gothic school were highly regarded by the French, their works being translated almost as soon as they were published. Balzac wrote a sequel to *Melmoth*; he was one of several prominent authors, including Sir Walter Scott, who gave praise and support to their Irish colleague. The original was adapted for the London stage, despite the Chinese-box complexity of its structure. That the terrible destiny of the Wanderer struck a responsive chord in Wilde is understandable; there is a touch of Melmoth in most artists, especially when the bills are due.

Maturin found his own respectable Protestant origins lacking in romance. Amateur theatricals became a lifetime preoccupation, and he invented an ancestor, the love-child of a female French courtier who escaped to Ireland after incarceration in the Bastille. When he became a curate in order to ensure a steady income, his preaching packed the pews of St Peter's in Dublin, but certain eccentricities of manner, combined with theologically suspect sentiments, barred his way to advancement. The picture he drew of Catholicism in *Melmoth* was marginally kinder than that in Lewis's *The Monk*, yet scarcely an advertisement for any of the major brands of orthodox Christianity. Damned if you do and damned if you don't appears to be the message.

The involved narrative, sprouting branches like some malign family tree, begins in 1816 with the arrival of student John Melmoth at the decaying mansion of his dying uncle. Asked to open a locked room, he sees within a portrait bearing the legend 'Jno. Melmoth, 1646' and is stricken with horror by the expression of the eyes. His uncle's assertion that the subject of the painting still lives adds to his disquiet. When the old man dies, among his effects is an ancient, discoloured MS. Alone in the shadowed chamber, in the sleeping, storm-swept house, John begins to read.

The Melmoth of the portrait, his appearance unchanged down the years, is committed to Satan's service. At moments of spiritual extremity, those unfortunates who fall under his burning gaze are given a choice between whatever Earthly nemesis awaits them or the false salvation offered by his Master. If he can persuade one victim to take on his pact with the Devil in exchange for illusory freedom, Melmoth will be released from his hellish servitude. The novel is the story of his century-long and ultimately doomed search for such a victim.

John Stanton (Maturin's inventiveness did not seem to extend to masculine first names), the English author of the MS., meets the Wanderer in Spain, a location much favoured by novelists of the period. European civilization's uttermost tip, a hand's breadth removed from the pagan darkness of Africa, it furnished an arena for the heightened passions, murderous feuds, ruthless banditry and Inquisitorial atrocities beloved by their public. An old woman tells Stanton of the appearance at a wedding of a strange Englishman and the three deaths which followed. Her description of the man is familiar to Stanton; they are destined to meet on two more occasions, the last with Stanton chained in a madhouse. From this point, the influence of the Wanderer spreads like an evil blight over the lives of young and old as he passes the barriers of time, space and the Inquisition's dungeons with supernatural ease.

Monsters are at their most fascinating when their nature is ambiguous. Melmoth is also a victim, destined for damnation more surely than those upon whom he preys. He is Satan's black hound, who will sooner or later be called to heel. Alone on an island off the Indian coast lives white-skinned Immalee, knowing nothing of her origins. She is Eve unawakened, Melmoth's spiritual opposite pole, and no more tempting quarry could be imagined. In the dual role of Adam and the Serpent, he invades her solitude, bringing news of the fabulous lands across the sea.

Through diverse circumstances, Immalee is reunited with her prosperous Spanish parents, taking the name of Isidora. Still the Wanderer seeks to seduce her, unaware that he pursues his own destruction. As the story comes full circle, he returns to John Melmoth's desolate mansion and is given a vision of the Inferno which awaits him.

Maturin died at forty-three, accidentally poisoned. Of his many published plays and novels, only *Melmoth* continues to exert its grip upon the contemporary imagination. If he left any unpublished masterpieces behind him, they will remain unread, for his papers met the same fate as the Wanderer, at the hands of his son.

First edition   London: Hurst, Robinson & Co; & Edinburgh:
Constable, 1820
First US edition   Boston: Wells & Lilly, 1821

7

EDGAR ALLAN POE
The Narrative of Arthur Gordon Pym

In recent decades, it has become increasingly difficult to disentangle the real Edgar Allan Poe from the creations of other writers' imaginations. Few authors have proved so irresistible to literary and cinematic myth-makers. Son of an American actor and an English actress, orphaned and adopted, a failed student, a discharged West Point cadet, married at twenty-seven to a cousin barely half his age, he was dead at forty. Titillating mystery surrounded his death. Biographers and critics could choose between drink, epilepsy, or that popular 19th-century nemesis, brain fever, to mention only the more plausible causes. Roger Corman, Richard Matheson, Ray Bradbury and Joseph Cotten, are a few of the names involved in re-creating the man and his fictions.

Poe was extremely popular in France, and the equally uncertain fate of the hapless Arthur Gordon Pym seemed to exercise a similar fascination upon Jules Verne. Unable to resist the lure, he completed—to his own satisfaction at least—the apparently unfinished story. His version appeared in 1897 as *The Sphinx Of The Ice-Fields*. The Antarctic remained a region of mystery, capable of accommodating the wildest of speculative fantasies, far beyond the time of Verne. In 1931, H.P. Lovecraft could, with confidence, use it as the setting for *At The Mountains Of Madness*, in which the cry of Poe's great spectral birds, 'Tekeli-li! Tekeli-li!' is echoed.

It is, of course, the very 'incompleteness' of the novel which completes its effect. The climax is vertiginous, sweeping the reader to the brink of the unknown at an ever-accelerating pace. To bridge the gulf which lies beyond would inevitably be anti-climactic. Even so, it must be said that the opening stages of the story can be hard going, as much for the reader as for Pym.

The omens, to put it mildly, are not auspicious. Young Pym, with the collusion of a friend, stows away aboard the *Grampus*, a ship described as 'an old hulk ... scarcely seaworthy.' The crew are well-matched, being recruited from the same school of seamanship as that of Lord Greystoke's *Fuwalda*, and consequently the body-count is high. Despite the wild oceanic setting and the unusual amount of violent action, Poe still finds opportunities to introduce the premature burial motif to great effect. The narrative, in fact, is crammed with the sort of incident common to the hag-ridden voyages of Gothic fiction, interspersed with lectures upon natural history and seamanship. But for readers willing to press on through these occasional Sargassoes, there are

23

better things to come.

Anyone who has read 'Ms. Found In A Bottle' will readily recognize similarities between the novel and this earlier short story. Both involve voyages, partly involuntary, to the *terra incognita* of the Antarctic, voyages in which storms of supernatural ferocity are encountered and the crews of doomed ships. Most significantly, enigmatic messages occur in each—in the short story, the single word 'Discovery' is written without conscious intent by the protagonist, while the novel describes gigantic hieroglyphs graven deep into the rocks of a strange black island. Both voyages reach a climax at which, hurled southwards by irresistible winds and currents, the characters face death, or revelation.

It is when Pym reaches black Tsalal that the novel finally shakes off the cobwebbed trappings of lesser Gothics, and begins to truly grip. Tsalal is one in a chain of islands set in a warm sea in the far south of the world. Soil, rocks, vegetation, all are black. The native islanders are black from toenails to teeth. They abhor that which is white, so that, when allowed aboard Pym's ship, a British schooner which rescued him and one other from the wrecked *Grampus*, they recoil from such commonplace objects as flour or the pages of an open book. The carcase of a strange white animal plucked from the sea by the British crew fills them with fear and horror. And in the end, their true attitude towards the white strangers becomes all too clear.

Hunted and starving, Pym and his companion thread their way through the pit-like depths of the inexplicable hieroglyphs. After further desperate encounters with the Tsalalians, they put to sea in a stolen canoe, and are borne south.

They enter a 'region of novelty and wonder'. Above all, it is a region of whiteness, but not the whiteness of the Antarctic as we know it. The sea is warm and free of ice. Ribbons of vapour burst from the milky-hued waters, amid wild, flickering lights. As if in a trance, they sail on, insulated from apprehension or fear. Finally, the entire southern horizon becomes a monstrous cataract of pale vapour, endlessly falling, from out of which fly gigantic birds. At the very foot of the cataract, at the brink of the unknown, a towering figure of snowy whiteness confronts them....

First edition   New York: Harpers, 1838
First UK edition   London: Wiley and Putnam, 1838 (anonymous)

8
CHARLES DICKENS
A Christmas Carol

'My dear,' says Bob Cratchit, mildly rebuking his wife for refusing to drink a toast to his employer, 'Christmas Day.'

Ebenezer Scrooge's downtrodden clerk, like all of the characters in *A Christmas Carol*, talks of Christmas Day as if it had existed from time immemorial. Charles Dickens was thirty-one when this short novel was published, and the concept of Christmas as we understand it was no older. It is a mark of his genius that he stamped his version of the feast-day so deeply into the national consciousness that no celebration of it passes without some reference to his name.

Equally enduring is the picture of Scrooge, the embodiment of grasping, grinding Victorian commerce, his very surname now synonymous with miserliness. So low is his spiritual temperature that the enshrouding London fog and nipping frost leave no mark upon him. Appeals from charitable Christian gentlemen meet a heart of flint; the seasonal good wishes of his nephew only reinforce his contempt for such meaningless gestures. The absence of his clerk upon Christmas Day is a legalized imposition, a raid upon his pocket.

This master of misanthropy receives his first hint of a come-uppance when his doorknocker metamorphoses into the face of his long-dead business partner, Jacob Marley. Clanking hard after it comes Jacob in his ghostly entirety, shattering Scrooge's attempts to resume his usual domestic routine. A ponderous chain drags behind the spectre, composed of all the apparatus of business which occupied his working life. A greater chain, he groans, is already attached to Scrooge. At Marley's instigation, Scrooge has been granted a chance to redeem himself before it is too late. He will be visited by three Spirits, from whom he may learn the error of his ways.

Not unnaturally, Scrooge would prefer to forgo salvation by ordeal and take his chances with the afterlife. He is given no choice. The Spirits of Christmas Past, Present and Future arrive on schedule to give him a conducted tour of his life as it was and as it might come to be. Along with him went the Victorian reader, presented with a kaleidoscopic vision of the middle and working classes celebrating the birth of their Saviour. It is a wholly secular vision, for all of its religious overtones; church and chapel do not figure in it.

Nor do Christmas trees, crackers, stockings or Santa Claus. As researchers have shown, these familiar trappings of the festive season were either unknown in 1843 or just beginning to infiltrate the upper reaches of society. Also, there is little that is Christian about them, for all the popular notion of

Victorian religiosity. The Spirit of Christmas Present, with his capacious robes and abundance of food and drink, is an early prototype of Santa Claus. To Scrooge's horror, the robes, when drawn aside, reveal the stunted children of Man, the girl Want and the boy Ignorance. Dickens, inspired by a visit to Manchester's satanic mills, had a point to make, and the ugliness of social injustice glowers through the bustling good humour of his tale.

A story-teller first and foremost, he never forgets the humanity of his central character. Through the Ghost of Christmas Past and the words of Scrooge's younger sister, we see him a virtual refugee from his unhappy home-life, spending a solitary Christmas at a boarding-school. His apprenticeship to a warehouse owner provides one of those scenes of festivity in which the energy of Dickens's prose leaves the reader almost as breathless as the dancers. The relief is only temporary. Gold becomes his ruling passion as all human connections beyond the counting-house fade away. Only a reputation for being a man of his word remains, and his word is unforgiving.

Because the timespan of the story is confined to one night, Scrooge's defensive shell of callousness crumbles with unconvincing rapidity. Admittedly, it is subjected to extraordinary pressures, particularly from the Spirit of Christmas Future. Dickens's relish for a good stiff dose of spectral horror drives the beleaguered miser from deathbed to graveyard and a preview of a friendless, unmourned passing. In death he becomes the helpless object of the profit motive at its starkest, at the hands of people who cannot afford the luxury of ethics. Is it a taste of things to come or one of several possible paths?

As with most of Dickens's novels, *A Christmas Carol* is probably best known through film, television or radio dramatizations. In an age which prefers the fuzzy reassurance of 'Goodwill to All Men' to the more exacting 'Peace to Men of Goodwill', his Victorian phantasmagoria tends to degenerate into a cosy fairy-tale, its darknesses glossed over or eliminated. 'This boy,' says the Spirit of Christmas Present, 'is Ignorance . . . beware, for on his brow I see written Doom.' That problem hasn't gone away overnight.

As *A Christmas Carol in Prose, being a Ghost Story of Christmas*
First edition   London: Chapman & Hall, 1843
First US edition   New York: Harpers, 1844

9

EMILY BRONTË
Wuthering Heights

To attempt to convey an impression of the darkness at the heart of *Wuthering Heights* is to face the fact that Charlotte Brontë did so first, and did it better. Editing the second edition of her younger sister's only novel, she wrote: 'It is moorish and wild, and knotty as a root of heath . . . in its storm-heated and electrical atmosphere, we seem at times to breathe lightning . . .' Of the dark-browed Heathcliff: '. . . he was child neither of Lascar nor gypsy, but a man's shape animated by demon life—a Ghoul—an Afreet.' Of the novel, again: 'He [it was published under the pseudonym 'Ellis Bell'] wrought from no model but the vision of his meditations . . . the crag took human shape . . . colossal, dark and frowning . . . yet . . . its colouring is of mellow grey and moorland moss clothes it.'

Charlotte, Emily, Anne and brother Branwell were the products of an unlikely literary forcing-house, Haworth Parsonage, in the West Riding of Yorkshire. Whatever help and guidance the people of Haworth got from the Rev Brontë, they saw little enough of his children by Charlotte's account. The surviving siblings (two older sisters had died in 1825) shared an intense, secretive life of the imagination nurtured upon the *Arabian Nights*, Sir Walter Scott and the wild sublimity of John Martin's haunted panoramas. Branwell's prospects as a painter evaporated in a fog of opium, alcohol and depression; in a group portrait of the four, he has painted himself out and hovers behind the sisters like an ectoplasmic presence.

Sickness and death were constant companions of the Brontës and their father's parishioners. The prospect from the parsonage windows began with the crowded cemetery. Infant mortality was high in the steep terraces of Haworth, as it was in most of Britain's burgeoning industrial centres. Tuberculosis flourished under the wide skies of the Yorkshire moorland. The Rev Brontë saw it carry off Branwell, Emily and Anne; a widower for forty years, he outlived all six of his children. Only Charlotte married, but she died during her first pregnancy.

It was amid these relentless reminders of physical decay and the intimations of a new age of regimented labour that *Wuthering Heights* was conceived. Charlotte, as enthralled as any anonymous reader by her sister's dark fancies, wondered whether: '. . . it is right or advisable to create beings like Heathcliffe . . . I scarcely think it is.' What sort of being he was is still debated.

Mr Lockwood, who rents Thrushcross Grange from Heathcliff, begins under a misapprehension about his temperament, but learns rapidly at the hands, paws and fangs of the Wuthering Heights household and their dogs. Trapped there by a blizzard, he is grudgingly allowed to stay overnight.

Heathcliff is unaware that he has been given a room which once belonged to Catherine, daughter of the late owner of the house, Mr Earnshaw. During a frightening dream, he puts a hand through the window to still the tapping of a tree-branch and instead touches the ice-cold fingers of a child. A girl's voice cries that it is Catherine Linton, come home from the moor. Screaming as he wakes, he arouses Heathcliff, who is simultaneously terrified and enraged. Wrenching open the window, Heathcliff calls out to the unseen presence.

Back at Thrushcross Grange, Lockwood wheedles more information out of an ex-servant of the Earnshaws, Mrs Dean. She recalls Mr Earnshaw returning from a visit to Liverpool, carrying a dirty, black-haired child he claims to have rescued from a solitary life in the streets. He christens it 'Heathcliff'. His son, Hindley, hates it, but Catherine, his daughter, soon befriends it. As her father's health declines, his regard for the foundling becomes obsessive.

The tension between Heathcliff, Catherine and Hindley intensifies as the years pass. When Hindley becomes master of the house, Heathcliff is relegated to the status of servant. The appearance of a rival for Catherine, Edgar Linton, precipitates a crisis. Heathcliff leaves, but returns mysteriously wealthy. Becoming Edgar's wife has not lessened Catherine's passionate affinity for her adoptive brother. It becomes obvious that a resolution of the triangular relationship cannot be found this side of the grave. Hollywood, baffled by an extra-marital affair unconsummated even by implication, compromised by showing the deceased lovers ascending hand in hand to a cloudy apotheosis, proving that Heaven and the Hays Code condoned infidelity so long as you got no fun out of it.

Speculation about Heathcliff is as endless as the question of the location of Dr Watson's war-wound. What was the unexplained purpose behind Mr Earnshaw's journey to Liverpool—sixty miles each way, *on foot*, from which he returned with a foundling and a few toys for his children? What was the child's strange influence upon his dying foster-father? Demon, changeling or social misfit, Emily Brontë's furious creation continues to haunt and provoke the imagination.

First edition   London: T. C. Newby, 1847
First US edition   Boston: Coolidge & Wiley, 1848

10
HERMAN MELVILLE
Moby-Dick

To enter into Melville's masterpiece is to become an Ishmael. You are caught up, as he was, in a pursuit not of your making, drawn resistlessly in the wake of Leviathan, plunged into a vortex and cast out again, spent. In the course of the quest you will have learned the perilous art of harpooning and butchering a creature with blood as hot as your own, but great enough to dwarf the reptilian monsters of antiquity.

'Anything down there about your souls?' asks the seaman Elijah, after hearing that Ishmael and Queequeg the harpooner have signed on board the whaler *Pequod* under Captain Ahab. Ishmael concludes uneasily that Elijah is 'a little damaged in the head'. On the morning on which he and Queequeg go to join their ship, Elijah crosses their path again, like a disciple of the Ancient Mariner, saying: 'Did ye see anything like men going towards that ship?' Queequeg has not seen them, but Ishmael admits to noticing some misty figures heading that way. Once aboard, they find no one but a sleeping rigger.

Ahab remains hidden until the *Pequod* is out to sea. When he appears, he lives up to everything that Ishmael has been told of him. A livid scar runs from out of his grey hair and down the full length of his face and neck, like the brand of lightning upon a stricken tree. An encounter with the white whale, Moby-Dick, has torn away one leg, to which a stump of whale-ivory has been attached. A 'grand, ungodly, god-like man', as Captain Peleg describes him, he has become moody and savage, living only to track down and destroy his enemy. It is as if the ivory links them by a form of sympathetic magic, binding his fate and that of his crew to his ever-receding quarry.

There was something of Ishmael in Melville. A decline in family fortunes and the death of his father in 1832 led him to seek work as a teacher, a bank clerk and finally a seaman. *Redburn*, his fourth novel, was inspired by his first voyage, to England. On his second he jumped ship in the South Seas and lived among the Polynesian cannibals. American friends persuaded him, on his return, to write of his experiences. The result was *Typee*. Its reception encouraged him to produce a sequel, *Omoo*. Marriage and fatherhood brought financial pressures; Melville's books were no bestsellers. For a time he sold fiction to magazines, a less risky source of income.

Moby-Dick, perhaps not so widely read as widely known is generally regarded as his finest work, with the possible exception of *Billy Budd, Foretopman*. Melville still had forty years to live when *Moby Dick* was published, but he gained little more from it in terms of fame or cash than from *Billy Budd*, which was published posthumously. The symbolism embodied in the white whale has probably generated more words than he ever wrote, but the ranks of the analysts have yet to present us with an Ahab.

The British and American public, confronted by a massive volume seemingly compounded of metaphysics and the mechanics of whaling, for the most part refused to dig deeper. Depressed and exhausted, Melville struggled on in obscurity. For twenty years he worked as customs officer, meanwhile composing verse, which, like *Billy Budd*, would not be read until after his death.

So long-drawn-out and anticlimactic a conclusion to his life is strangely at odds with the energy which suffuses the near 700 pages of *Moby-Dick*. The sense of space it conveys is vast; no galaxy-spanning epic of SF so captures a feeling of depth, distance and the *weight* of Time. Melville's prose gives an Old Testament solemnity and grandeur to the awesome details of the whaling business: the carving of immensities of flesh, rendering down of rivers of blubber, demolishing of cathedrals of bone.

Before Time began, says Ishmael–Melville, the whole world was the whale's. Who can show a pedigree like Leviathan? Ahab's harpoon had shed older blood than the Pharaoh's. But soon he is quoting the Nantucket captains, who even then foresaw the whale's extermination. Not unreasonably for a man of his time, he finds the prophecy implausible. Quartermain may have felt the same way about elephants.

'To be enraged with a dumb thing seems blasphemous,' declares Starbuck, mate of the *Pequod*.

'All visible objects,' Ahab replies, 'are as masks ... If man will strike, strike through the mask! How can the prisoner reach outside except by thrusting through the wall? To me, the white whale is that wall.... Sometimes, I think there's naught beyond. Talk not to me of blasphemy ... I'd strike the sun if it insulted me.'

Nothing in Ahab's life so becomes him as the manner of his dying. It is magnificently arrogant, supremely nihilistic. If there can be such a thing as inverted blasphemy, Ahab is guilty of it. He seeks to usurp the prerogative not of God but of Lucifer.

First edition, as *The Whale*   London: Bentley, 1851
First US edition, as *Moby-Dick: or, the Whale*   New York: Harpers, 1851

11-
J. SHERIDAN LEFANU
Uncle Silas:
a Tale Of Bartram-Haugh

Uncle Silas begins with a defensive foreword by the author which, at this remove, only serves to show how critical attitudes can change. The term 'sensation novels', apparently applied to LeFanu's books, is rejected by him; he points out that Sir Walter Scott's work had not been so labelled, despite its generous quota of crime and bloodshed. Readers whose sensibilities have been bludgeoned by today's meat-market school of horror writers may find the blood and violence in *Uncle Silas* barely detectable. Earlier Gothic writers, conversely, might consider the corridors of Bartram-Haugh woefully lacking in clanking chains and headless nuns.

LeFanu was no stranger to the business of professional criticism. During his writing career he was both journalist and editor, as well as an outstanding teller of fantastic tales in a country noted for them, Ireland. Stories such as *The White Cat of Drumgunniol* mine the rich lode of Irish legend and superstition, but *Uncle Silas* is set, for the most part, in rural Derbyshire. This is the countryside of the squirearchy and their huge, rambling houses, to which the surrounding landscape and its inhabitants are little more than appendages. Bartram-Haugh is a peculiarly inhospitable example of the type, reflecting the character of its reclusive master, Silas Ruthyn.

The narrator is Maud Ruthyn, adolescent daughter of Silas's older brother. Though she has never met her uncle, a portrait of him as a young man has fixed him firmly in her imagination, aided by guarded hints from her father regarding his brother's dissolute youth. The comfortable tranquillity of her life at Knowl is enlivened by this romantic figure, until other and less welcome events intrude. Her undemonstrative but affectionate father, a widower, is visited by Dr Bryerly, a disciple of the Swedish philosopher-theologian Swedenborg. Mr Ruthyn left the Church of England to become a Swedenborgian, an act deplored, if little understood, by his household and Maud. Acutely class-conscious, they are not reassured by the enigmatic Doctor, who dresses like an artisan while enjoying the status of a gentleman. Afterwards, Maud's father tells her that he may have to go on a journey, but he will not reveal his destination.

It is with Mr Ruthyn's announcement that Maud is to have a new teacher that a great grotesque enters the story. Madame de la Rougierre first appears in the moonlight like an apparition, cackling and gesticulating, to Maud's justifiable alarm. Closer acquaintance does not improve her. Tall, sallow, hollow-cheeked, draped in purple silk, she careers through the narrative, dispensing a mixture of hypocrisy, spurious benignity and vindictiveness, fuelled by brandy. Only when she is caught rifling his desk does the remote Mr Ruthyn see what has long been plain to everyone else and send her packing. Fortunately for the reader, she returns.

The air darkens. Maud's father takes the journey he warned her of—he dies of heart disease. His will makes Silas her guardian, until she reaches twenty-one. She must leave Knowl till then and reside at Bartram-Haugh, taking only her maid, Mary Quince. From her home, with its legends of haunted galleries, Maud goes to a truly haunted house, of which her uncle is the presiding spirit. The silver-haired, spectral presence of Silas Ruthyn dominates the narrative from this point onwards; his ambivalent attitude towards his niece, his recurrent laudanum-induced 'illnesses', the hostile aura radiating from his servants, induce an atmosphere of uncertainty and dread.

When he is not sunk in a laudanum stupor, Uncle Silas is scheming to marry off Maud to his raffish son, Dudley, so as to restore the family fortunes. Dudley, an associate of the sporting fraternity and a handy man with his knuckles, is less accomplished in the role of suitor. He and his sister have none of their father's social graces; motherless, they have been left to their own devices, picking up such education as they can. It becomes plain, even to Dudley, that marriage is not on the cards. Silas, long ostracized by county society since the suspicious disappearance of a colleague and guest, does not baulk at murder as an alternative. Maud, though feeling increasingly threatened by her guardian's restrictions upon her movements beyond Bartram-Haugh, does not suspect his darker pupose. Only her much older cousin, Lady Monica Knollys, and the mysterious Dr Bryerly are sensible of the real danger.

The shadows thicken in the dusty, deserted corridors of Bartram-Haugh as Silas spins his intricate web of deceit and avarice. Maud, seeking the room in which the alleged murder was committed, stumbles upon a secret yet more sinister. LeFanu tightens his grip upon the reader's nerves, screwing up the tension page by page, springing surprises like a diabolical conjurer. If Maud, in retrospect, seems a little too naïve, even for her age and sheltered upbringing, in the presence of so palpable an evil, the fault is a minor one. *Uncle Silas* remains a classic of its kind, as even Swedenborgians might agree.

First edition   London: Bentley, 1864
First US edition   New York: Munro, 1878

12

LEWIS CARROLL

Alice's Adventures in Wonderland
Through the Looking-Glass

Immortality, if contracted in infancy, is usually incurable. The symptoms can include anything from social embarrassment to psychological destruction. Life becomes a permanently tilted seesaw, on which no amount of adult striving can counterbalance the weight of that small alien figure at the other end. It can even be contagious. A Sunday Supplement magazine carried an advertisement offering prints of two photographs of Victorian children at £137 the pair. The photographer was the Rev Charles Lutwidge Dodgson, aka Lewis Carroll, who conferred immortality upon Alice Liddell with book and camera. And, by association, upon any other pre-pubescent girl who posed for him.

The Church, as a shelter for the talented, the intellectual or the simply eccentric, was still a thriving institution in his lifetime. Dodgson, math-ematician, writer and accomplished amateur photographer, is only one of its better-known disciples. Alice's father, Henry Liddell, domestic chaplain to the Prince Consort, compiled the massive *Greek Lexicon*, the first truly efficient linguistic tool for translating from the Greek. In a society engaged in aping Hellenic art and culture, not least as an acceptable language for the expression of eroticism, it sold out quickly. The chaplaincy was not Liddell's only link with Britain's blue blood; he was kin to a baron, an earl and the family of a future queen, Elizabeth Bowes Lyon.

According to some researchers, Dodgson may have proposed marriage to his well-connected Alice. Fewer eyebrows would have been raised by the age disparity than might be imagined; the forcible transition from childhood to adult responsibilities occurred at more than one level of Victorian society. Their relationship had begun in Oxford in 1856. Alice was almost four when Dodgson and a friend came to photograph the Liddells' home, the Deanery. At his suggestion, she and her sisters were included in the foreground of the picture. Six years and many meetings, stories, jokes and photographs later, came the momentous boating trip and picnic which saw the birth of *Alice*.

The fact that the story was extemporized while Dodgson was occupied in rowing a boat may account for the episodic nature of the early chapters. After the slow, dream-like fall down the rabbit-hole, there follows a sequence of changes in size brought about by magical drinks or stones which meta-morphose into cakes. These events have an air of having been devised to keep things moving, with no clear notion of a destination. The constrictions of the subterranean setting (the original MS, half the length of the published version, was entitled *Alice's Adventures Underground*) are soon abandoned in favour of something resembling the upper world.

Appearances could not be more deceptive. The fauna, consisting, among other creatures, of March Hares and Dormice, Gryphons and Mock-Turtles, show an alarming tendency to talk back, volubly and aggressively. Words, following the example of the venerable Father William, stand on their heads to confound commonsensical Alice. If Tenniel's illustrations sometimes make her look like an adult in children's dress, her behaviour reinforces the image. She is, in miniature, one of those nineteenth-century ladies who outfaced the heathen in far, strange corners of Empire.

By the time the first 'Alice' book had wedded the Reverend and the Dean's daughter in the public's mind, Dodgson was no longer welcome at the Liddell home. Could the hypothetical proposal have been responsible for this? Whatever the reason, he contrived to keep in touch with the children. Alice was nineteen when the sequel, *Through the Looking-Glass*, appeared. She received a specially bound copy to take its place beside its predecessor.

Six years had elapsed between the two books. Many of the original readers were children no longer and a new generation of potential readers had sprung up. Those adults who had shared in their children's enjoyment in 1865 greeted *Looking-Glass* with enthusiasm, perhaps finding an additional intellectual pleasure in the fact that it was based upon chess-moves. In just over a month, sales had reached 15,000 copies. The name 'Lewis Carroll', adopted when the young Dodgson began contributing short pieces to magazines, was now world-famous.

The sequel has the feel of a more considered work, the difference being apparent in the opening pages. Carroll, no longer catering for an audience surrounded by the distractions of a river trip, had less need of literary fireworks to hold their attention. Tenniel had agreed to illustrate it, not without some reluctance, for Carroll could be an exacting taskmaster where his book's appearance was concerned, despite his diffident manner. The result was another set of superbly grotesque visualizations, including an horrific Jabberwock. *Looking-Glass* is as rich as *Alice* in memorable characters and quotable lines, many of which have become indispensable parts of the English-speaking world's vocabulary.

On the far side of the Looking-Glass, Space and Time are mutable, for those who know the secret. To quote Alice and Humpty Dumpty:

"One can't help growing older." "*One* can't . . . but two can. With proper assistance, you might have left off at seven."

Alice's Adventures in Wonderland
First edition   London: Macmillan, 1865
First US edition   New York: Appleton, 1866

Through the Looking-Glass, and What Alice Found There
First edition   Macmillan, 1871 (but dated 1872)
First US edition   New York: Macmillan, 1872

13
EDWIN A. ABBOTT
Flatland

Most readers, if asked to name a nineteenth-century mathematician, clergy-man and fantasist, would probably plump for Lewis Carroll. Without doubt, his *Alice* stood head and pinafore above the competition, but competition there was. Almost twenty years after Alice fell for a White Rabbit, Edwin A. Abbott introduced the denizens of Flatland to our three-dimensional world, in the guise of 'A Square'. Despite Abbott's religious affiliations, his book treats the Church and Victorian society in general with some irreverence.

Among his gifts was that of knowing when to stop. The main text of *Flatland* runs to just under 100 pages: just enough to leave the reader wishing for more. Brevity is not a quality usually associated with the Victorians or, for that matter, with today's fantasy millers, but Abbott's slender joke is never spun out beyond its innate capacity.

Like Alice, 'A Square' falls out of his own world into a baffling, even terrifying, place where natural laws seem to be set at naught. Unlike her, he becomes so enamoured of Spaceland and its hints of multidimensional spaces beyond, that he is reluctant to return to depthless Flatland. When he does so, he cannot resist the urge to expand upon the glories of the Solid state, and is arrested for preaching sedition. In gaol, he passes the years by writing *Flatland, A Romance of Many Dimensions*.

To imprison anyone in this world of two dimensions, or to enclose them for any purpose, it is only necessary to surround them with a line. All structures are exercises in planar gometry, their forms defined by social custom. Society is as rigidly ordered as the shapes of the beings who comprise it. The concept of a third dimension, of *height*, exists but is not publicly discussed. Unknown to the general populace, a manifestation of Higher Space occurs once every millennium, in the High Council chamber. The Counsellors studiously ignore it. The entity responsible is the Sphere, who transported 'A Square' into Spaceland.

The narrator belongs to the professional classes, being a lawyer with a talent for mathematics. Professional men are Squares; professional gentlemen are Pentagons. Soldiers and lower-grade workmen are Isosceles Triangles with narrow bases; the middle class are Equilateral Triangles. The nobility begin as Hexagons, rising in eminence as the number of their sides increases, until they are Polygonal. When they are sufficiently many-sided to be indistinguishable from Circles, they become members of the priestly order.

As for women, they are all Straight Lines. Intelligence being a function of the individual's angle, with the acutely angled Soldiers ranking lowest on the scale and the Circles highest, it can be appreciated that someone devoid of angles is in a bad way mentally. Women are, therefore, much deadlier than men. Movement in Flatland is governed by complex rules, their prime purpose being to avoid impaling fellow-citizens upon one's apex. Straight Lines combine brainlessness with two murderously sharp points; add to this their tendency to hysteria and a woman becomes a force to be reckoned with.

It is hardly surprising that the preface to the second edition includes a somewhat tongue-in-cheek apologia on behalf of 'A Square' regarding his attitude to the fair sex.

Abbott's solution to problems of recognition (plane figures see each other edge-on, appearing merely as straight lines) is ingenious; their leading edges are luminous. Where the edges recede, as from the apex of a triangle, the luminosity fades with distance. Once, in a past age, this distinction was almost obliterated by an artistic revolution. Chromatistes, a pioneer in a markedly unaesthetic society, experimentally painted his house and family, creating a wholly new means of identification. So universal was its appeal that soon only the extremes of society—women and Circles—remained colourless. There was a violent reaction against this seditious movement. Chromatistes was slain amid a general massacre of the multicoloured. Orthodoxy reasserted itself and the practice of painting was forbidden.

Flatland, surprisingly, has weather. A slight gravitational pull towards the south enables rain to fall across the surface. What happens to the water after that is not too clear. The source of daylight, on the other hand, is something that even the wisest Circle has been unable to determine. Some future Galileo will doubtless discover it, and suffer accordingly, since it involves the Third Dimension. 'A Square', a respectable lawyer, became intoxicated with the view from Spaceland to such a degree that he could not restrain himself from uttering heresies.

Flatland is one of those rare fantasies which educate, painlessly, while they entertain. Geometry textbooks might profit from a touch of the same leavening wit. The same degree of social comment would surely have them blue-pencilled, and not only in Victoria's Britain.

As by 'A. Square'
First edition   London: Seeley & Co, 1884
First US edition   Boston: Roberts, 1885

14
HENRY RIDER HAGGARD
She

One of the incidental pleasures of Victorian fantasy lies in the picture it can present, unwittingly, of the writer's view of his world. In *She*, Rider Haggard confronts his readers with pages of classical Greek, old English, and medieval Latin, en route to the action. Did he believe he was catering for a classically-educated public numerous enough to ensure a profit? Or were his publishers willing to indulge the author of *King Solomon's Mines*, hoping that the masses would simply skip the erudite passages? In the end, they were no obstacle to sales, which rose to 25,000 within a few weeks.

What the readers got was a novel-length exercise in the macabre. If it is true that fantasy attracts us by making our deepest fears palatable, even enjoyable, then *She* caters admirably for our fear of death. Along with the macabre element runs an allied strain of misogyny, a not unfamiliar quality in Haggard's characters.

The story is narrated by Horace Holly, a Cambridge student whose sole friend has committed suicide, leaving a five-year-old son, Leo Vincey. Holly, a misogynist at twenty-two owing to a disastrous and expensive affair, takes on the guardianship of the child at his friend's request. Modern readers may doubt his suitability for the rôle when, discovering that an elderly don is luring the golden-haired child to his rooms with gifts of sweets, he forbids the relationship on dietary grounds. Leo, however, attains the age of twenty-five unscathed, and is shown the mysterious legacy left by his father.

The strange story revealed by the documents and relics comprising the legacy, of an ageless woman ruling a hidden land in Africa, is irresistible to Leo. Holly reluctantly accompanies his ward, together with an equally misogynistic manservant, Job. The voyage ends in shipwreck, but the travellers discover that their arrival was foreseen. They are taken inland by the Amahagger, a race of surly cannibals, who prove to be subjects of the legendary She described in the legacy.

Amahagger women are free to choose their own husbands, a custom which distresses Job, and eventually leads to tragedy for Ustane, the girl who chooses Leo. A comical episode involving Job and a marriage-minded lady ends in the murdering of the European's Arab companion and the wounding of Leo, before Billali, She's representative, can quell the cannibals.

Holly, Job, Ustane and the dying Leo go with Billali to the mountain stronghold of She. During the trek, Holly saves Billali from drowning, an incident which has important repercussions, but which he describes in almost farcical terms. The mountain, when reached, is the entrance to a veritable subterranean world, part natural, part the prodigious creation of an extinct pre-Egyptian race, the Kôr. With the stone won in its excavation a city was built, itself now fallen into ruin, and the farms of She's subjects have been walled about. At this point, the combination of Haggard's love of Africa with his interest in agriculture threatens to swamp the story. Within the mountain, in millennia-long seclusion, lives Ayesha, She-who-must-be-obeyed.

Lives, or is buried? Holly's first sight of the robed figure of Ayesha reminds him of 'a corpse in its graveclothes'. The terrified Job describes 'a corpse a-coming . . . down the passage' as She approaches with her eerily graceful walk. Her palace is part of the burial and torture chambers of dead Kôr, in which she preserves the body of Kallikrates, the Greek whom she murdered two thousand years ago because he loved another woman. The mummified dead of the ancient empire are all about her, in their thousands. So plentiful are they, and so accustomed are the Amahagger to their presence, that they are burned as torches to light the weird and gloomy festivals of the cannibals.

Thus entombed by her own choice, She, despite her occult powers and intelligence, has resigned herself to awaiting the reincarnation of the slain Kallikrates, who alone can absolve her from guilt by acknowledging her love. Leo, of course, is the living double of Kallikrates. When Ayesha has healed his wounds and used her powers to dispose of Ustane, she reveals that the source of her ageless beauty lies in a flame springing from the depths of the Earth. To persuade Leo to bathe in the fires, she goes before him, repeating her two-thousand-years past immersion. Everyone knows what happens next . . . but the scene never loses its fascination. Two millennia of spiritual death manifest themselves in one awful moment.

The world may have been spared Ayesha's long-brewed plans for conquest —but one can only regret that she never achieved her ambition to confront that other durable She, Queen Victoria.

As *She; a History of Adventure*
First edition   New York: Harpers, 1886
First UK edition   London: Longmans, 1887

15
ROBERT LOUIS STEVENSON
Dr Jekyll and Mr Hyde

Faced with a resolutely virginal expanse of white paper, an author might well envy Stevenson's ability to dream whole chapters of a story. Whether the screaming nightmares which accompanied the experience were an acceptable price to pay is another matter. Tuberculosis, that devouring muse of so many creative artists, dictated the manner of his adult life, driving him to seek relief in other climates. It was during a long spell of illness that he dreamed the opening episodes of the most famous tale of addiction since *Confessions of an Opium Eater*.

In its present form the story represents Stevenson's second attempt to translate his nightmare into words. After reacting angrily to criticism from his wife, he cooled off, agreed that she was right and promptly burned the original 40,000-word manuscript. It may be that Mrs Stevenson *was* right, but it is hard not to deplore that impetuous act. That first version might have been closer to the raw material of his dreams.

As his friend Henry James remarked, whatever Stevenson thought of women in his everyday life, he seemed to find them an encumbrance in his fiction. Anyone coming to *Dr Jekyll and Mr Hyde* with memories of numerous film adaptations will be struck by their total absence, save in minor roles. The doctor is a tall, well-built man of fifty who possesses a 'quarter of a million sterling' and a large, tastefully appointed house, yet there is no mention of a wife, fiancée, mistress or any other form of female companionship at any stage of his life. This deficiency applies to every one of the chief figures. When Jekyll speaks of his secret pleasures, which he describes as 'undignified', we are left to imagine them for ourselves. Mr Hyde's unrestrained pursuit of evil is no more specific than 'drinking pleasure ... from any degree of torture to another'. Shades of Dorian Gray.

Jekyll's dilemma, as he sees it, is not that his misdeeds are grievous; he does not find them so. What he cannot bear is that they must exist in tandem with his loftier aspirations. He dreams of having two identities, each pursuing its individual bent untroubled by man's duality. Long researches, condemned by a fellow-doctor, Lanyon, as 'unscientific balderdash', uncover a chemical key to the problem. Drug-induced modifications of personality are common currency today, but they didn't prove acceptable to some critics in 1886. Jekyll establishes that the body is a projection of the spirit; separate out the baser component of the spirit and allow it to become dominant and the body will reflect the change. After the tranformation he is smaller and younger-looking and feels 'a heady recklessness ... I knew myself ... to be ... tenfold more wicked ... a slave to my original evil.'

Jekyll's servants have instructions to allow Hyde the run of the house. Stevenson points up the dichotomy in the doctor's character by situating the house in a row of properties which are going down the social scale; only his retains its air of dignified prosperity.

Enfield, a friend of Jekyll's lawyer, Utterson, sees Hyde knock down and trample a young girl who collides with him one night. With the help of some neighbours, he forces him to agree to compensate her family for the fright she has received. Hyde leads them to a door in an otherwise featureless housefront, from which he re-emerges with a cheque in Jekyll's name. Stevenson, without describing Hyde in physical detail, suggests the abnormality of undiluted evil through the fear and murderous rage it arouses in the people who apprehend him. Passing that door some time later with Mr Utterson, Enfield tells his story without mentioning Jekyll's name, only to learn that the lawyer already knows of the connection. The tale unravels to its horrific yet pathetic conclusion.

The impact of *Dr Jekyll and Mr Hyde* upon the Victorians was immediate and lasting. Published in January, it had sold 40,000 copies by July. Several plays were based upon it. It became the subject of sermons. Queen Victoria may or may not have been amused by it, but she read it. No doubt there were some who saw, beyond the fascinating struggle between darkness and light, a wider application to society as a whole. Trampling was one of the lesser brutalities undergone by London's pre-pubescent girls in return for the gold of respectable Jekylls.

Stevenson and his family sailed for America in 1887, unaware of how fame had preceded them. The ship's pilots who came aboard as they approached New York introduced themselves as Jekyll and Hyde. Reporters surrounded Stevenson before he could disembark. He was showered with requests to write articles for what he considered to be absurdly large fees. Fees he would probably have described as of *Arabian Nights* extravagance were to be spent in putting his nightmare on celluloid. Filmland's interest has flagged in recent years, but good and evil are still marketable commodities. There will be a revival.

As *Strange Case of Dr Jekyll and Mr Hyde*
First edition   London: Longmans, 1886
First US edition   New York: Scribners, 1886

16
RICHARD GARNETT
The Twilight of the Gods

The *fin-de-siècle* era wasn't all Aubrey and Oscar and *The Yellow Book*, even if it ended with Oscar's exit to France—not that he ever contributed to *The Yellow Book*. Many who did established minor reputations, devoid of sensationalism or cause for ridicule. For Richard Garnett it provided a means of expressing a lighter and less conventional side of his personality. In public life he bore the shelf-long titles of Superintendent of the Reading Room and Keeper of the Printed Books at the British Museum Library.

Paper-making was the business of the Garnett family, who had been long established in the Yorkshire town of Otley, a handful of miles from the Brontë's Haworth. Richard quickly graduated to the other end of the trade, where people were paid for making little black marks upon the stuff. The majority of his seventy-one years were spent behind the scenes in one of the world's greatest accumulations of the printed word. If he is watching events at the Library from some bookish Elysium, the spectacle of its struggles to prepare for the Third Millennium must be a melancholy one.

Even a partial acquaintance with Victorian fiction will show that the public were expected to have some familiarity with the Ancient World, its history, theology and literature. In this respect Garnett went far beyond a mere grounding in the classics; his erudition was regarded as formidable by his contemporaries. Thus *Twilight*, though light in tone, carries a considerable freight of references and allusions likely to be partly or wholly lost upon modern readers. While this may rob the language of its full richness, it should not impair enjoyment of his wry, cynical humour. Love, hypocrisy and mendacity are human constants, whatever the Age.

The number of stories in the collection varies considerably from edition to edition. There were sixteen in the 1888 original and more were added in 1903. An illustrated hardcover (1924), with an introduction by T. E. Lawrence, no less, had twenty-eight, as had an American edition of 1926. Later paperback reprints reverted to the original sixteen. Lawrence was only one of a roster of Garnett enthusiasts which included Flecker, H. G. Wells and Swinburne. Anyone who has shared a long hut with a couple of dozen other adolescent National Servicemen may boggle at the thought of entertaining them with readings from *Twilight*, but Lawrence claimed that his squaddies loved it. Perhaps the alternative was *The Seven Pillars of Wisdom*.

Christianity gets a bad press in Garnett's stories. Paganism has its failings too, but it is allowed to deliver the goods now and again. Among those dealing with the Church and the Devil, 'The Demon Pope' is almost a condensed novel and is reminiscent of the images used by Fellini and Bunuel.

'Madam Lucifer' begins: 'Lucifer sat playing chess with Man for his soul. The game was evidently going ill for Man. He had but pawns left, few and struggling. Lucifer had rooks, knights, and, of course, bishops . . .'

In the title story, Prometheus is freed from his chains and mistaken by a band of Christians for a miraculously preserved martyr. Finding it a hazardous office, he retires with his Greek lady to run a homely wayside house for disenthroned Gods. There is humour in the author's footnotes, as with 'The Elixir of Life', to which he adds that the magazine in which it appeared expired immediately afterwards. To show that Homer could nod, he confesses that 'The Poison Maid' may have been an unconscious plagiarism of Hawthorne's 'Rapaccini's Daughter'. An occupational hazard for a widely read writer.

Garnett's urbanely subversive style belongs to a well-established tradition. Examples of it persisted into the next century in the pages of *Punch*, the stories of Saki and the work of Americans such as Clark Ashton Smith. There are dialogues in *Twilight* which would not sound out of place in the historical fantasies of Sprague de Camp. Garnett's children carried on the tradition of service to literature, which had begun with his own father, who preceded him at the British Museum. His son Edward was a novelist and publisher's reader whose wife, Constance, did the first English translations of Tolstoy, Chekhov and Dostoevsky. Their son, David, is remembered for two highly individual fantasies, *Lady into Fox* and *A Man in the Zoo*.

It may be, as de Camp speculated in *Amra*, that the unfashionable erudition discernible behind the wit and playful wickedness of the stories causes publishers to shy away. If they feel that the market no longer has a place for it, that is the public's loss. To anyone out there who is willing to take a chance, please make it the full twenty-eight, with or without illustrations.

First edition   London: T. Fisher Unwin, 1888
Expanded edition   London and New York: John Lane, 1903

17

WILLIAM MORRIS
The Story of the Glittering Plain

Seated in his Morris-designed chair, between walls adorned with Morris-designed wallpaper, the affluent aesthete of the late Victorian era could savour the sensuous pleasures of handling a novel written, designed, printed and published by Morris, while across its bold black lettering fell many-coloured rays filtered through Morris-made stained glass. As the joyless jargon of another day would put it, it was the total Morris experience.

If the description suggests a dilettante, it is 100 miles from the reality. The Arts and Crafts Movement, of which Morris became the leading figure, was formed by artists and craftsmen dissatisfied with the policies of the Royal Academy. Their own policy was to create artifacts which combined beauty and usefulness. For Morris, this was part of a philosophy which, in an ideal world, would embrace the whole of human society. In pursuit of that ideal he learned many crafts, and learned them well.

The heedless, turbulent, fecund human race, enthralled by steam, enchanted by electricity, preferred or had thrust upon it the iron marvels displayed in the Crystal Palace. A sympathetic critic has said, truly, that a Morrisonian civilization could never have supported Earth's swelling population. If the heirs to the Crystal Palace had shown any evidence of being able to do so, the criticism would carry more weight.

Ironically, his talent for verse and fiction obscured Morris's other activities in the eyes of many contemporaries. To them he was a poet who had a number of rather eccentric hobbies. He was among the first to come under the spell of the Icelandic Eddas and responded with characteristic thoroughness by learning how to translate them from the original. In 1871 he went to Iceland and toured its volcanic terrain—no light undertaking. He can claim to be the founder of the Heroic Fantasy genre by having put his swordsmen and sorcerers into wholly invented worlds. Which should also qualify him for the role of patron saint of the computer games industry. If the worlds have a markedly Nordic atmosphere, that is one of the minor failings of a pioneer.

Hallblithe of the House of the Raven is the hero of *The Glittering Plain* and his betrothed is the Hostage of the House of the Rose. 'Hostage' is not used in the customary sense of an enemy held for ransom or military advantage. As he sits before his house, smoothing a spearshaft, three weary strangers ride up. They ask if this is the Land of the Glittering Plain. Hallblithe, rather curiously in view of what we later learn about the fabulous nature of the Plain, knows nothing of it. The strangers ride away, looking dejected.

Hardly have they gone when the daughters of the Rose and the Raven come running from the shore, crying that sea-raiders have abducted the

Hostage. Hallblithe dons his hauberk, buckles on his sword, takes up his shield. He doesn't need to ask for them—his sister brings them to him as if accustomed to the routine. In Morrisland, everyone knows what a man's gotta do.

A boat with a black sail is waiting, occupied by a massive red-haired man dressed in black. Hallblithe reluctantly accepts his offer to take him in the wake of the raiders. The redhead, who says he is called Puny Fox because he has six larger brothers, whistles up a wind to blow them to the Isle of Ransom. Puny Fox, as may be already obvious, is an avatar of Loki. On the isle, in a hall known as The House of the Undying, Hallblithe learns that he has been deceived; the Hostage has been taken to the Land of the Glittering Plain.

He is allowed to sail to the Land on a ship which is carrying an ancient, white-bearded Ransom chieftain, for reasons he cannot understand. When they arrive, only he and the old man are put ashore. Incredibly, a brief spell in the Land transforms the chieftain into a warrior in the prime of life. For so long as he remains there, he will be young.

Young Hallblithe, too preoccupied with his lost love to consider the pros and cons of immortality, has an audience with the King of the Land. He is given good counsel, or so it seems, but immortals can deceive as readily as ordinary men. With the help of the chieftain he searches for the Hostage, and the more he learns of the Land, the less enticing it looks. In desperation, he builds a boat and escapes, only to be driven ashore on the Isle of Ransom.

Whatever the virtues of the great medieval epics and the sagas, they did go on a bit. Life in pre-television Iceland was probably like that. Morris was initiating a new genre while following a tradition in which tight plotting and logical consistency did not figure prominently. His strength lay in devising a prose-style as clear and strong as his typefaces, which felt archaic but avoided the florid excesses of his imitators. Hallblithe really swings into action only as he extricates himself and the Hostage from the Isle of Ransom, but life isn't all *Sturm und Drang*, even for heroes.

As *The Story of the Glittering Plain, which has Been Called the Land of Living Men, or the Acre of the Undying*
First edition   Hammersmith (UK), 1891
First US edition   Boston: Roberts, 1891

18
OSCAR WILDE
The Picture of Dorian Gray

Britain scattered the English language abroad with a liberal hand. All too often it came clumping back like Frankenstein's Monster, trampling syntax and pronunciation underfoot. When it did return enhanced and reinvigorated, it was from a quarter which owed us little.

The tramcar interior sequence in *Odd Man Out*, with the entire Abbey Theatre Company struggling to turn their best profile to the camera, could have represented the Irish literary scene. Any Irishman could write a book, or be even more eloquent about the book he intended to write. And if local competition was too fierce, there were richer pickings across the Irish Sea. It helped if you could adapt your public persona to the English media's love for the self-destructive Celtic genius.

Oscar Fingal O'Flahertie Wills Wilde gained a reputation as a classical scholar before coming to Oxford from Trinity College, Dublin. London's literary and theatrical heartland was only a step away and he went after its luminaries with an alacrity which belied his languid aesthetic posturing. The lily in his medieval hand might more appropriately have been a length of lead piping.

Recognition of a kind came with Gilbert and Sullivan's comic-opera *Patience*. Audiences instantly identified the image-conscious poet, Bunthorne, with Wilde. Instead of being discomfited by the parody, he thrived on it. By 1888 he was married and had two sons, for whom he had written *The Happy Prince*, but these concessions to domesticity had not lessened his capacity for outraging society. A storm of protest followed the incomplete serialization of *Dorian Gray* in *Lippincott's Magazine* in 1890. The book, from Ward, Lock & Co, was in no wise harmed by this prior publicity. In a coat-trailing preface, Wilde declared: 'There is no such thing as a moral or immoral book. Books are well written, or badly written. That is all.'

He wrote no other novels. His play *Lady Windermere's Fan*, staged in 1892, was the first of a string of theatrical triumphs, though the critics were largely against it. Among those in favour was another ex-Dublin man, Bernard Shaw, whose own plays would soon be rivalling Wilde's for their skilful use of wit and paradox in presenting their arguments. Both writers flourished amid controversy and in their different ways attracted publicity by their unconventional philosophies of life. *Dorian Gray* provided a forestaste of Wilde's fate and must have been a source of acute satisfaction for moralists, who could look back at it and say: 'I told you so!'

Of the novel's three main protagonists, artist Basil Hallward, Dorian Gray and affluent aesthete Lord Henry Wotton, the third is most obviously representative of the author. Good-looking, witty, possessed of exquisite taste, in demand at all the best dinner-tables, he is Wilde with all of life's niggling imperfections removed. A chance introduction to Dorian in Hallward's studio presents him with a new and beautiful vessel into which to tranfuse his cynical doctrines. Hallward, besotted with the purity and grace of his young model, is resentful of Lord Henry's interest, wishing Dorian to remain uncorrupted by his worldly influence. His portrait of the youth, he feels, is the finest thing he has ever painted and contains as much of himself as it does of the sitter.

Narcissus was no more enchanted by the beauty of his own image than is Dorian. He wishes that he could remain forever young in body, while the picture would bear the ravages of age. For this, he swears, he would give his soul. Lord Henry's substitute for eternal youth is to see himself reflected in the malleable personality of Dorian. Hallward, who has little to offer but devotion, sees his fears realized as the younger man is captivated by Lord Henry's effortless charm. With loving care, Wilde was fashioning the rod with which society would later beat him.

Alone for once, Dorian visits a theatre and becomes infatuated with the adolescent actress playing Juliet. She returns his love, but in doing so loses her instinctive, untutored talent. In becoming herself, she ceases to be the girl he desired and he abandons her. She commits suicide. When next he looks at the picture, there is a cruel yet indefinable twist to the mouth of the figure.

Lord Henry sends him a book, a nameless volume almost phosphorescent with the bloom of decadence. Possibly the first of that long shelf of shunned works which includes *The King in Yellow* and *Necronomicon*, its real-life original is usually assumed to be Huysman's influential *A Rebours*. Dorian reads it and his fate is sealed.

Hidden upstairs in the nursery in which he spent much of a desolate and loveless childhood, the picture degenerates into unspeakable hideousness, while years of vice and indulgence leave no trace upon his face or body. But Dorian, as might have been said about Wilde, hasn't got the courage of his lack of convictions. There comes a day when he stands before his portrait and raises a knife.

At its heart, *Dorian Gray* is a moral tale. If Shaw and Wilde were fond of shocking the bourgeoisie, they did so from within their audience's charmed circle, not as outsiders. In the end, Wilde got the elbow because he wasn't cynical enough.

First edition   London: Ward, Lock, 1891
First US edition   New York: Ward, Lock, 1891

19
BRAM STOKER
Dracula

Like overhanging Upas trees sprouting from the rich graveyard soil of
Gothic fantasy, *Frankenstein* and *Dracula* cast baleful shadows far beyond their
native century. Myriad imitations have flourished, and continue to do so, in
rank profusion among their writhing roots. The film industry endlessly re-
cycles them, while contriving never to be faithful to the originals. Actors
found whole careers upon playing the Monster or the Vampire, or sometimes
both.

Yet they each have a long ancestry; man-like monsters lurch through
Europe's medieval legends and Dracula's blood-kin flourished in print before
Stoker produced the definitive version in 1897. Half a century earlier, the pro-
digiously prolific James Malcolm Rymer had filled 800 pages of Lloyd's
penny dreadfuls with the gory deeds of Varney the Vampire, British aristocrat and fiend.

Speculations on the roots of the vampire legend are many and various,
ranging from bloodsucking bats through human psychological and genetic
abnormalities to the concept, stemming from Stoker's syphilis-hastened
death, of Dracula as a social disease with teeth. The latter idea could also be
seen as one more attempt to saddle the Victorians with the obsessions of our
enlightened age, which, sexually speaking, has painted itself into a corner.
Whatever its basis, fear of the undead clings tenaciously to the popular
imagination.

Much has been written in recent years to the effect that Count Dracula had
a historical counterpart in Vlad the Impaler, an Eastern European nobleman
whose name speaks volumes. To this unlovely reputation, Stoker added the
attributes of the vampire, but he was not content to rely upon purely supernatural causes. Deep within Dracula's mountain fastness lie '. . . caverns and
fissures . . . volcanoes . . . waters of strange properties . . . gases that kill or . . .
vivify'. So a dash of pseudoscience is added to the recipe; the Count, like *She*,
taps the heart of the planet for his power. His human opponents employ the
advanced technology of the time, notably the phonograph and the typewriter,
in coordinating their campaign against the undead. There is a strong
emphasis upon the collection and dissemination of information. The Count
himself is a formidable forward planner, as he masterminds his solo invasion
of Britain through a firm of solicitors, thus involving the luckless Jonathan
Harker.

Not inappropriately, then, the story is told in the form of letters, diary
excerpts and phonograph cylinder recordings. The constant shifts of viewpoint as the several characters recount their versions of events might seem to

work against the creation of suspense or terror, but this does not happen; the method is skilfully exploited. Jonathan Harker, newly risen from clerk to solicitor, travels to Transylvania to conclude negotiations with his firm's client Count Dracula. He keeps a record of the journey—customs and costumes, exotic recipes to present to his sweetheart, Mina Murray, descriptions of the wild and gloomy scenery—which changes gradually to expressions of fear and disquiet. Finally, imprisoned in the isolated Dracula castle, oppressed by the half-comprehended menace of the Count and his three female consorts, Harker is driven to a pitch of desperation beyond the reckoning of his unhuman captor.

The action switches to the port of Whitby, where, through Mina and her friend Lucy Westenra (the foreign surname is a pointer to later tragedy), we are introduced to some of the principal male characters. Here, below the ruined abbey and the cliff-perched graveyard, the Count's storm-driven ship runs aground, its dead steersman still lashed to the wheel. Now the many strands of the story begin to interweave. Lucy knows Dr Seward, supervisor of a lunatic asylum; the unaccountable behaviour of an inmate, Renfield, is eventually traced to the influence of Dracula, whose newly acquired house abuts the asylum grounds. Lucy falls ill, with symptoms so alarming and mysterious that Seward asks the advice of his old mentor, Dr Van Helsing. Van Helsing recognizes the vampiric influence and the battle begins, but Lucy cannot be saved. In the end, her fiancée, Arthur Holmwood, drives the stake through her heart and releases her spirit from the tomb.

A shaken Jonathan Harker is brought home by Mina and joins the ranks of the Dracula-hunters. Deaths multiply as the Count stalks the night, now as a great black hound, now as a bat, now as a pale, creeping mist. Remorselessly, his plans for establishing bases in London, from which to ravage the capital, are thwarted by Van Helsing and his loyal band. But Mina, now Mrs Harker, is left unguarded, and Dracula still has the power to strike at the heart of his foes.

Bram Stoker was a man of the theatre; though he wrote numerous novels, his theatrical reputation might well have outweighed his fiction without *Dracula*. Yet, had he never written anything else, this curdled brew of blood and necrophiliac voluptuousness would have been sufficient to secure for him lasting fame.

First edition   London: Constable, 1897
First US edition   New York: Doubleday, 1899

20
HENRY JAMES
The Turn of the Screw

In the 'Everyman' edition, *The Turn of the Screw* is more of a long story eked out by wide margins than a novel. The fact that this edition originally combined it with *The Aspern Papers* shows that publishers J. M. Dent once thought so too. Even on the occasion of its first publication in Britain, following American magazine serialization in 1898, it was half of a two-story volume. James himself deprecatingly described it to H. G. Wells as 'essentially a pot-boiler'. Few small pots can have been boiled to such effect.

Likewise, few supernatural tales can have originated in a conversation with the Archbishop of Canterbury. Edward Benson, the incumbent at that time, related to James an account of children in a country house plagued by seemingly supernatural visitations. The situation, sketchily outlined as it was, lodged itself in the writer's imagination, later to flower into one of the best-known ghost stories in the English language. Though it has several times been dramatized, even to the point of a screen 'prequel' giving a version of the events prefiguring the novel's central situation, the strength of the story lies in what is *not* told. This ambiguity is at its heart; readers and dramatists must interpret it according to their own lights.

We are eased into the story in the leisurely manner of the time—the narrator learns of it from a friend, as a result of a Christmas Eve fireside session of anecdotes. The friend, in turn, heard it from the governess who figured in the events she described. He committed them to paper and has decided to reveal them, forty years later. There is more than a hint that he was in love with her, at a distance; she was several years his senior. She too may have felt an equally hopeless attraction for the uncle of the two children she was engaged to teach. These fireside speculations are, so to speak, a storm warning; rougher weather lies ahead.

The children, ten-year-old Miles and his younger sister, Flora, are orphans. Their father's bachelor brother accepts responsibility for them to the extent of providing a home at his country estate and putting the boy to school. He declines any personal involvement, leaving their upbringing to the housekeeper, Mrs Grose, and a governess, Miss Jessel, while he resides in London. Miss Jessel, though young, dies. The new (and never named) governess, fresh from a country parsonage, is impressed by the comparative splendour of her employer's lifestyle and delighted by Flora's beauty and charm.

A letter from Miles's headmaster disturbs this sunny mood. The boy, due to come home soon on holiday, has been forbidden to return to the school. The actual arrival of Miles deepens the mystery, for he is outwardly as fair and intelligent as his sister. Showing the letter to the housekeeper, the governess discovers that she cannot read. The letter is never fully explained to Mrs Grose and so we never learn the exact nature of the boy's offence.

Strolling through the grounds of the estate, idly imagining a chance meeting with some handsome man, the governess suddenly sees a stranger watching her from a tower. She says nothing of this to anyone else, until the same man appears again, frighteningly closer, at a terrace window. Describing him to Mrs Grose, she learns that he was the late master's valet, Peter Quint. Was—because Quint is as dead as Miss Jessel. The nature of the relationship between the pair begins to obsess the younger woman's imagination. She becomes convinced that they are exercising an unwholesome influence upon the children from beyond the grave. The every word and action of Miles and Flora begin to seem like acts of deception designed to disguise this from the world of the living. So strong is her conviction that she is able to persuade Mrs Grose of its plausibility, though the housekeeper cannot see the spectral visitors.

At this point, the reader of today, accustomed to fast and readily available communications, may wonder why outside help was not sought. Specifically, why was the minister of the nearby church not called upon for spiritual aid and advice? (Significantly, upon their last attendance at church before the climactic tragedy, the governess does not enter, remaining in the churchyard among the graves.) The answer could depend upon whether her experiences are to be regarded as objective or subjective. Do the phantoms of Peter Quint and Miss Jessel exist outside of her mind? Is the subtle corruption of their presence really the worm gnawing at the innocence of her charges or is she visiting her own repressions upon Miles and Flora? Who, in the end, is responsible for the tragic outcome?

The Turn of the Screw draws no diagrams. Rather, it provides a screen upon which the reader can project his or her innermost fears and fantasies. It would be fascinating to know precisely what it was that Henry James may have seen upon that screen.

Printed by Heinemann for copyright purposes but not published, 1898
First published edition, in *The Two Magics*   London: Heinemann, 1898
First US edition, in *The Two Magics*   New York: Macmillan, 1898

21

G. K. CHESTERTON
The Man Who Was Thursday

Olde England drowsed in the glow of an everlasting summer afternoon, while the smoke from myriad cottage chimneys climbed straight up to Heaven. The ploughman's lunch had not yet been capitalized and the comfortably crooked roads led to the doorways of tree-shaded inns. Roistering goodfellowship was the order to the day. A man was as good as his neighbour, within reason.

And what became of this green idyll of cheese and ale and good stout walking-boots? Why, nothing. It still stands four-square to the winds of actuality, a dream of the past seen through the murky glass of the Industrial Revolution. A dream which gripped the imagination of Gilbert Keith Chesterton and permeated his work. It colours the sunset skies which arch over his fantasy of London; the meteorology is the message.

Seen from the viewpoint of a society lurching like some roughed-up beast towards the Third Millennium, the spectacle of middle-class literati of the balmy Edwardian era looking back to a medieval Golden Age is paradoxical. Chesterton might have appreciated the irony, being addicted to paradoxes to a degree which could verge on the irritating. In *Thursday*, however, they are controlled with masterly skill, tumbling out one from another like Russian dolls.

Bomb-throwers are not the figures of fun they once were, though they survived two world wars in that capacity, as British screen comedies testify. The tight little island of 1908 could still laugh and shudder at foreign anarchists and even regard them as a species of hero. Taking these bogymen as his protagonists, as did so many novelists of the day, Chesterton stood their philosophy upon its head. There are echoes of another Gilbert in the surface absurdity of the narrative; Sullivan would have found ample material for inspiration here.

The church of Saffron Park lies on the sunset side of London. On the evening when the yellow-haired poet Gabriel Syme meets the poet of Saffron Park, Lucius Gregory, the sunset looks like the end of the world. The two cross swords on the subject of anarchy, about which Gregory professes to be in earnest. Soon he is hustling Syme off to meet the Supreme Council, seven anarchists named after days of the week. Gregory hopes to be elected to the vacant role of Thursday. He exacts a promise of silence from Syme about what he sees and hears. Syme, at the meeting-place, exacts a similar pledge from Gregory, before revealing that he is a Secret Service agent.

When the vote is taken, Gregory loses. Syme becomes Thursday. Silenced by his pledge, Gregory can only depart, fuming. The President of the

Council, Sunday, was not present, but even in his absence he dominated the meeting. Meeting him later, at breakfast on a balcony overlooking Leicester Square, Syme finds Sunday's sheer size almost incomprehensible: '. . . he was abnormally tall and quite incredibly fat. His head, crowned with white hair . . . looked bigger than a head ought to be.' The model for Sunday is not far to seek. Chesterton's trousers were once described as resembling a tunnel on the London Underground.

At the breakfast, the planned assassination of the Czar is openly discussed. No eavesdropper, says Sunday, will credit with serious intent any group who publicly profess their anarchy. Syme is ready for a desperate struggle when the President declares that they are harbouring a spy, but it proves to be Tuesday, masquerading as Gogol, a Pole. Following this meeting, Syme flees through a snowbound London in a hilariously nightmarish chase episode, pursued by Friday, the incredibly decrepit Professor de Worms. Cornered in a tavern, he is astounded to discover that Friday is also a Secret Service spy. Both of them were interviewed for their posts by the same unidentified man who spoke to them in a pitch-dark room.

The game of revelatory roulette is now under way. One by one, the deadly conspirators show their blue identity cards, proving themselves to be Secret Service infiltrators. Only the overwhelming Sunday retains his credibility; no one doubts his implacable devotion to the anarchist cause. In a desperate attempt to prevent the Czar's assassination in Paris, Syme and his companions cross to France, where they become embroiled in a series of fights and flights and confusions of identity until their *bona fides* are established.

Returning to England, they chase the gigantic President through the streets of London, as he flees by cab, fire-engine, elephant and balloon, tantalizing his pursuers with enigmatic messages. Finally, tattered and exhausted, they find themselves being conveyed by carriages to a great house, where they are to be Sunday's guests at a party.

Now their true identities are revealed, as they linger in the garden with Sunday, after the other guests have departed. There are other means than guns and bombs for overturning the established evils of the world, other anarchists who gathered in subterranean rooms before going out to establish a new philosophy of life. And a leader beyond the understanding of men, who once spoke out of darkness.

First edition   Bristol: Arrowsmith, 1908
First US edition   New York: Dodd Mead, 1908

22
WILLIAM HOPE HODGSON
The House on the Borderland

At Ardrahan in County Galway, in Western Ireland, stood a house, the Old Rectory. In 1887 it became the temporary home of the Rev Hodgson and his family. R. Alain Everts, in the magazine *Shadow*, describes the impact of an English Anglican minister upon an Irish Catholic community. It was not a happy meeting. There were disputes, including a physical attack upon the Rev Hodgson, and the orchards on the Rectory estate were despoiled. Hope, a schoolboy at that time, did not forget the experience.

In 1908, *The House on the Borderland* was published. The author, in the guise of editor, says that the MS, was: 'discovered . . . in the Ruins . . . south of the village of Kraighten, in the west of Ireland'. The House, or its ruins, is surrounded by extensive gardens in which fruit-trees and shrubbery, long untended, have run wild. The whole area is dreary and desolate, a rural wasteland scattered with decaying cottages. Rural Ireland, then, has been fashioned into a fit setting for the brooding presence of the House.

Two tourists arrive in Kraighten in 1877 on a fishing holiday. Some miles from the village they discover a huge water-filled pit, overhung by a spur of broken rock. Buried among the tumbled stones on the spur is a battered diary, which describes a vast structure which once stood upon a natural dome covering the pit. This House, of which the nameless diarist and his sister were the last tenants, disappeared, together with the dome, in a mysterious catastrophe, leaving only the fragmentary ruins. Only the oldest inhabitant of Kraighten can recall the House as it stood or the arrival of the occupants. So forbidding is the atmosphere of the ruined gardens around the Pit that the tourists, after reading the diary, resolve not to return to the spot.

The diary forms the major part of the novel. Hodgson, again in editorial guise, says of it: 'Of the simple . . . account of weird and extraordinary matters, I will say little . . . The inner story must be uncovered, personally, by each reader, according to ability and desire . . . yet I can promise certain thrills, merely taking the story as a story'. Which may well be the most understated introduction since *Moby-Dick*. Hodgson's imagination opens up endless vistas of time and space and rushes down them, headlong, leaving the reader breathless in his wake. Savage struggles with the swine-like creatures who swarm from the depths of the Pit; astral journeys to a red-lit mountainous amphitheatre in which monstrous gods look down upon a gigantic counterpart of the House; a pilgrimage through time to the death of the Solar System; a meeting with the spirit-form of his lost love beside a haunted sea—these are only some of the experiences which befall the reclusive diarist.

What is the relationship between the House and its astral twin? Why is structural damage to the one duplicated in the other? To what degree are the Recluse's adventures subjective, engendered by his retreat from the world and his obsession with the memory of his lover? It is his sister Mary's re-action, or rather lack of reaction, to the Swine-folk which casts doubt upon the reality of her brother's account. She seems unaware of their existence and is frightened by his (to her) unaccountable actions in defence of the House. He, in turn, cannot understand her lack of caution. And when he takes his involuntary journey into the future, his dog, Pepper, dies of accelerated old age, while the fabric of the House crumbles and the Recluse becomes a bodi-less entity. Yet when the clock of time reverses, returning himself and the House to their former state, Pepper remains dead and there is no evidence that his sister shared in the experience at all. The logic could be that of dreams, were the destruction of the House not an independently attested fact.

Hodgson employed the Swine imagery in at least one other story, *The Hog*, in which the eponymous monster rises into our everyday world from a shadowy gulf. At least one commentator has equated the recurrent Swine and Pit motif with a distaste for carnal love. The traditional link between Irish peasants and pig-keeping, when added to the actual ravaging of the Rectory orchards, suggests a less Freudian interpretation. As Hodgson says, there is an underlying story which the reader may decipher to his or her own satisfac-tion. Whatever the answer, *The House on the Borderland*, with its dizzying leaps through outer and inner space, remains a unique vision. It is good to see Hodgson's work once more receiving the attention it deserves.

As *The House on the Borderland, from the manuscript discovered in 1877 by Messrs Tonnison and Berreggnog, in the ruins that lie to the south of the village of Kraighten, in the west of Ireland*
First edition   London: Chapman and Hall, 1908
First US edition, as *The House on the Borderland and Other Novels*   Sauk City (Wisc): Arkham House, 1946

23

MARJORIE BOWEN
Black Magic

If the name of Margaret Vere Long rings no bells, think of George R. Preedy, Marjorie Bowen, Joseph Shearing or Robert Paye. Between 1909 and 1950, she was all of them, and possibly more. Under these pseudonyms, primarily that of Marjorie Bowen, she produced over 150 stories of the supernatural. Her talent for interweaving historical romance with diabolism is shown to great effect in her first published novel, *Black Magic*.

Distrust and misunderstanding have bedevilled relations between the various Christian sects throughout history, and the Catholic Church has received its share. Above all, the Papacy, with its combination of celibacy and spiritual infallibility, has provided a fertile ground for speculation. To imagine a woman invading the Vatican, that stronghold of male supremacy, to visualize her femininity concealed within the embroidered robes of Papal office, has been an enduring fantasy down the centuries. Hence the legend of Pope Joan.

In the fiery and fragmented Europe of the ninth century, kings and princes held the power of life and death over their subjects. But the royal knee was still bent to the Pope. To be Defender of the West meant being Defender of the Faith. Rome, no longer military dictator of a sprawling empire, was spiritual ruler of millions. Through her streets seethed a cosmopolitan horde of soldiers, adventurers, merchants, pimps, artists and pilgrims. She was the dream-city of the Western world, and nowhere more so than in the imagination of Dirk Renswoude, alone in a crumbling mansion in Flanders.

As Dirk patiently applies gold-leaf to a carven devil, two strangers arrive. Balthasar of Courtrai, a young nobleman seeking fortune and adventure, travels with scholarly Thierry, who journeys to the great universities of the south. Balthasar also seeks word of Ursula, his wife, whom he has never seen, for they were married by proxy. Dirk tells him that she died; her grave is in the mansion's courtyard. Of the two, Thierry shows the more concern. Balthasar is frankly relieved to be free. Dirk and Thierry soon discover that they share mutual interests. Hesitantly at first, then with amazement and joy, they reveal their fascination with black magic.

From the beginning, their relationship has a strangely sexual intensity. As their circumstances change, each becomes in turn the dominant or submissive partner, but it is Dirk who proves the bolder, and Thierry the waverer. Forced to flee from a college when Dirk employs witchcraft to kill another student, they take refuge in the castle of Jacobea, a noblewoman to whom Thierry is greatly attracted. Dirk, anxious to dispose of any competitor for

55

Thierry's affections, discovers that Jacobea is desired by the castle's steward, Sebastian, though he has a wife, Sybilla.

Leaving the castle, they meet a monk who is carrying gold which he has collected in order to found a monastery. They steal it in order to buy their way into Frankfort University, where they can pursue their study of the black arts. Dirk is visited by a masked woman, who threatens to make public her knowledge of his past unless he uses his powers to help her in murdering her husband. After she leaves, he divines her identity by sorcery. She is the Empress of the West, Ysabeau; her lover is Balthasar, who would be Emperor. Now Dirk begins to discern, on the horizon, the realization of his own ambitions, which are to Balthasar's as the sun to a candle.

In Marjorie Bowen's prose, the fields and towns of medieval Europe shimmer in a burning haze of sunlight or cower under the stifling purple pall of unnatural storms. Lightning forks and flickers about the characters as they act out their complex loves and hatreds. The interiors of cathedrals and villas swim in the sumptuous, many-coloured radiance of stained glass, reflected from gold, silver and crystal. Flowers mass on glistening marble, scattering petals on rug-strewn floors, drugging the air with languorous perfume. Gowns and doublets, armour and hose, blaze with orange and purple, crimson and green; great gems glitter from settings of precious metals. It is a hectic, high-key world, into which black diabolism fits without incongruity.

The men and women who inhabit it are strongly drawn, their emotions and intrigues in no way overwhelmed by their exotic setting. Balthasar schemes his way overwhelmed by their exotic setting. Balthasar schemes his way to the throne and reigns with his lover and Empress, the stormy Ysabeau. Dirk, after a terrifying display of Satanic power within the shadow of St Peter's, achieves his ultimate ambition, to be Pope. He has resolved to make Thierry Emperor, and so Balthasar must be cast down. Hell is released upon the city; criminals roam unchecked through the streets, nameless monsters stalk the night. Ysabeau and Balthasar make a courageous stand against the Devil-Pope before being driven into exile. Thierry, at last aware of the true identity of Dirk, finds that all power has a price, which even Popes and Emperors must pay. Amen to that.

As *Black Magic; a tale of the rise and fall of Antichrist*
First edition   London: Alston Rivers, 1909
First US edition   New York: Hodder, 1913

24
MAX BEERBOHM
Zuleika Dobson

Looking back, through Time or Space, has a foreshortening effect. Those deceptively close-ranked distant hills have their counterpart in historical events, especially when there is ample documentation of the period still available. From today's viewpoint, the celebrated writers of the latter half of the nineteenth century scarcely have elbow-room; as the end of the century approaches they are packed like rush-hour commuters. A title or a name recalls a dozen others by association, and one of the most evocative is *The Yellow Book*.

The sulphurous cover of the Bodley Head's periodical, launched in 1894, established yellow as the colour of all things bizarre and decadent. Oscar Wilde, in 1891, had written of a nameless book in yellow covers which corrupted Dorian Gray. Robert Chambers's 'The Yellow Sign' in 1895 told of a cryptic symbol which marked out for death those unfortunates who read another mind-rotting volume, *The King in Yellow*. Poster designers took up the eye-catching colour with enthusiasm, though it had the disadvantage of fading quickly. Max Beerbohm, in the company of Arthur Symons, Sickert, Le Galliene and, of course, Aubrey Beardsley, was featured in the first issue of *The Yellow Book* without noticeably adding to the abundant corruption of the times.

But then, as Holbrook Jackson pointed out in 1913 in *The Eighteen Nineties*, it was also the age of bicycles, knickerbockers and 'Ta-ra-ra-boom-de-ay!' To hold a lily while cycling down Piccadilly might have defeated even Bunthorne. W. S. Gilbert wasn't alone in finding the attitudes of the Wilde bunch risible. The *fin-de-siècle* decade was still in full flower while Beerbohm and others were dissecting its pretensions. In a period when 'new' was the favourite prefix, Beerbohm declared that he could no longer keep abreast of the younger writers and summed up his life in *The Works of Max Beerbohm* (1896). He was twenty-five. The forty-year-old Bernard Shaw refuted this when he relinquished the post of drama critic on the *Saturday Review* to: 'The younger generation . . . the incomparable Max.'

It was during the 'new' career which post-dated his *Works*, and which included several years of broadcasting with the BBC, that he wrote *Zuleika Dobson*. For this, he drew upon his experiences as an Oxford undergraduate at Merton College, where his talent for satire had attracted attention. He was also something of a caricaturist, and produced a set of illustrations to accompany the novel's text showing a willowy, elongated Zuleika.

To Oxford on a sunny afternoon came doom for a generation of flannelled undergraduates. It alighted from the train, radiant in white, twinkling with diamonds, the cynosure of all eyes. It was Zuleika, granddaughter of the Warden of Judas College. She was not strictly beautiful and her figure was less than Greek, but young men found her irresistible. As a governess in Notting Hill, she was taught the art of conjuring by the family's smitten elder son. Shortly thereafter, she took it up professionally, using his box of tricks. Whenever she asked her audiences for the loan of a hat, they would rise as one man.

She went to Paris and Berlin, causing a prince to be imprisoned; to Italy, becoming the target for a Papal Bull; to Russia and Spain, where a great matador died because he was watching her and not the bull. She wowed them in New York, Chicago, San Francisco. Her grandfather, who had never approved of the marriage which produced her, relented and invited her to Oxford. Now, as their landau rattles along below the dreaming spires, the stony visages of Roman emperors watch her pass and sweat bursts from their brows, but the omen goes unheeded.

Of all the lovesick swains, only one resented his fall and concealed the symptoms, and he was the one with whom she fancied herself to be in love. He was the Duke of Dorset, whose magnificent exterior was equalled only by his academic achievements. Before her arrival, he had conducted a deeply satisfying affair with his reflection, and he was thrown into turmoil by this intrusion. When he confessed his condition, Zuleika rejected him; he had lost the charm of unavailability. His response was to announce his intention of drowning himself during the collegiate boat races.

The result of this splendid gesture would have amazed the most self-centred of men. With cries of 'Zuleika!', his fellows hurled themselves into the rain-lashed waters, to be followed by the entire student population of Oxford, drifting pallidly downstream between upturned boats while their stricken elders lamented from the banks.

What if all of Europe's youth were to follow Oxford's example, Zuleika mused, as she checked train services to Cambridge. They did, Zuleika, they did.

First edition   London: Heinemann, 1911
First US edition   New York: Boni, 1911

25
EDGAR RICE BURROUGHS
A Princess of Mars

Looking at bookshop shelves lined with colourful paperback editions of his novels, seeing a thousand jokes and cartoons which work only because of the world's familiarity with his most famous character, Tarzan, and watching endless repeats upon television of films based upon his creations, it is difficult to accept that only the pressure of poverty drove Edgar Rice Burroughs to become a professional author. Do we really owe Amtor, Barsoom and Pellucidar to his failure as a businessman? What outlet other than fiction could there have been for the fantasies bubbling up in the brain of this Victorian self-exiled from Chicago to California?

The unforeseen success which attended the publication of his fantasies in the shape of *Under the Moons of Mars* (later *A Princess of Mars*) seemed to simultaneously please and discomfit their author. For many years, his expressed attitude towards his work was a mixture of defensiveness and self-mockery. At the same time, his business instincts acquired a sharper edge, though Hollywood remained impervious to it. It is to the movie moguls that we owe the false image of Tarzan as a loveable tree-dwelling oaf.

Only recently have serious moves been made regarding the filming of another series, one which Burroughs acknowledged as his favourite. Barsoom, known to our astronomers as Mars, gave birth to his weirdest romances. Serialized in *All-Story Magazine* and destined to make those issues into collector's items, *Under the Moons of Mars*, despite its imperfect construction, is a thrilling adventure, erotic, eerie and bloodthirsty by turns. The sequels were rarely so highly charged but were never less than entertaining. Barsoom stamped itself so ineradicably into the mental universes of younger writers that whole shelves of interplanetary swashbucklers can be credited to its influence. Leigh Brackett and Ray Bradbury are among its more talented fans.

John Carter, hero of the first three Barsoomian novels, is a man of mysterious antecedents, the more so because Burroughs never reveals them or tries to relate them to his life on the red planet. By Carter's own account, he cannot recall having any childhood. He has the appearance of a man of thirty and has always done so. When his first-person narrative begins, he is an ex-Civil War captain who has located a rich seam of gold in Arizona. Burroughs had vivid memories of Arizona, gathered as a young trooper of the Seventh Cavalry, when outlaws and Apaches still robbed and roamed. Carter's partner, Powell, is killed by a band of Apaches, who then pursue Carter. Taking refuge in a mountain cave, he is overcome by a paralysing vapour. Conscious but unmoving, he sees the Apaches flee in terror from some presence behind him.

Fear spurs him to a supreme effort of will. Climbing to his feet, he sees his uniformed body still prone on the cavern floor. He has taken on a new form, outwardly identical to the old. Naked, he walks out into the Arizona night and is drawn irresistibly to the brilliant red disc of Barsoom. Beyond the suggestion of an affinity between the warrior and the God of War, there is no attempt to rationalize these events.

Barsoom, as Carter first knows it, is divided between a handsome red-skinned race, cultured but warlike, and tribes of gigantic four-armed green nomads, devoted to battle and torture. Ochre moss covers the uplands and the hollows where vanished oceans once rolled, and immemorially ancient cities slowly crumble into decay. He materializes, naked and unarmed, among the green men and quickly establishes his martial superiority, aided by Barsoom's lesser gravity. The Tharks, as they are called, capture a beautiful red princess, Dejah Thoris. Carter rescues her and, naturally, falls in love with her. Just as naturally, the path to consummation is strewn with traps, obstacles and cultural misunderstandings. Swordplay, treachery, intrigue and marvels heaped upon wonders surround him as he treks across the dying wildernesses of her world, his blade seldom unbloodied.

Establishing what came to be a personal tradition, Burroughs ends the novel on a cliff-hanger. The atmosphere plant, which generates the air upon which Barsoomian life depends, is failing. Carter makes a desperate attempt to reach its heavily protected interior, but falls unconscious, leaving a red man to struggle towards the control room. He awakens upon Earth, in his original body.

The pace did not slacken in the sequel, *The Gods of Mars*. If anything, it quickened. *The Warlord of Mars* completed the trilogy and established Carter at the apex of a society of fighting men. The Barsoomian series, ten titles in all, is of variable quality, but the level of invention remains surprisingly high. Most of Burroughs's more memorable grotesques are native to the red planet. Though imitators have run the formula ragged since the astonishing paperback revival of his work in the 1960s, the originals remain untarnished. As John Carter was wont to declare: 'I still live!'

First edition   Chicago: A. C. McClurg, 1917
First UK edition   London: Methuen, 1919

26
EDGAR RICE BURROUGHS
Tarzan of the Apes

The popularity of the world's bestselling fictional hero presents a paradox in that most of the people who think they know him, know only his screen shadow. Its most pretentious manifestation, *Greystoke*, has at least the virtue of returning the Apeman to approximately his correct point in time. Burroughs was a child of the Victorian Age, albeit an American one, and his style reflects the lingering influence of that era; his near-contemporary, H. G. Wells, was by contrast rushing headlong into a fantastic future. A puzzled Burroughs was belatedly accused, in 1918, of deriving his inspiration for *A Princess of Mars* from Wells's *The War of the Worlds*, which he had never read. Charges of plagiarism were to be made against him throughout his long and inventive career, though not by the authors who were his alleged sources. Ironically, he became in turn probably the most openly plagiarized novelist of the twentieth century.

To reinforce the credibility of *Tarzan*, Burroughs introduces 'himself' as narrator, a device he used frequently. In this capacity, he learns of the disastrous African voyage of the recently wed Lord and Lady Greystoke in 1888, a story backed up documents illegally borrowed from the British Colonial Office. An interesting point made by 'Burroughs' is that he has falsified the names of the people involved. Thus Tarzan is not, nor ever has been, John Clayton, Lord Greystoke. And 'Jane' was never Jane. Burroughs's grip upon his readers' imaginations is such that this simple literary device has sparked off orgies of speculation.

Sent to investigate the activities of a foreign colonial power, the Greystokes are marooned by mutineers on an unexplored African shore. They build a substantial cabin, but Lady Greystoke dies soon after the birth of her son and her husband is killed by a huge ape. Their orphaned baby is taken by a female ape as a replacement for her dead infant. Larger and more intelligent than gorillas, these anthropoids are the first of a host of species known nowhere beyond the bounds of Burroughsian Africa. Which does not mean that he ignored research or knowledgeable advice. When a critic pointed out that *Tarzan of the Apes* featured that non-African cat, the tiger, the error was quickly corrected. Like all good story-tellers, his fantasies were built upon a foundation of fact.

Civilization's highest type, as Burroughs the Anglophile saw him, is brought into conflict with the forest primeval. The theme is heredity versus environment. Under no illusions about the probable fate of a real child in such circumstances, he provides Tarzan with a foothold by picturing the apes as a link between the human and the bestial. In a series of brilliantly realized episodes, Tarzan's climb to maturity recapitulates the evolution of mankind. Most effective of all is the boy's discovery within the cabin of a picture-book once intended for his education in some tropical outpost. Squatting beside the mouldering skeletons of his parents, he laboriously deciphers the illustrations. His hairless skin ('Tarzan' means white-skin in the language of the great apes) assumes a new significance. He is a Man. The distinction is confirmed by the discovery of his father's hunting-knife.

His new status is put to a fearsome test when a gorilla attacks him. At ten years of age, Tarzan is as strong as a fully grown man, but is saved only by his accidental use of the knife. From here on, his intelligence, increasing strength and foresight makes his assumption of tribal leadership inevitable. Tragedy strikes when Kala, his foster-mother, is killed by native hunters. He turns his formidable powers against these new, human, enemies. These passages have been described as racialist, which is to ignore the logic of the situation; Tarzan has no knowledge of human customs, laws or ethics. Fortunately, he picks up from the natives the habit of wearing a loincloth before his first meeting with Jane Porter.

Burroughs never outgrew the use of coincidence to keep things moving and only his vivid imagination muffles the creaking of the plot as yet another crew of mutineers dump Jane and Tarzan's cousin, Cecil Greystoke, on the beach, together with coloured servant Esmeralda and Professors Porter and Philander. Tarzan rescues Jane from the attentions of a lustful ape and learns that no gentleman would take advantage of a girl's distress. Circumstances part him from the castaways and lead him to the rescue of Lieutenant D'Arnot, a French naval officer captured by cannibals. D'Arnot teaches him to talk, in French, and guesses the significance of his dead father's diary. This is also in French, a custom of the English aristocracy, supposedly intended to thwart the curiosity of their servants.

Tarzan is on the way to Paris and his inheritance. Jane, back in the USA, has agreed to marry a wealthy suitor to pay off the family debts. All seems set for the Apeman to swing in, grab the girl and save the old homestead—except that Burroughs was seemingly born with a talent for keeping readers in suspense. Tarzan's saga had hardly begun and even his creator's death, in 1950, was not allowed to end it.

First edition   Chicago: A. C. McClurg, 1914
First UK edition   London: Methuen, 1917

27

ARTHUR CONAN DOYLE
The Lost World

In the 19th century, monsters invaded the world. Grotesque beyond any dra-
gon-dream, they multiplied until the very boundaries of Time could no
longer accommodate them. History's horizons had to be pushed back beyond
Biblical limits to give them breathing-space. For they were protected by more
than spines and scales and bony plates. They were armoured with intellectual
respectability. They were classified and categorized. They were dinosaurs.

With one bound, fiction-writers were free to exploit the distant past to a
degree previously unknown. Only the yawning gulf of years separating the
last dinosaur from the first apeman presented a momentary difficulty. Writers,
impelled by ignorance or inflamed imaginations, ignored it, or resorted to
inventing environments in which prehistoric creatures could linger to await
the coming of modern man. Conan Doyle was not the first of these, but *The
Lost World* established his pre-eminence.

The thunder of antediluvian feet has, if anything, grown louder since his
day. In the imaginations of young and old, the dinosaur today competes suc-
cessfully with the gaudiest of extraterrestrials. Following closely upon *The
Lost World* came *The Land That Time Forgot*, regarded by many as Edgar Rice
Burroughs' finest imaginative work. Together, they tower over the flood of
monster tales which poured from the presses to entertain later generations.
Doyle, however, outstripped all rivals in the matter of characterization. The
outrageous Professor Challenger ranks second only to Sherlock Holmes in
the Doyle pantheon. An unlikely monster in himself, Challenger's massive
ego and almost equally massive physique carried him through a series of fantastic, if lesser, adventures subsequent to the novel.

The volcanic plateau which is the setting for *The Lost World* is located in an
unspecified area of the Amazonian forest. By 1912, Africa may still have been
dark enough to conceal Tarzan and his tribe, but only South America, among
known lands, could offer a convincing hiding-place for evolutionary discrepancies on a large scale. It continued to be a happy hunting-ground for
speculation by certain newspaper feature-writers until long after World War
Two, and is still good for the odd column. A plateau closely resembling
Doyle's fictional creation actually exists, but regrettably without similar
inhabitants. Or, in view of current concern over the destruction of the rainforest, perhaps not so regrettably.

A good deal of the verve which sustains the novel's pace before the main
set-pieces springs from the author's own literary and medical background.
The bickering professors and the brawling, irreverent medical students may
be caricatures, but they are based upon living models. The dinosaurs and

their world are, of necessity, fictions founded upon others descriptions and suppositions, and so draw heavily upon the imagination and literary skill of the novelist who seeks to imbue them with life. Doyle succeeds in painting vivid impressions of the prehistoric forest, now hushed and gloomy, now splashed with colourful, riotous life. His staging of the various encounters with the monstrous *fauna* is memorably theatrical, reaching a peak with the pursuit of the narrator, Malone, across the moonlit plateau by a tyrannosaurus.

In an age when ecology and conservation are catchwords, the cheerful slaughtering of wildlife by Rider Haggard's intrepid adventurers dims, momentarily, their heroic auras. Challenger, Summerlee, Malone and the hunter of slave-traders and big game, Lord John Roxton, inflict little damage upon the dinosaurs, though this is largely due to the slow-witted giants being impervious to anything short of a sustained barrage. Where the modern reader's sympathies may be sorely stretched is in their treatment of the ape-men who form one of the tribes dwelling on the plateau; the other tribe consists of native Indians seeking refuge from the world below.

Doyle derives some humour from the resemblance between the hirsute Challenger and the apemen, but the likeness—intentionally or otherwise——goes deeper than the skin. The apemen are hairy, beetle-browed, cunning and ogreishly strong. Their customs include that of throwing prisoners off the plateau's edge, to be impaled upon towering bamboo stalks. They are dexterous in the use of ropes and knots. They wreck and loot the explorer's camp. They exhibit, in short, many all-too-human traits while parodying the human form. The Indians display a properly respectful attitude to Europeans, and are rewarded by being classed as a particularly highly-evolved type by the Professor. When they appeal for help, the resultant slaughter of the apemen is carried out with scarcely a qualm. Challenger shows no scientific detachment in this respect. Only Malone, who, as a journalist, had often wished to cover a war, begins to appreciate something of its horror.

At the close of the novel, Roxton and Malone prepare to return to the Lost World. Time is running out for the dinosaurs, as, in the world of Conan Doyle, it would soon run out for countless Malones.

As *The Lost World; being an account of the recent amazing adventures of Professor George E. Challenger, Lord John Roxton, Professor Summerlee, and Mr E. D. Malone of the "Daily Gazette"*
First edition   London: Hodder and Stoughton, 1912
First US edition   New York: Doran, 1912

28
WILLIAM HOPE HODGSON
The Night Land

Sooner or later in most reviews of The Night Land, the reviewer complains that its pseudo-archaic language is a stumbling-block for the reader. Why use a mock-medieval mode in telling a story of the far future? The fact that the narrator begins by recalling a past life in an unspecified pre-industrial society is scarcely a justification. One possible answer is that Hodgson may have hoped thereby to distance his invented age from his twentieth-century public. Whatever the reason, the difficulties have been greatly exaggerated. Anyone willing to make the effort will find that the manner of the telling heightens the atmosphere of a remote and alien Earth.

Hodgson himself had a personality to match that of any of his fictional heroes. Like many other writers from the closing decades of the Victorian era, his life ended in the holocaust of the First World War. It was typical of him that he refused to be relegated to civilian life after being injured while on military service. With some effort, he persuaded the Army to re-enlist him, and was killed in 1918 by German shellfire, at the age of forty. According to one biographer, R. Alain Everts, heroism went hand in hand with hypochondria and a disquietingly boisterous sense of humour. A physical culture enthusiast, he thought nothing of startling his neighbours by appearing outside an upper window, precariously elevated on stilts.

There is, then, a solid foundation for the courage and prowess of the nameless protagonist of The Night Land. He needs them, for Hodgson's future world will test such qualities to the limit. The Sun is dead and the airless surface of the Earth is shrouded in snow. At the bottom of a stupendous rift in the rocky crust, legacy of some past catastrophe, volcanic warmth and a trace of atmosphere linger. Here huddle the last human communities, wrapped in unending night. Scientifically implausible now, the novel was written at a time when the Sun had not yet been accorded the inconceivably long life-expectancy it enjoys today.

The home of the larger of the two known communities is the Great Redoubt, a metal pyramid subdivided into 1,320 levels, each with its own population and function. Of this colossal structure, only the merest tip projects above ground level. This tip, with its crowning observation tower, is eight miles high. The whole concept is strikingly similar to the never-implemented plans for gracing London with huge pyramidal necropolises, complete with towers at their apex. Far off in the night is the Lesser Redoubt, the exact location of which has been forgotten. The span of time which has elapsed since its founding is many times greater than the whole present history of civilization; the very sea it overlooked has vanished.

And then, after an immeasurable age of silence, a telepathic message is received from a girl living in the Lesser Redoubt. Elation struggles with caution. The Night Land swarms with sentient and semi-sentient entities capable of telepathic communication, almost all of them inimical to human life. For aeons they have besieged the metal mountains, seeking to destroy the inhabitants, physically and spiritually. To the Earth's last humans, the loss of the soul is an ever-present danger, infinitely worse than physical death. Though he came from an actively religious family, Hodgson resolutely affirmed his atheism throughout his short life, yet his horrors have a strong spiritual component.

The Lesser Redoubt, monster-encircled, is about to fall. The youthful hero, who alone is capable of receiving the girl's desperate telepathic pleas, finds that she shares his memories of an earlier life. He sets out, armoured in body and spirit like any paladin of Arthur's court, to fight his way to her across leagues of haunted darkness. In place of a sword he carries the Diskos, a weapon with a spinning blade, attuned to the personality of its wielder. It will make a light for him in the darkest places, but a light can attract things which roam the night.

Logic and evolution have played no part in shaping this future world. Hodgson's monsters crouch in the gloom of a dying Earth, all the more fearsome for being half-seen. They are creatures of the unconscious, vast dim forms from the nightmare-spawning shadows beyond the lamps of Reason, their powers and purposes never clearly delineated. Only the lesser and purely physical menaces can be met with muscle and the biting fire of the Diskos.

The Night Land is an odyssey in which mankind's lapse from spiritual integrity is linked inescapably with the onslaught of nameless forces, from the dark gulfs which were always on the borderland of Hodgson's imagination. There is no scientific miracle waiting in the wings, no hint of salvation. At best, the struggle will continue for so long as human resolution endures.

It is pointless, though irresistible, to speculate upon what heights of Fantasy Hodgson might have scaled had the war not intervened. What is undeniable is that he left behind two classics of the genre, of which *The Night Land* is one.

As *The Night Land; a love tale*
First edition   London: Eveleigh Nash, 1912
First US edition, in *The House on the Borderland and Other Novels*
Sauk City (Wisc): Arkham House, 1946

[1915]

29

CHARLOTTE PERKINS GILMAN
Herland

A single-sex Utopia would appear to raise more problems than it solves, not least that of being short-lived. *Herland's* Herland, with its wholly female population, is such a state. Men do not play even a subordinate role in Herland society; there have been none for many generations. Nor has there been any scientific development making male participation in parenthood redundant. A virgin birth, 2,000 years ago, was the solution.

Cut off by war and volcanic upheaval from all outside contact, with their menfolk destroyed, Herland's population faced extinction. And then, spontaneously, one woman conceived and brought forth a child. Unlike a more widely publicized virgin birth of approximately the same date, Herland's is a continuing phenomenon. The first mother's children were all female and all eventually conceived. This process, invariably producing females, continued until every inhabitant was a direct descendant of the original single parent. A sf writer at some later date would probably have included references to genes, dominant mutations and the like, to strengthen plausibility, but this is not Charlotte Gilman's purpose. This sudden outbreak of parthenogenesis is the response of the female principle to a desperate need.

Having set up her Utopia, she proceeds to put its principles to the test by having it invaded by three men. It might have been more revealing had the invaders included a woman; as it is, the men embody three kinds of male response, from wealthy chauvinist pig, Terry, to romantic idealist, Jeff. Van, sociologist-narrator, maintains a balance between these extremes. Terry has financed the expedition, including the use of an aircraft to reach the plateau. They have all fantasized about the nature of Herland, according to their respective temperaments. They are all due for a shock.

The good humour which pervades so much of the book is in startling contrast to the same writer's evocation of mental torment in *The Yellow Wallpaper*. One after another, masculine preconceptions are sent tumbling, yet somehow without bitterness. Ann J. Lane's fascinating introduction nevertheless makes clear the links between madness and Utopia, springing from the unhappiness in Charlotte Gilman's private life. Soon after her birth in Connecticut in 1860, her father deserted the family. Charlotte worked to support herself during most of her adult life. Married at twenty-four, she suffered acute depression after the birth of her daughter and eventually moved to California, leaving her husband and child. Reunited later with her daughter, she became a professional writer and lecturer, her theme being women's autonomy, free from the roles prescribed for them by men.

In 1909 she began to publish a monthly magazine, *The Forerunner*, which featured *Herland* as a serial, and somehow maintained it for seven years with a minimum of advertising revenue. Racked by cancer, she took her own life in 1935, by the use of chloroform; in Herland, anaesthesia was used to subdue the rebellious men.

Motherhood, not surprisingly, is the motive power which drives this community of women. Moreover, it is motherhood in a peculiarly intense form; born parthenogenetically, originating from a single ancestor, they are one vast family of sisters. This raises the question of uniformity, both physical and psychological, but this has been avoided by imaginative education, which develops individual skills and inclinations. Education begins almost at birth and unobtrusively embraces all aspects of life, so that the very young are never conscious of the process as something imposed upon them. Management of their limited natural resources is a vital part of the scheme; Herland's food supplies are sufficient, but only because of a far-sighted agricultural policy in which tree cultivation plays a major role. Here, Charlotte Gilman draws so attractive a picture of hardworking intelligence and enterprise that the Women's reluctance to venture beyond the plateau becomes unconvincing and must simply be accepted for the sake of the argument, as with most Utopian fiction.

Herland, of course, is less an idealized picture of a woman-oriented society than of a system designed to realize the maximum potential of every individual, of whatever sex. Such a system still evades us, as we struggle to keep the present imperfect educational establishment functioning. More advocates with the talent and humour of Charlotte Gilman are needed, though to modern ears her voice lacks the requisite shrillness.

She may also, in this post-Kinsey era, be felt to have skirted some of the implications of a single-sex society. Kinsey, however, had fewer intentional laughs.

First edition New York: Pantheon, 1979
First UK edition London: Women's Press, 1979

30
FRANCIS STEVENS
The Citadel of Fear

To induce the suspension of disbelief is generally held to be an indispensable
part of the writer's craft, all the more so when dealing with *outré* events. In
practice, this rule has been broken many times, and with success. Anyone
who has enjoyed late-night television revivals of horror films from the period
of 1930 to 1950 will agree that mere plausibility is not everything. *The Citadel
of Fear*, though antedating the heyday of Karloff and Co by several years, has
the authentic air of delirium fitted to midnight viewing. Why it appears to
have been overlooked by Hollywood is a minor mystery.

None of the above is any reflection upon the quality of the writing.
According to Sam Moskowitz's introduction to a later edition, Francis
Stevens was by some believed to be a pen-name for A. Merritt. Others, while
acknowledging similarities of style, maintained that she was the superior
writer. Oddly, her description in *Citadel* of the evil, sentient statue of Nacoc-
Yaotl could be said to prefigure the Luciferean mask which is the dominating
image of Merritt's *The Face in the Abyss* (1923).

At thirty-two, a widow with a young daughter and an invalid mother to
support, she began to sell stories to such magazines as *Argosy* and *All-Story
Weekly*. Despite a fair degree of success, her known writing career spans no
more than four years, from 1917 to 1920. From 1940 onwards, partly at the
suggestion of Merritt, *Famous Fantastic Mysteries* began to reprint her work,
but by that time Gertrude Bennett, aka Francis Stevens, had disappeared
from the literary scene so completely as to be untraceable.

As with Merritt's *The Moon Pool*, the hero of *Citadel* is of Irish descent.
Though his name is Colin O'Hara, he is referred to as 'Boots'. Happily, this
unheroic appellation is dropped after the ninth chapter. Together with an
older partner, Archer Kennedy, he discovers a fertile valley in the seared
wilderness of Mexico's *Collados del Demonio*, the Hills of the Fiend. At first
sight it is a cultivated Eden. Further investigation reveals it as a deceptive
gateway to something ancient and sinister.

In this singular garden stands an equally improbable hacienda. The owner,
Biornson, reluctantly gives them shelter, but imprisons them in their room at
nightfall. O'Hara's muscles prove equal to the challenge. Beyond the cultivated land, they enter a forest of giant ferns, where huge luminous moths
flutter through the night. Biornson overtakes them and O'Hara has to inter-
vene to prevent Kennedy from killing him. A pack of white wolves attack the
pair, followed by white-skinned men who dwarf even the massive O'Hara.
They are overpowered and again imprisoned, this time in a strange city.
Biornson comes to their cell and tells O'Hara that they are in Tlapallan, the

land of Quetzalcoatl, and that it hides a secret too dreadful to be described. He is the sole survivor of a lost scientific expedition who married a local girl and decided to stay.

Escaping again, Kennedy and O'Hara penetrate to the heart of Tlapallan, where a gold-rich city stands above a fiery lake. Kennedy, seeking to evade attendants, comes face to evil face with the statue of Nacoc-Yaotl. Or is it a statue? Crouched in the shadow of the god, he learns the mind-numbing secret at which Biornson hinted. O'Hara, separated from his partner, knows nothing of this. He is soon embroiled in the simmering feud between the devotees of Nacoc-Yaotl and Quetzalcoatl, inadvertently supporting the latter. Unwittingly, he has set the two factions on the road to war. He is escorted forcibly into the desert, to find his way to civilization or die. Kennedy remains as a prisoner.

Fast-forward fifteen years. In the USA, O'Hara is telling his sister, Cliona, of his recent return to Tlapallan and the lifeless desolation which he found there. On the following night some monstrous creature invades Cliona's house. Driven off by a barrage of pistol shots, it leaves ruin and an incredible welter of blood behind it. Then a white ape attacks O'Hara. Fighting it off, he pursues it to the high gates of a mysterious house. The tenant, who gives his name as Chester Reed, explains that he is conducting animal-breeding experiments; the ape had somehow escaped. There is a girl in the house, said by Reed to be his mad daughter, who bears a strong likeness to the women of Tlapallan.

Reed proves to be a much-changed Kennedy. In his house of horrors, Nacoc-Yaotl broods over nameless creatures which Kennedy has created by use of techniques learned in Tlapallan. Living flesh can be dissolved, reduced to basic protoplasm, and remoulded into any desired shape by the power of thought. At the lurid climax, this Fortress of Fear is brought crashing to destruction, as O'Hara, assorted gods and police detectives slug it out with the spawn of perverted science.

No account of Francis Steven's work should omit her sense of humour. The golden objects stolen from the ruined city by Kennedy, at the cost of untold sweat and toil, turn out to be of solid copper, gold-plated.

First edition   New York: Paperback Library, 1970

31

DAVID LINDSAY
A Voyage to Arcturus

In the heady days of the Third Programme, when the state of the ratings was solely the concern of HM Navy, the BBC broadcast a dramatization of *A Voyage to Arcturus* which lasted five hours. At the time, radio was probably the only medium adequate to the task. Today, the cinema's greatly developed technical resources might well make effective use of the same material, given a touch of genius in the director. The upsurge of interest in fantasy and SF which raised cinematic spectacle to new heights, and dragged obscure works blinking into the light, is responsible for the present availability of Lindsay's novel.

Between the publication of *Arcturus* and Lindsay's death, in 1945, he wrote several other books, including two which were published posthumously. Few readers could readily name them. *Arcturus* itself is not an ingratiating work; the shelf it occupies is a short one, reserved for titles more often to be found in lists than in reader's pockets. The message it spells out is no comforting one.

Beginning with a seance (someone in need of a subject for a thesis might profitably choose the seance in fiction between the two World Wars), Lindsay sets his three protagonists in motion towards Tormance, a fictitious satellite of the double star Arcturus. A wealthy merchant, Faull, has hired a medium and all the trappings of a theatrical performance to entertain his guests. Backhouse, the medium, deplores these frivolities, but there are to be further distractions. Two latecomers, Maskull and Nightspore, enter as the seance is about to begin. A materialization is achieved—the figure of a young man, which moves about the room. A third man, a stranger, bursts in and interrogates the ectoplasmic presence. He then 'kills' it, with horrifying results. Nightspore obviously knows the newcomer, addressed as 'Krag'. Together with Maskull, they leave.

Maskull is induced to travel to Tormance. A crystalline spaceship awaits them at the top of an isolated tower. He attempts to climb the stairway leading to it, but is defeated by what seems to be an abnormal gravitational force. Only when Krag slashes Maskull's arm and spits upon the wound does ascent become possible for him. Krag is Pain; without pain, nothing of worth can be achieved. As the ship speeds into interstellar space, Maskull falls into a profound sleep. When he awakes, he is on Tormance, alone. Nightspore, Krag and the ship have vanished.

He begins his journey of self-discovery and, ultimately, self-negation across the bizarre landscapes of Tormance, under the punishing glare of the binary star's component suns, white Branchspell and weirdly blue Alppain. Already he has undergone the first of many metamorphoses, the growing and discarding of new organs with which to interpret his changing environment. It is a metaphysical odyssey, an amazing voyage through inner space, into a world of abstractions embodied in living shapes.

This world has a Satan, in the form of the shadow-figure Crystalman; everything which diverts the individual from the pathway to sublimity, be it pleasure, love or even beauty, is his domain. He stands before the brilliance of the true world Muspel, discolouring its purity. To paraphrase the vision of Nightspore:

> A dim, vast shadow, somehow throwing out a scent of disgusting sweetness. The fierce light streaming through it became split, as by a prism. What had been fiery spirit was now a mass of crawling, wriggling individuals, jostling and fighting and even devouring each other. They never saw beyond the Shadow. When direct movement wearied them, they fell again to killing, dancing and loving.

The shadow-world, then, is our world (and would 'killing' and 'dancing' have been juxtaposed at any time other than the years immediately following the First World War?) Our object all sublime is sublimity itself, and all other concerns are mere distractions. It is an awful goal, and Lindsay offers no convincing argument for seeking it. Like so many purveyors of high objectives, he makes the alternatives sound unduly fascinating and preferable but can scarcely hint at the nature of the Grail. Certainly, the price to be paid is measured in pain, of body, mind and spirit. In James Hilton's *Lost Horizon*, one character half-jokingly compares Shangri-La to an Oxford college; *Arcturus* has overtones of institutions featuring cold baths and hard beds. Perhaps this is why sublimity is strictly for the boys. To paraphrase again:

> But cannot women see the Muspel-light?'
> 'On one condition. They must forget their sex. Womanhood and love belong to life, while Muspel is above life.'

Lucky girls.

Still, it is not necessary to have ambitions of a transcendental kind to be enthralled by the fertility of Lindsay's imagination, the ever-changing landscapes of Tormance, the host of strange beings who help or hinder Maskull as he marches towards his ultimate metamorphosis. The journey is sufficient in itself.

First edition London: Methuen, 1920
First US edition New York: Macmillan, 1963

32
E. R. EDDISON
The Worm Ouroboros

Eric Rucker Eddison's most popular novel is part of an extensive and intricate romance in four volumes concerning an enormous Englishman, Edward Lessingham, the goddess Aphrodite and a supporting cast of millions. It differs from the three others, the Zimiamvian trio, in being more nearly pure adventure, while being told in the same exuberant, classically influenced prose.

Eddison was a highly competent civil servant who lived in an imaginative sphere far removed from Whitehall. His inner world was conceived on a grand scale and his heroes were of corresponding stature. They fought against villains of equal might who were rather more interesting as persons. Both factions conducted themselves with a lack of inhibition which Conan the Cimmerian might have found unnerving.

Apart from the presence of Lessingham, the link between *Ouroboros* and the Zimiamvian novels is extremely tenuous. He is the owner of a house in the north-west of England which is a gateway to other realities. Sitting outdoors one evening, he feels the influence of the planet Mercury and knows that he will have a visitation. A chariot drawn by a winged horse arrives at his bedroom window and bears him away. It is difficult to decide whether Lessingham is present in the flesh or as a dream-projection of himself; when he reaches his destination, he passes through objects as if either he or they were immaterial.

The Mercury Eddison describes cannot be the sun-scarred innermost planet. Lilies and Irish yews grow in the garden where Lessingham lands and the starry night could be a continuation of the terrestrial night which he left. It has been conjectured that it is the Mercury of the astrologer rather than the astronomer. Whichever, Lessingham fades from the narrative after the principal players have been introduced.

Eddison names his imaginary nations with an offhanded disregard for the misleading associations attached to such well-worn labels as Demons, Witches, Goblins and Ghouls. There is no apparent rationale; the Witchlanders practise witchcraft, but so do the others. Perhaps he just liked the sound of the words, which is almost certainly the case when he gave names to his characters. They are a fine, full-blooded crew with a truly aristocratic disregard for the wider social implications of their deeds. Seldom has any author conveyed so convincingly the sheer joy of being consciously a hero.

Gorice, King of Witchland, demands that the lords of Demonland, Juss, Goldry Blusco, Spitfire and Brandoch Daha, swear fealty to him. Goldry challenges him to a wrestling-match; if he loses, he must renounce all claim to

Demonland. Enraged by Gorice's ungentlemanly tricks, Goldry breaks his neck. This only worsens the situation. Another Gorice, a sorcerer of limitless ambition, succeeds to the throne and begins to brew up trouble for the heroes.

The chapter in which Gorice and the nerveless, melancholy traitor Lord Gro summon up a sending to blast the Demonland fleet is unrivalled as a description of demonic power barely contained. By the signs of the Crab, which adorns his iron crown, and the worm Ouroboros, which, tail in jaws, encircles the world, Gorice seizes Goldry and imprisons him in a city of brass on the stupendous heights of the mountain Zora Rach. An epic climb through regions of soul-shrivelling horror brings Juss to his rescue. By the magic of the ever-young Queen Sophonisba, herself a refugee from the depredations of Witchland, Goldry is restored to full awareness. Meanwhile, back in Demonland, Gorice and his allies are carving up the country.

The nobles and royalty of Eddison's novels are not the standard cut-out-and-colour figures prevalent in Swords and Sorcery. In the midst of battle they find breath to scheme and plot, love and murder, suffer personal tragedies and crises of conscience. Of them all, Lord Gro is the most fascinating. A doomed romantic, he is cursed with the ability to see and empathize with the motives of both sides. When the tide of war turns against one faction, be they Witches or Demons, he deserts to their colours. His behaviour points up the meaninglessness of the actions which give purpose to the lives of the warrior-lords, and is not appreciated on Mercury.

To assume that a writer shares the beliefs and attitudes of his characters is a frequent cause of misunderstanding. Sometimes, however, it is difficult to avoid the conclusion. Eddison writes of battle and slaughter with an enthusiasm which suggests a frustrated swashbuckler behind the neat civilian exterior. We can only thank Fate that he was assigned to the Board of Trade and not the War Office.

The Icelandic Eddas, with their endless tallies of feuds, deaths and betrayals, gripped his imagination in childhood. Eddison's response was unusually fervent, to the extent of setting himself to learn Icelandic. The insight thus gained into the Norseland psyche led to the writing of his Viking novel, *Stybiorn the Strong*. He does not hesitate to incorporate his other literary preferences into *Ouroboros*, where his Mercurians quote from Shakespeare, adding weight to the theory that it is all a dream of Lessingham's.

The great flaw in *Ouroboros* occurs when the Demons, bored with the fruits of victory, ask the Gods to turn Time back upon itself so that they can fight the war over again. It's the sort of behaviour that makes you think the cuckoo-clock makers have a point after all.

As *The Worm Ouroboros; a romance*
First edition   London: Jonathan Cape, 1922
First US edition   New York: Boni, 1926

33
DAVID LINDSAY
The Haunted Woman

If Hillary, after climbing Everest, had returned to find that everyone had been looking the other way at the time, he might have felt as David Lindsay did after *A Voyage to Arcturus* was published. It was remaindered with less than 600 copies sold. The mountain being too steep and the air too rarified for popular consumption, the only recourse was to descend to the plains. Brighton and its environs formed the territory of his next novel, and his characters were recognizably denizens of the 1920s.

Arcturus had baffled and upset the critics, but they had admitted to being faced with something out of the ordinary. By resorting to an outwardly conventional romantic entanglement between contemporary people, Lindsay sent them off in quite another, but equally wrong, direction. He was not writing a ghost story or a tale of star-crossed lovers; at least, not in the way in which some of them interpreted it.

It is debatable whether the supernatural justification for the strange house in *The Haunted Woman* is any more necessary than the crystal spaceship which took Maskull to Arcturus. Runhill Court incorporates part of a Saxon structure, Ulf's Tower. The upper rooms are reputed to have been removed by trolls, together with Ulf. Another version of the name is Elves' Tower. The story of Ulf, which is never challenged, is of a quite different order of fantasy, and may well have misled reviewers who were taking the novel's events at their face value. The tower as a means of access to new levels of consciousness has its counterpart in *Arcturus*.

Isbel Loment is the most powerful of the four main protagonists; to some degree, the lives of the three others are determined by her thoughts and actions. Men are strongly attracted to her, but her innate passion and intelligence has not yet been given full rein. Her peripatetic life as a ward of a wealthy aunt, drifting from hotel to hotel, is coloured only by her engagement to Marshall Stokes, an underwriter. (Lindsay worked for some years with a firm of underwriters.) When Marshall meets Judge, a widower who is thinking of selling his house, Runhill Court, Isbel's aunt is interested. Marshall and the women go to view the property.

Judge has a secondary reason for letting Marshall see the house. He has had the disorienting experience of entering a lost room, one of those mentioned in the legend. Marshall, he hopes, can offer some reassurance or at least a second opinion. Upstairs in Runhill Court, Isbel hears an almost musical vibration, apparently emanating from the fabric of the building. A visiting American artist warns her that the house could be very dangerous for someone of her peculiar temperament.

On a second visit with Marshall, who intends to enter the attic, the East Room, from which Judge gained access to the supposed missing portion of Ulf's Tower, she suffers a disabling headache and remains downstairs in the huge hall. Suddenly she sees a previously unnoticed stairway. Ascending, she finds a panelled chamber with three other doorways. Choosing the middle door, she enters another room, furnished with an oval mirror.

Her reflection startles her. The woman in the mirror displays a sexually passionate and tragic personality which she recognizes as her unawakened self. Trying another door, she finds herself back in the hall, where Marshall shortly joins her from the garden, saying he has been looking for her. The staircase has disappeared. She remembers nothing of what happened after she climbed it.

Judge accompanies her on her third visit, with a mutual acquaintance, Blanche. Blanche regards the pair's relationship with jealous hostility. Left alone again, Isbel climbs the stairs, which have reappeared. To her alarm, Judge enters the hidden chamber. He is equally confounded, having been in the East Room. Though they cannot understand the distortion of space this entails, they are aware of the strength of their mutual attraction. Afterwards, neither of them can remember the meeting.

So the theme of *Arcturus*, and of Lindsay's whole life, it might be said, resurfaces. Colin Wilson has labelled it as the 'two worlds' problem; at certain moments we may experience an intensity of being which raises our perceptions to another plane, as if our real selves had broken through the prison-wall of the everyday. But the breakthrough cannot be sustained and we sink back into our mundane half-life.

Isbel, Judge and Blanche return to Runhill Court. This time, Blanche finds them together in the lost room, but she also has changed and does not resent their love. She opens the third door, which they have always feared. From a window, she sees a beautiful summer landscape in which a man in medieval costume is playing a stringed instrument. The man turn his head and she sees his face. Not long after they leave Runhill Court, she dies. Her death is a warning; we cannot live long on the heights.

Lindsay died in 1945, partly because of blood-poisoning due to self-neglect. The cumulative effect of years of incomprehension and rejection no doubt hastened his end.

First edition   London: Methuen, 1922
First US edition   Hollywood (CA): Newcastle, 1975

34

DAVID GARNETT
Lady into Fox
A Man in the Zoo

Writers in general are a source of alarm and despondency for their nearest and dearest. To take to the typewriter, ignoring a family tradition of asset-stripping or gun-running, sets parents rummaging through their ancestry for evidence of instability. And, considering the handful of writers whose incomes have reached subsistence level, their concern is understandable.

Some, however, have the literary life thrust upon them. If your grandfather wrote *The Twilight of the Gods* and was superintendent of the British Museum Reading Room, your father was a critic and biographer and your mother a translator of Dostoyevsky, then to dig ditches would appear perverse. David Garnett, in effect, did just that when his stance as a conscientious objector led to his becoming a farm labourer during the First World War. Afterwards, together with journalist Francis Birrell, he ran a Soho bookshop, an occupation which at that time was considered respectable. Both partners were associated with the Bloomsbury Set; after the death of his first wife, Garnett married Angelica Bell, daughter of Vanessa.

The hazards of marriage were a major preoccupation of his fiction, in which the female partner figured as an unknown quantity. In *Lady into Fox*, the hero's wife literally becomes a vixen; in *The Sailor's Return*, she is an African Negress settled in an English village; a non-fictional biography, significantly, deals with Pocahontas. Josephine, in *A Man in the Zoo*, is a fairly conventional middle-class girl, but the indeterminate nature of their relationship drives her boyfriend to take refuge in Regent's Park Zoo.

Publishing these two short novels in combination emphasizes that they are, in some ways, mirror-images of each other. In the first, Richard Tebrick marries Silvia Fox (interestingly, Angelica's aunt, Virginia, married a Woolf) in what seems to be an ideal Victorian partnership. Then, suddenly, she is transformed into a small, reddish vixen. Tebrick takes ruthless measures to keep the metamorphosis a secret, out of devotion to her. In the second, John Cromartie, entangled in an uneasy relationship with Josephine Lackett, resorts to the bizarre expedient of offering himself to the Zoo as an exhibit. By assuming the identity of a captive animal, he can retreat from the larger prison of the world into the security of a cage. Paradoxically, this gives him greater public exposure than ever before.

Distancing himself from human involvements has not freed him from emotional hazards. The unprecedented crowds before his cage in the Ape

House inspire jealousy in his neighbours, the Orang-outan and the Chimpanzee. At the suggestion of a keeper, he allows one of the lesser big cats, a Caracal, to share his quarters. Incautiously, he comes within reach of the Orang-outan. Though valiantly supported by the Caracal, he loses a finger in the resulting savage struggle. For a while, the bond between man and cat seems about to parallel that between Tebrick and Silvia, but here there is competition in the form of Josephine. Surviving the illness and nightmares consequent upon the attack, Cromartie returns to his cage, only to learn that the Ape House is to become a Man House, displaying racial types. The Orang-outan goes first, replaced by a Negro, Joe Tennison.

Tebrick has attempted to divorce himself from the community, but his odd conduct draws unfavourable attention. He and his vixen take refuge in the cottage of Silvia's old Nanny, Mrs Cork, who recognizes her in her new guise. Step by step, Silvia withdraws from her conventional wifely persona. In the beginning, distressed by her 'nakedness', she had worn an adapted jacket. Soon, she tears this to rags, a preliminary to the destruction of her entire wardrobe. Rejecting tea and bread and butter, her appetites become wholly carnivorous. Tebrick, in constant fear of hunting packs as Silvia roves the fields and woods in search of bloody meat, slides gradually into unwashed, unshaven, solitary disarray. There comes a day when he finds his wife proudly mothering a litter of cubs.

Tenaciously, he clings to the one relationship that still has meaning for him. He becomes an 'uncle' to the cubs, coming to cherish them for their individual personalities, at times running clumsily with them upon all fours. At the furthest point of her recession from respectability, Silvia has found her greatest fulfilment. But the huntsmen are not to be denied. Tebrick, like Cromartie, must pay for his alienation in blood.

For Cromartie, his self-imposed exclusion ends on a happier note. Josephine, driven to distraction by the strange course of their affair, offers to join him in his cage. Benevolent though they are, the Zoo authorities draw the line at the public exhibition of married couples. And so, departing from the Zoo, Josephine and John become just another strolling pair of lovers in the Park, the Caracal forgotten. Parables, morality tales, or modern Aesop's fables, Garnett's stories defy any attempt to pigeon-hole them, and are all the better for it.

Lady into Fox
First edition   London: Chatto & Windus, 1922
First US edition   New York: Knopf, 1923

A Man in the Zoo
First edition   London: Chatto & Windus, 1924
First US edition   New York: Knopf, 1924

35
LORD DUNSANY
The King of Elfland's Daughter

Edward John Moreton Drax Plunkett, 18th Baron Dunsany, enjoyed a rare advantage when portraying the warrior-lords so beloved by Heroic Fantasy writers. He was one. Of noble Anglo-Irish lineage, he fought in the Boer War and the First World War. Also, his physique was of that elongated type popularly associated with blue blood. An ex-soldier from north-eastern England, recalling him, said that horses appeared to shrink to pony-like dimensions when Dunsany was in the saddle. He was also remembered for his generosity with the universal battlefield currency, cigarettes.

That the literary imagination could resist being coarsened and stultified by the horrors of trench warfare seems little less than miraculous. Yet more than one fantasist such as Dunsany emerged from the mud and blood with their dream-worlds intact. When he compares a witch-fire to 'the evil pool that glares where thermite has burst', the anachronism is as startling as Tolkien's reference, in *The Lord Of The Rings*, to an express train.

While Dunsany's writings are not short of references to huntin', shootin', and fishin', their very quantity and quality distance him from the stereotyped image of the landed gentry. Though his first book, *The Gods of Pegana* (1905), was published on a vanity-press basis, he had sold seven collections of short stories by 1916. Several novels and scores of shorter works followed; the anecdotal adventures of that durable club-man Mr Jorkens alone filled five volumes. His influence upon the genre has been enormous, but his style is deceptively difficult to emulate.

Dunsany's Elfland adjoins 'the fields we know', all but its highest peaks hidden by a smoky wall of accumulated twilight. This functions as a warning rather than a barrier, for it can be penetrated from either side. The peril, for human intruders, lies in the deadly fascination which Elfland exerts upon them. There, time is measured by no Earthly clock. Elvish folk only become conscious of the ageing process when they venture into the lands of men. Men who enter Elfland find that, however brief their stay, years will have passed when they return to their kin. Those who live near the frontier never look to the East, where it lies, and will not speak of it. A few wild creatures, such as foxes and unicorns, stray between the realms.

The men of Erl, whose land is perilously close to the East (Dunsany's fictional cover slips only once, when he refers to Erl's 'English grass'), are tired of their uneventful lives and ask to be ruled by a magical lord. Their ruler accedes to this request, with misgivings, and sends Alveric, his son, to seek the Elf-king's daughter, Lirazel. With the help of Ziroonderel, a friendly witch, Alveric acquires a magical black blade.

Armed with this and his father's sword, he crosses the twilight frontier. In the changeless light of Elfland, he is attacked by the trees of an enchanted wood. His father's sword proves unequal to the task, but the black blade swiftly defeats their magic. Beyond the wood, across flowery lawns, rise the silvery towers of the royal palace. Before the palace stands Princess Lirazel.

Four armoured knights advance to her defence. Having learned nothing from experience, Alveric again uses his father's sword, and again has to resort to the witch's weapon. The knights' blood flows thick and slow, crawling over their glittering armour. Instant lovers, Alveric and Lirazel flee to Erl, barely avoiding the Elf-king's retributory rune-casting.

In time, they have a son, Orion. The folk of Erl have a magical lady. For a while, everyone is contented. Then a messenger arrives from Elfland, where only moments have passed since their elopement. Lirazel's father has sent a troll to deliver to her a powerful rune. Presently, her growing awareness of age and her failure to comprehend the ways of Earth leads her to unleash the rune. Half-unwillingly, she is whisked back to Elfland. Alveric sets out to find her, but the King withdraws the boundaries of his land, beyond human reach.

Deserted by both parents, Orion's upbringing is left, in the true upper-class tradition, to the lower orders. Like his stellar namesake, he becomes a hunter. Any sympathy which his plight might arouse could well be dispelled by his notions of sport. Discovering unicorns, Orion's first, second and third impulses are to run down and slaughter them and tote their severed heads home as trophies. Finding it difficult to pursue several of them single-handed, he induces a number of trolls to act as beaters and dog-handlers. These episodes display the typically schizophrenic attitude of the huntin' fraternity, lauding the power and grace of their prey before gorily dismembering it. It is hard not to conclude that Orion and his stupefyingly self-centred parents deserve each other. Only Dunsany's gifted use of the language, and a strong vein of humour, render all of this palatable.

Magic, as a term, has today been robbed of its magic. It needs a Dunsany to recall what it once meant.

First edition   London: Putnams, 1924
First US edition   New York: Outnams, 1924

36
A. MERRITT
The Ship of Ishtar

Abraham Merritt was that rarity among pulp-magazine writers, the man who could afford to give it up. From the age of eighteen, when he became a newspaper reporter, journalism was his fulltime career until his death in 1943. In the perverse way in which such things happen, his secondary interest, fiction, brought him a degree of fame far beyond anything journalism had to offer. Six years after his death, Popular Publications produced *A. Merritt's Fantasy Magazine*; it ran for only five issues, but was the first pulp to be named after an individual author.

Merritt's explorations in Central America and his seemingly limitless knowledge of myth, legend and folklore enriched the texture of his fiction. Many readers, deluged by multicoloured torrents of descriptive prose, found it entirely too rich. To what degree he could actually visualize the scenes he described is debatable. The vast backdrops for the action of *The Moon Pool*, for instance, could bring on chromatic indigestion if translated into terms of paint and canvas. But as time passed, his prose became tighter, more disciplined, without sacrificing its exotic hues. *The Ship of Ishtar* found him at the peak of his powers. It is the most fully realized of all his fantasies.

By a happy coincidence, *Ishtar* appeared in the same year as that cinematic classic of the genre, *The Thief of Baghdad*. In an ideal world, Douglas Fairbanks and his designer, William Cameron Menzies, would have gone on to collaborate with Merritt. Fairbanks would, doubtless, have rewritten the ending, but for Merritt that would be no new experience. Not everyone approved of his disregard for the 'happily ever after' formula.

Ishtar's John Kenton is that familiar figure of the fictional 1920s, the disillusioned First World War veteran. Independently wealthy, once a keen archaeologist, he has lost his love for the past and sees no palliative for his restless spirit in the future. Then, from a dig in Babylon which he had financed, comes a block of stone, bearing a partly effaced inscription referring to the goddess Ishtar. But is it stone? Gripped by an irresistible impulse, Kenton breaks it open. Within, imprisoned for 6,000 years, is a ship, a ship of ivory and crystal upon a crystal and turquoise sea. From the bows to the mast, the deck is of ivory; from mast to stern, of ebony. Tiny figures stand on the sloping deck or man the oars in the rowers' pit. Kenton tries to pick them up, but they are immovable. Inexplicably, more and more details become visible as he watches. The figures begin to move. His New York apartment fades, dissolves. He is on the Ship of Ishtar, on a timeless sea.

The Ship, created by the gods of Assyria, symbolizes the eternal struggle between Ishtar, Goddess of Love, and dark Nergal, Lord of the Underworld.

6,000 years ago, Zarpanit, High Priestess of Ishtar, and Alusar, Priest of Nergal, fell in love; for this unforgiveable act they were set aboard the Ship to sail for ever, separated from each other by an intangible barrier dividing ivory deck from ebony. So powerful was their love that it defied even the edict of the Gods, and, united in death, they passed from the Ship. But Sharane and Klaneth, lesser servants of Ishtar and Nergal, remained, with their respective followers. Into this supernatural stalemate falls Kenton, to the alarm and bewilderment of all.

Immediately, he is embroiled in the deadly struggle. Both factions suspect him of being an agent of the opposition or a spy sent by the God of Wisdom, Nabu, for some mysterious purpose. To Kenton's own bafflement, he is intermittently swept back through space and time to his own apartment, where only minutes have elapsed for every day spent in the world of the Ship. He allies himself with Sharane and her warrior-maidens, but also forms friendships with two of Klaneth's crew who were recruited from his own world, the ape-like Gigi and the cynical Persian, Zubran. Inevitably, he and Sharane become lovers.

Kenton leads an assault upon the acolytes of Nergal and takes command of the Ship. Klaneth survives and disappears, rescued by his dark lord. Now the core of their strength is a formidable quartet—Gigi, Zubran, Kenton and a gigantic Norse oarsman, Sigurd. The Ship sails on, past golden isles riotous with blossom and brilliantly plumaged birds, islands where the cities are thronged by men and women from many lands and eras. Then Klaneth re-appears in a great bireme, crammed with warriors, and in a bloody battle succeeds in capturing Sharane.

The novel reaches its climax as Kenton storms the seven-tiered temple of the god Bel, in a magnificently staged *tour de force* of colour and action, to her rescue. But he must return, once again, to his world of slow-marching hours. And his final reckoning with Klaneth is still to come.

Send us a reprint, Gods.

First edition   New York and London: Putnams, 1926

[1925/1926]

37

FRANZ KAFKA
The Trial
The Castle

As in some shadowy horror film of the Karloff school, fog clings and curls about the two best-known novels of Franz Kafka. Visually, at least, the films share with the novels their Mid-European roots, if not their preoccupations. At the centre of each narrative is K., the nameless and perhaps partly autobiographical protagonist. Is there one K. or two? *The Trial* ends with his death, and it predates *The Castle*. Students of Kafka's life and works maintain that neither novel was completed. The very order of the chapters in *The Trial* is held to be incorrect as published. The situation is appropriately ambiguous and wholly Kafkaesque.

Literary detectives could scarcely hope for a more fruitful source of clues than 'Letter to his Father', from *Wedding Preparations in the Country* (1909), Kafka's account of his early family life. Repeatedly, he strives to stand back, to view his father whole and in relation to the rest of his world; helplessly, he falls back to the centre of the maze where his father looms, blocking all exits, overshadowing all paths.

The figures of authority, or those figureheads who symbolize authority, who dominate the halls and corridors of Kafka-land, talk and gesture and deport themselves in mysterious ways. Between them and K., a host of lesser functionaries is interposed—everyone, eventually, is in some capacity a servant of The Authorities—ostensibly to interpret for him the language he so stubbornly misunderstands. All of these things are reflected in the character of Kafka senior as portrayed by his eldest son. He is not the first, nor the last, parent of a writer to find unsought-for immortality as an ogre.

K. of *The Trial*, a competent and respected young bank official, is arrested in his rooms by two men dressed in black. Their first act, after notifying him of his arrest, is to eat his breakfast. It is his introduction to a hitherto unsuspected world in which Justice and the Law appear to intersect as randomly as sub-atomic particles. No crime is specified. No crime is ever specified. Nor is the offender gaoled. He is allowed to go about his business at the bank, but the Law has not forgotten him.

The K. of *The Castle* is no solid citizen established within a prosperous society. He is an outsider, a Land Surveyor summoned by the lord of the eponymous Castle. His arrival in the village below the Castle is unauspicious. There is no record of his being asked to act on the lord's behalf. There is almost unanimous agreement on the undesirability of a Land Surveyor. His attempt to go directly to the Castle is thwarted by snow, misleading streets and the hostile reticence of the villagers. Like an exhausted mountaineer, he retreats to the lower slopes, to regain his strength and plan his route afresh.

As if embedded in a universe of cottonwool, the two K.s thresh about, seeking a purchase upon reality. But the reality surrounding them is encoded in a language in which everyone, save themselves, seems fluent. As they cease to integrate with society, their status dwindles. K.-2 seeks an audience with the enigmatic Klamm, an inhabitant of the Castle who spends much time in the village, but Klamm evades him. Sharing with Kafka and K.-1 a propensity for getting involved in inconclusive love-affairs, he has by now become engaged to a village girl, Frieda. He takes the post of school janitor, temporarily abandoning land surveying. There being no house available, the pair move into a classroom and set up home. As there are only two classrooms, they are forced to move back and forth between them as the teaching schedule dictates.

With this episode, and many others, Kafka comes closer to the Marx Brothers than to Karloff. The novels could be described as tragedies enacted in a series of farcical incidents. For K. the bank official, the farce ends and his uncertainties are brutally resolved. For the surveyor turned janitor, still gamely floundering on when his tale ends in mid-reel, the farce continues but judgement has been indefinitely suspended.

Kafka suffered from tuberculosis, a common enough complaint of his time. To this, perhaps, may be attributed the recurring sickness and lassitude which afflicts several of his characters. He died of it in 1924, leaving instructions regarding the burning of his papers, which were of truly Kafkaesque ambiguity. They were ignored. K. would not have expected it to be otherwise.

The Trial
First edition   London: Gollancz, 1937
First US edition   New York: Knopf, 1937
(originally Der Process   Berlin: Die Schmiede, 1925)

The Castle
First edition   London: Secker, 1930
First US edition   New York: Knopf, 1930
(originally Das Schloss   Munich: Wolff, 1926)

38
JOHN BUCHAN
Witch Wood

Buchan's reputation as a chronicler of the doings of tweedy, athletic patriots has tended to obscure other aspects of his fiction. The three more or less inaccurate films based upon *The 39 Steps*, which reached their nadir with Richard Hannay dangling from the hands of Big Ben, as if the director had just caught up with Will Hay's *My Learned Friend*, probably helped to perpetuate the error. Strangeness does manifest itself, however, even in such epics of derring-do as *The Courts of the Morning*, where the Poison Jungle might well have sprung from the pages of A. Merritt. In *Witch Wood* it is his talent for the historical and supernatural which comes to the fore.

A knowledge of seventeenth-century Scottish history will help in reading *Witch Wood* (Buchan's studies, *Cromwell* and *Montrose*, cover the period), but isn't strictly necessary. Like so much of Scottish history, it was a time of turmoil. In the tiny parish of Woodilee, the great events, wars and political struggles, are as distant as the moon. News of the wider world filters in via packmen and other travellers. The essential matters—crops, cattle, births and deaths—are the main concerns of everyday life. And the advent of a new, young minister is a major event.

The Rev David Sempill comes to Woodilee with high hopes and fond memories of boyhood holidays spent there with his grandfather, a miller. To be Woodilee's minister is the fulfilment of his dreams. He has not been long established, however, before he begins to see the parish with other eyes than those of childhood. The forest encircles Woodlilee, a remnant of that ancient wood which once covered Britain. For some, it bears the name 'Melanudrigill', a name of old and evil repute. Though his housekeeper, Isobel, warns him against venturing into the 'Wud' at night, he rides out to visit a sick parishioner and takes the forest path.

Buchan builds up an atmosphere of foreboding, of lurking, undefined malice, almost entirely by the use of light and landscape. In Sempill's first passage of the 'Wud', the Black Wood, no tangible enemy is seen but the threat is there. The night-sounds of the forest are disquieting rather than reassuring. Naturally courageous and buoyed up by a sense of vocation, Sempill is not deterred from completing his errand of mercy. It is the death of the woman he rode to see, and the distress of her husband, which stays with him afterwards, not memories of a haunted trail. He is young and conscious of his limited experience of the harsher facts of life.

Life for the new minister is destined to become more complex and perilous than he could have dreamed, and soon. The outer world intrudes upon Woodilee with warfare and religious controversy, and he becomes personally involved. Always having had a secret wish to be a soldier and adventurer, he is drawn to the mysterious Montrose, who is regarded by the local Kirk dignitaries as a bloody-handed agent of the enemy. Even more shockingly, he stumbles upon Satanic rites in progress in the Black Wood. While seeking to break up the gathering, he is beaten unconscious. Recovering, he resolves to root out the coven members from among his flock.

Increasingly, Sempill becomes the odd man out, and his view of the world and his mission is transformed by a rapid succession of events. The ministers of the Kirk regard him, almost unanimously, as a heretic and bring him to trial; his parishioners obdurately resist his exhortations to abandon their Satanic master; only a handful are willing to pit themselves against the dark power of Melanudrigill. In a vale not far from the Devil's altar, he meets Katrine, niece of an aristocratic neighbour. They fall in love, a love which ends in tragedy. He spies upon another meeting in the wood, to identify the coven members, but his evidence is rejected by a hostile Kirk, the more so as one of the accused is a prominent churchman.

And then, falling impartially upon the just and the unjust, the young and the old, comes the Plague.

Together with Katrine, Mark Kerr, an officer of Montrose's now defeated army who has taken on a new identity with David's help, and a few others, Sempill fights the dreaded scourge. The terrible isolation of a pre-industrial village, the fear which keeps the outer world at a distance and the devasting effects upon a farming community of sickness are impressively realized. The Plague passes, but there is a reckoning to come; someone must be held responsible for such a visitation. A disgraced minister is an obvious target for Divine wrath . . . Sempill finally confronts the leader of the witch-cult, but he has lost his own vocation; what action must he take?

Witch Wood holds little for the tomato-ketchup school of horror enthusiasts; its supernatural elements are firmly rooted in the life of the countryside and the unchanging weaknesses and strengths of humanity.

First edition   London: Hodder & Stoughton, 1927
First US edition   Boston: Mifflin, 1927

39
CHARLES WILLIAMS
War in Heaven

Charles Williams was a member of that donnish literary fraternity which included C. S. Lewis and J. R. R. Tolkien. All three shared an interest in Fantasy, with an emphasis upon exploring the nature of religion and morality. Tolkien, a Catholic, has been criticized, rather short-sightedly, for the alleged absence of religion in *The Lord of the Rings*. Lewis and Williams, both Anglicans, made Christianity the central theme of their fiction, though elements of Tolkien's invented mythology crept into Lewis's Dr Ransom trilogy.

War in Heaven concerns a struggle for possession of the Holy Grail, or Graal, embodied in the form of chalice. It opens in a manner deceptively similar to the kind of period murder mystery anathematized by Raymond Chandler. Most characters have three-syllabled surnames and snobbery is rampant. Anyone below middle-class status is either comical or contemptible; the first murder victim's social standing (low) evokes more comment than his condition.

The body in question is discovered beneath a table in the offices of a London publisher, Stephen Persimmons. Under the management of Stephen's father, Gregory, the firm had published unprofitable works on occult subjects; Stephen continued to produce religious titles, though of a more orthodox nature. To Inspector Colquhoun, conducting the murder investigation, this information is at first of only incidental interest.

Then the unpleasant Sir Giles Tumulty, author of *Sacred Vessels in Folklore*, asks for a paragraph purporting to give the location of the Graal to be deleted from his MS. A visting Archdeacon, Julian Davenant, sees the uncorrected MS and is surprised to find that the Graal reposes in his parish church in the village of Fardles. Unknown to him, Gregory Persimmons has just bought a country house near Fardles, to which he invites one of the staff, Lionel Rackstraw, with wife, Barbara, and child, Adrian.

Davenant, who might have given Father Brown a few pointers, cannily says nothing about the Graal. Back at Fardles, he transfers the undistinguished-looking chalice from the church to the rectory. Objects, even such an object as this, have no hold over him, but he is worldly enough to foresee the upheaval it could cause.

Upheaval begins that very afternoon, in the shape of Gregory. Spinning a tale about a priest who needs altar furniture for a mission church, he asks for: '. . . the extra chalice . . . you didn't often use'. Davenant politely refuses. Shortly afterwards, the church is broken into and despoiled. A stranger appears at the rectory gate, asking for work and food, none too convincingly.

The Archdeacon resolves to stow the chalice in a bank-vault in the nearest town. Setting off for the railway station, he is waylaid, stunned and robbed.

Gregory, the thief, has acted upon information given him by Tumulty. He wants to use the Graal as an instrument to further his occult activities; his particular purpose is to raise Adrian as a disciple of Satan, after disposing of Lionel and Barbara. Tumulty tells him where to obtain a certain ointment, which, when applied by an initiate, can put him in touch with Satanic forces. Misapplied, it can condemn the user to an Earthly Hell. He goes to a dingy chemist's shop off the Finchley Road, in a street described as: 'One of those . . . terraces of slime which hang over the pit of Hell'. A rare Lovecraftian passage.

With the help of a Catholic duke, the resourceful Archdeacon recovers the chalice from Gregory's house in an episode more comical than dramatic. At one point in the novel, two characters express admiration for the Jeeves stories. Plainly they are speaking for the author, who at times slips into a Wodehouse-like style. It is a measure of his skill that he can go on to re-create the requisite atmosphere of supernatural menace after such sequences.

Gregory returns to Finchley Road and meets Manasseh, a Jew deeply versed in the black arts. Manasseh's sole aim is destruction—of Heaven itself, if such an end can be achieved. Using Gregory as a focus, he launches an attack upon the Graal, but is defeated by Davenant and his allies. Barbara, however, has fallen victim to Gregory's witchcraft and is beyond their help. Adrian is left in great spiritual peril. A stranger enters the game, calling himself Prester John, to the mystification of both parties. Meanwhile, the police succeed in connecting the murder with the devilish clique.

Manasseh captures the Graal and the Archdeacon, who is to have the role of sacrificial victim. The shop disappears, apparently withdrawn from normal space, leaving the police baffled. Within, the struggle between Darkness and Light rages, and the world's fate trembles in the balance.

The situation was not new, even then, nor its inevitable outcome. The difference is that Williams was a believer, and it shows.

First edition   London: Gollancz, 1930
First US edition   New York: Pellegrini, 1949

40
THORNE SMITH
Turnabout

Europe and America reeled, shell-shocked, out of the trenches in 1918 and blundered into a minefield of sex, jazz and bootleg liquor, re-emerging just in time to sign on for the second round. Or so popular fiction would have it. Writers seized upon the more exploitable aspects of the age and distilled from them a new kind of humour. The wisecrack, America's substitute for the stiff · upper lip, was born. Hollywood bought it by the ton, processed it and fed it to the millions who queued six nights of the week at the picture palaces. They would have queued on the seventh too, had the Law allowed.

To sex, liquor and jazz, Thorne Smith added a touch of the fantastic. The results, almost inevitably, found their way to the cinema screens and were preserved for future audiences by the voracious appetite of television. Though the filmmakers of the day had to tone down the more risqué incidents of Smith's stories, they were adept at verbal and visual innuendo. What remained, enhanced by camera wizardry, was sufficiently titillatory. Players such as Roland Young and Constance Bennett will be for ever associated with his characters.

The turnabout in question is one of gender. Tim Willows, an early example of Advertising Man as hero, is given an Egyptian statuette as a wedding present by his dissolute Uncle Dick. Five years on, Tim and his wife Sally, are beginning to view each other with critical eyes. Sally, waiting with mounting exasperation for her husband to summon up sufficient resolve to remove his socks, speculates about local Lothario Carl Bentley. Soon she and Tim are locked in one of those inconsequential and acerbic dialogues of which Smith was a master. Mr Ram, the Egyptian figure, watches from the bookcase and decides that the time is ripe for teaching them a lesson.

Things begin to go askew independently of Mr Ram. During a drunken party, Tim finds Carl embracing Sally in the kitchen and cools his ardour with a rolling-pin. Convinced that the blow was fatal, the couple, after a rambling and gin-fuelled discussion, decide to park the body in the basement. When victim and 'murderer' come face to face on the commuter train next day, both are disconcerted, though Carl little suspects that a sore head will soon prove to be the least of his worries. Tim is equally unaware that it is to be his last working day at the Nationwide Agency. In a way.

Rolling out of bed on the following morning, he finds that Sally has unaccountably got between him and the bedroom mirror, blocking his view of himself. Also, her reflection is silently mimicking his requests for her to move aside. Only when his own body suddenly hurtles out of the bathroom, shrieking, does he grasp the awful truth. The reflection is his own. Mr Ram has granted their frequent wishes to swap lives, in the most literal way.

Sally, at first revelling in her masculine strength, threatens to submit Tim to a fate worse than death. Her elation wavers when she realizes that she must now take his place at the Agency, to keep them from the breadline. Meeting the unfortunate Carl on the train, she turns his journey into a nightmare by professing ardent love for him. She goes on to create havoc at the office by unthinkingly walking into the ladies rest-room. Her husband, rising late, wrestles with the mysteries of the feminine wardrobe *circa* 1933. His efforts, plus some bold experiments with make-up, produce an effect which stuns the domestics and Sally's friends alike.

The incidents become progressively more outrageous. Separately, the two are disrupters of the status quo; together, with a little help from a hip-flask, they devastate such worthy occasions as church suppers. Tim gets a kick out of disabling lecherous males, but his murderous reactions are reserved for his doctor, when pregnancy sets in.

Light-hearted as the novel is, it still makes some pertinent comments upon the routine indignities inflicted upon women in a man's world. There is worse to follow for Tim, as his childbearing female neighbours enthusiastically regale him with tales of obstetrical horrors. He carries the additional burden of knowing that his former body is responsible for his plight. Carl, as always, suffers. Making a pass at 'Sally', he finds himself, clad only in an inadequately buttoned union suit, being chased along the main street by the gun-toting object of his affections.

Tim has been composing most of the advertising copy supposedly written by Sally. Fortuitously faced with the task of writing a piece about union suits, he is inspired by the Carl Bentley debacle to produce the sort of advertisement he has often longed to read. It appears in print. Sally–Tim is fired, to no one's surprise.

To say that all ends more or less happily, after further confusion and scandal, is not to give anything away. Smith, in a tongue-in-cheek postscript, describes himself as one of America's greatest realists. Certainly it is his shrewd eye for society's foibles which firmly underpins even the wildest of his fantasies.

First edition   Garden City (NY): Doubleday, 1931
First UK edition   London: Barker, 1935

41
THORNE SMITH
The Night Life of the Gods

Take a tall, lean, sardonic scientist who spends most of his time in his private laboratory; a scientist who plays it by ear, achieving his goals by unorthodox means; a scientist who invents his own drinks, has an incredible capacity for alcohol and sings tunelessly while he works. Hands up all of the Henry Kuttner aka Lewis Padgett fans who recognize Galloway Gallagher. You're wrong. Any Thorne Smith fan knows that we're talking about Hunter Hawk, who preceded Gallagher by a decade, alliteration and all.

One of the ways in which the worlds of Hawk and Gallagher differ is in the use made of them by their respective authors. It is the difference between the devotee and the dilettante of SF and Fantasy. Gallagher is Kuttner's affectionate parody of a hackneyed figure, the eccentric scientific genius. He inhabits a future constructed during the years immediately before and after Hiroshima, a future which proved accurate in numerous respects, though oddly free from the shadow of nuclear Armageddon. Much of Kuttner's fiction, even at its lightest, carried an implied threat lurking in the wings.

Smith's Hawk is fixed firmly in the short hectic era between 1919 and 1934. Like Kuttner, Smith died in his mid-forties. He made little distinction between magic and science; ghosts, gadgets and errant gods alike served to disrupt what passed for the social order, though their effects were not lasting. Gallagher was a working researcher, if an erratic one, while Hawk had independent means. Smith's barbs were aimed at the speakeasy society, the suburban swingers whose activities, suitably sanitized, provided material for Hollywood screenwriters. Anything that was spilled as a result was less likely to be blood than bathtub bourbon.

Gladys Lambert, Hunter Hawk's sister, imposes her family upon his reluctant hospitality after Mr Lambert's business goes broke. The only likable member of her otherwise obnoxious clan is her daughter, Daphne. A real affection exists between niece and uncle, surviving even the frequent explosions caused by his experiments. These are resented by the others for the damage inflicted upon what they already regard as their own property. Like the nervous associates of The Man in the White Suit, they cannot foresee that the real trouble will begin only when the explosions stop. Hunter has perfected the ideal anti-relative device—a ray which turns living flesh into the semblance of stone.

After Ian Fleming had taught the world to love the pleasures of Bondage, an invention with such peculiar possibilities would have involved any fictional scientist in Cold War capers. In 1934, it could have furnished a diversion fot Bulldog Drummond, when he wasn't whipping moneylenders or strangling gorillas. Smith's imagination didn't work that way. Scarcely has Hunter petrified the Lamberts, all save Daphne, before he meets Ludwig Turner, one of the Little People (about Barry Fitzgerald size), and his dangerous dark-eyed daughter, Megaera. Meg has had 200 years in which to perfect the gentle art of getting what she wants, and what she wants is Hunter. She is also impressed by his petrification ray, the more so because she has the complementary ability to bring statues to life. A little time and a lot of alcohol later, they unleash their powers in the hushed galleries of New York's Metropolitan Museum.

Surrounded by stony deities, their next move is only too predictable. Rather than relying upon their own knowledge of the habits and personalities of the Olympians, they animate Mercury, the gossip-monger of the Gods. He selects a group guaranteed to liven up any party. Manhattan is about to play unwitting host to Bacchus, Neptune, Hebe the cup-bearer, Apollo, Diana and her bow, Venus and valiant Perseus, who refuses to be parted from the head of Medusa.

Clothing is the first necessity, meaning that a boisterious bunch of near-naked Greek divinities has to be transported to an outfitters on Broadway, leaving that normally *blasé* thoroughfare reeling. Shelter, food and drink, particularly drink, come next, leading to a surrealistic episode in a fish restaurant in which Perseus insists upon setting Medusa's head next to his plate and plying her with wine until she bursts into maudlin song. Those indispensable straight men, New York's cops, come in for some rough handling as the Gods leave a trail of gratified and petrified diners, swimmers who have sunk, literally, like stones, and one inconvenienced but adaptable clergyman behind them, before being besieged behind the walls of Hunter Hawk's home.

As the forces of law and reaction close in, Hunter concludes that America no longer has a place for free spirits. He and Meg are as anachronistic as the Gods. In a rare passage which suggests a corrosive core to Smith's flippancy, he has Hunter declare: 'I leave the field to the filthy, criticising, vice-coveting tribe that . . . sets the standard of life.' It could be an epitaph.

First edition   Garden City (NY): Doubleday, 1931
First UK edition   London: Barker, 1934

42
A. MERRITT
Dwellers in the Mirage

A monstrous Luciferean face weeping golden tears; a ship of the Gods breaking from a stone cocoon 6,000 years old; a city of sentient metal sledge-hammered into ruin by rebellious colossi—these and many other memorable images from Merritt's pen influenced younger writers such as Jack Williamson, Henry Kuttner and Hannes Bok. Williamson's *The Alien Intelligence* (1929) drew compliments and advice from his exemplar. Artist-author Bok, as deft with words as with a brush, completed fragmentary narratives left after Merritt's death. The prolific and versatile Kuttner wrote an exciting parallel-Earth novel, *The Dark World* (1946), his cover version of *Dwellers in the Mirage*.

The mirage in question is no desert illusion but a freakish phenomenon hiding a lost land within an Alaskan valley. When Leif Langdon and his Cherokee Indian partner, Jim Two Eagles, go gold-prospecting and hear drums in the north, the sound revives haunting memories for one of them. Three years before, during a scientific expedition to the Gobi Desert, Leif had listened to the drums of Uighur tribesmen summoning a dreadful entity from beyond this world. Clad in faded ceremonial robes generations old, the Uighur hailed Leif as the reincarnation of their ancient hero, Dwayanu.

Yellow-haired, tall and massively muscled, he is the epitome of the migratory warriors who had stormed out of the heart of Asia to become the feared Norsemen. To the Uighur, he is the one who will restore their greatness and reunite them with the legendary lost colony founded by their distant fore-fathers. Above all, he is the summoner of Khalk'ru, the Annihilator. In that capacity, not suspecting what was to come, he saw a young girl sacrificed. This hateful memory has haunted him ever since he fled the Uighur temple. Yet something compels him to retain the massive ring which bears the image of Khalk'ru set within a yellow stone.

Jim Two Eagles, like so many ethnic persons in fantasy, is acutely conscious of his tribal traditions. As he accompanies Leif towards the drum-loud Alaskan hills, he is receiving warnings from the spirits of his ancestors, but he will not desert a friend. Where the drums beat, they find a valley ringed by sheer cliffs, with a floor of glacial rubble. As they watch, the rubble becomes a field of black, pyramidal stones, only to dissolve into a blue lake. They guess that layers of cold and warm air, and trapped carbon dioxide, form a ceiling over the valley which generates mirages. Only which is the illusion and which the reality?

Once below the mirage, the valley is stranger than they could have imagined. Towering trees, giant ferns and exotic flowers proliferate in the green-tinged dusk. Golden-skinned pygmies, led by a girl from the outer world, Evalie, inhabit this wild garden. Leif and Jim, in rescuing a chained pygmy warrior, discover that his language is derived from the same Mongolian roots as Jim's Cherokee dialect. The rescue brings them into conflict with Lur, the witch-woman of the Ayjir; the Ayjir stronghold, Karak, is at the other end of the valley. The clash reawakens the dormant ego of Dwayanu within Leif, which the pygmies sense, and fear. Stronger and stronger grows Dwayanu's influence, flooding his mind with atavistic memories.

He goes to Karak, where the Ayjir are reluctant to accept his new persona. In a trial of speed and strength he defeats red-haired Tibur, the hammer-thrower, at his own deadly game. Their scepticism is shaken. When he tells them that he has visited the Uighur homeland, their doubts return, for they believe that the world beyond the valley is a howling desert, destroyed by the wrath of Khalk'ru. Sight of the ring bearing Khalk'ru's symbol does not wholly convince them. Only Lur, the beautiful witch-woman, is willing to form an alliance with him, but her motives are suspect. Leif is caught between the need to maintain supremacy over Dwayanu and his desire to tap the other's knowledge of these arrogant, devious warrior-aristocrats.

As Dwayanu, he confronts the Annihilator. In this valley, Khalk'ru's presence is overwhelming, infinitely more terrifying than in the crumbling temple in the Gobi. A colossal yellow disc, an amber portal twenty times the height of a man, is his doorway into the world of life. His incredible body recedes into the nothingness beyond the lens, while writhing black tentacles reach through to grasp the chained sacrificial victims. Even as Leif–Dwayanu summons him, the Ayjir plot to sacrifice the reborn hero to their alien god. Then the long strife between the valley peoples comes to a head, as Evalie and her golden-skinned allies storm the fortress of their oppressors.

Can the Annihilator be banished from Earth? Will it be Leif or Dwayanu, Lur or Evalie, after the final reckoning? The ending, on a note of regret, lingers in the memory.

First edition   New York: Liveright, 1932
First UK edition   London: Skeffington, 1933

43

CLARK ASHTON SMITH
Zothique

To be young, consumptive, commercially unsuccessful, resident in a garret and surrounded by one's great but unsold works, was the romantic vision of the artist's life. Artists themselves, always susceptible to their own fictions, subscribed to it in spirit. It had the useful virtue of casting a glamour over unswept floors, peeling paintwork, last week's unwashed crockery. Clark Ashton Smith, one of Fantasy's great romantics, may never have lived in a garret, but he was no stranger to dust.

The sixteen stories and one poem making up *Zothique* were written and published between 1932 and 1951. Taken in sequence, they form a fragmented history of Earth's last continent, in a remote age when science has been forgotten and magic reigns supreme. Verse and the short story were Smith's chosen vehicles; his sole attempt to write a novel was abandoned after a few thousand words. He was the master of the short, intensely vivid narrative, in which the borderline between poetry and prose is frequently blurred.

These chronicles of far stars and distant epochs were for the most part written in a wood and tarpaper cabin standing amid blue oaks near Auburn, California. Paintings and carvings, Smith's own handiwork, shared the interior with the hundreds of books which overflowed from shelves and boxes. A visitor, George Haas, recalled that when Smith picked up one volume and blew on it, the resulting cloud of dust in the hot enclosed air almost choked them. Not surprisingly, much of his writing was done outdoors, under the sheltering oaks.

Though accounted a brilliant poet by his contemporaries, his verses were largely ignored by the wider world. An admirer of Baudelaire, he taught himself French within a year in order to read his poems in the original language and translate them. He was for a time associated with the San Francisco circle, referred to in Leiber's *Our Lady of Darkness*, which included such luminaries as Jack London and Ambrose Bierce, but his own death in 1961 at the age of sixty-nine went almost unremarked. It took a change in the reading public's response to Fantasy to bring his work back into the limelight, where it belongs.

The upsurge in the market was heaven-sent for imitators of Tolkien, Burroughs, Howard and other established names. Smith was a tougher proposition. His mordant humour and fondness for irony, expressed in an incredibly rich vocabulary replete with archaisms, real or invented, defied even superficial imitation. As lovers of the macabre, he and his long-time correspondent H. P. Lovecraft ran a close race; if Death had ever decided to hire a good PR man, Smith would have filled the bill. His characters differed most markedly from Lovecraft's in that they acknowledged the existence of sex. It was this, combined with his fondness for sombre colours, which probably inspired the joke about his favourite girlfriend being Funereal Violet.

Lin Carter, in editing *Zothique*, has worked out the chronological sequence of the stories from internal evidence. Thus 'Xeethra' (1936) is the true beginning of events, while 'The Empire of the Necromancers' (1932) was the first to be published. In the latter, a grotesque duo of necromancers is unleashed upon the myriad tombs of ancient Cincor, a land '. . . drear and leprous below the huge, ember-coloured sun . . . peopled only by the bones and mummies of a race that the pestilence had slain . . .'

Plagues figure prominently in the history of Zothique, magic apparently being no sure antidote for their ravages. The dead take on the qualities of the landscape—shrunken, dimmed but enduring. Awakened to a sere semblance of life to indulge the whims of the dreadful pair, they are still capable of recalling their heritage of sorcerous lore and wreaking a hideously apt revenge.

Love and lust have not relinquished their place in human affairs while civilization ebbs, though their character reflects the mood of Earth's twilight. Prince Yadar, in 'Necromancy in Naat', finds 'a shadowy love and a dim contentment' with the beautiful Dalili, their future assured by the fact that they are already dead. 'The Witchcraft of Ulua', princess of Tasuun, is employed to break down the resistance of her youthful and virginal cup-bearer, Amalzain. As anyone but Ulua might have guessed, nocturnal visitations by worm-nibbled succubi stiffen nothing but his resistance. Shepherd-girl Rubalsa, assailed by 'The Black Abbot of Puthuum', emerges unscathed from his eldritch attentions and lives to choose her own mate, an almost cloyingly sentimental conclusion by Smithian standards.

The apex of incarnadined horror is achieved with 'The Dark Eidolon', the tale of a childhood injury avenged on a scale which would tax the visual resources of a major studio. Not for the first or last time, Smith crams enough colour and *outré* incident into a short story to fill the average novel. His wizardry surpasses that of his fictional sorcerers; his words are incantations; his images, like the hieroglyphics of Vergama, burn in the mind's eye and engage the imagination long after the last page has been turned.

First edition New York: Ballantine, 1970

44
GUY ENDORE
The Werewolf of Paris

To a generation of New Europeans, the significance of Paris for Anglo-Saxon travellers of an earlier vintage must be hard to grasp. Until London raised her skirts, stepped up the noise level and invented a whole new range of souvenir junk, the French capital had been a synonym for sexual licence when seen from the grey cliffs of Britain or the small-town Main Streets of Middle America. Robert W. Chambers, an American writer who pre-dated Endore, went there in 1886 as an art student. The result was a series of stories reflecting the many moods of the city: frothy, romantic, haunted, horrific. Endore's novel begins in a manner reminiscent of Chambers in a lighter vein as the narrator, an American literary researcher, unwillingly agrees to act as escort to a fellow-countrywoman, Eliane.

Following a squabble when she insists on stripping in an all-night restaurant, Eliane leaves with one of the customers. The narrator, walking home, is accosted by an apparent prostitute. He declines her offer, whereupon she confesses to being a nymphomaniac who uses the profession as a disguise. Disturbed by her manifest distress, he passes on and meets two scavengers sorting through their harvest of discarded treasures. Among these is an MS which proves to be a written defence, by one Aymar Galliez, of Sergeant Bertrand Caillet at his court-martial after the siege of Paris in 1871.

We are already in murky waters before the MS, the main body of the novel, has been examined. Endore, as the author of a fictional biography of de Sade and a translation of Hanns Ewers's sensational *Alraune*, was no stranger to the subject of aberrant sexual behaviour. Obviously, he was also familiar with the real-life court-martial of Sergeant Victor Bertrand, known as 'The Vampire', whose necrophiliac outrages horrified Paris in 1849. The remarkably lenient verdict, a sentence of one year's imprisonment, was, however, scarcely the stuff of drama.

The novel's preamble tells of a feud between two families, the Pitamonts and the Pitavals. Captured after murdering two Pitavals while disguised as a monk, Jehan Pitamont is bricked up in a well and fed on raw meat. Gradually he loses the power of articulate speech and can only howl like a wolf.

The scene shifts to nineteenth-century Paris, where Aymar's aunt, Mme Didier, employs an orphaned servant-girl, Josephine. After being seduced and made pregnant by a priest, Father Pitamont, the girl becomes promiscuous and has a covert affair with Aymar. When Pitamont's son is born, he has hair upon his palms and eyebrows which meet across the bridge of his nose. Mme Didier declares these characteristics to be the marks of the wolf.

At the moment of her death, the infant, though not present in the room, gives voice to animal-like cries.

From Paris, the household moves to the family farm, where Aymar's scepticism regarding his aunt's beliefs falters in the face of the boy Bertrand's odd behaviour. Farm animals are being slaughtered as if by some beast of prey. As wolves are no longer present in the area, locally owned dogs are suspected. But old superstitions and traditional remedies reassert themselves as the butchery continues. Aymar, finding Bertrand prostrate and bleeding, is shocked to discover that his injury results from a silver bullet. The boy confesses to having vivid dreams in which he becomes a wolf. Aymar takes desperate measures, barring the window of Bertrand's room and locking him in at night. For a while, the dreams and killings cease.

The respite is only temporary. When they recur, Aymar, inspired, puts him on a diet of raw meat. Matters return to normal, until Bertrand and other local youths go to Paris to sit their educational examinations. During a visit to a brothel, he savagely attacks a girl, leaving her scarred by bites. Aymar punishes him, but the situation has gone beyond control. Bertrand, after committing incest with his not wholly unwilling mother, kills and partly devours another youth before fleeing to the anonymity of Paris.

Though the capital is about to be laid under siege by the Prussians, Aymar doggedly pursues him. Reluctant to explain the improbable nature of his mission to his old Republican comrades, he scans the newspapers for reports of unusual murders. He is soon convinced that Bertrand is at large. The afflicted youth, in fact, has joined the National Guard under the alias of Caillet and is carrying on a doomed affair with the rich and beautiful Sophie Blumenberg. As her awakened sexuality drives her to ever greater excesses, she allows him to feed upon her blood, until her body is a cicatrized record of their mutual need.

While Prussian armies tighten their grip upon Paris, Aymar observes the growing inhumanity of his fellows on and behind the barricades, and wonders if the acts of the werewolf are still distinguishable from those of the mass. And as food supplies dwindle, strange meats become acceptable to all. In the end, Bertrand Caillet's fate involves no silver bullets; it is one which society can still mete out to its misfits.

First edition   New York: Farrar & Rinehart, 1933
First UK edition   London: Hamilton, 1963

45
JAMES HILTON
Lost Horizon

To add a phrase to the language is something granted to few writers. James Hilton did it twice. 'Goodbye, Mr Chips' has been exploited by countless comedians, while 'Shangri-La' rivals 'Utopia' as a synonym for perfection upon Earth. Both of the novels which featured them were filmed, and eventually became victims of the musical remake syndrome. *Lost Horizon*, that most urbane of Utopian adventures, suffered most from the transformation.

By 1933 the number of plausible locations for lost lands was rapidly decreasing. Hilton set his demi-paradise in a valley tucked deep within towering mountains fringing the Tibetan plateau. Sheltered by precipitous rocky walls, the Valley of the Blue Moon is warm and fertile, a green anomaly amid the glacial peaks. The inhabitants are a mixture of Tibetan and Chinese blood, but 'cleaner and handsomer than the average of either race'. A vertical mile above them perches the lamasery of Shangri-La, residence of the intellectual and administrative elite and a treasure-house of art and literature from many lands and eras. Many of the lamas are white Europeans.

Four passengers, fleeing by 'plane from a revolution-torn Indian state, are kidnapped by their pilot. After a cold and interminable flight, they crash-land in a high, windswept valley. The pilot, a Chinese, dies of his injuries. As the four debate their next move, a party of Asiatics appears. The leader invites them to a nearby lamasery, Shangri-La. There is no alternative but to accept.

Of the four, Conway, a British Consul, adapts most readily to the situation. The others—Barnard, an American businessman, Mallinson, a younger colleague of Conway, and Miss Brinklow, a missionary—find it less acceptable. Their desire to return to the outer world is met with courteous unhelpfulness. Yes, a party of porters may be coming to the valley, sometime. No, they would be unlikely to agree to escort strangers back across the mountains. Meanwhile, is there not much to see, to enjoy, to learn? The very air is at once stimulating and soothing.

Gradually, they become accustomed to the pace of life in the Valley of the Blue Moon and to find employment for their various skills and talents. All save Mallinson, to whom it is a prison. He hero-worships Conway and is appalled by the effect it is having upon someone he regards as a man of action. Desperate to find someone who shares his misgivings, he befriends Lo-Tsen, a beautiful Manchu girl younger than himself, or apparently so.

Mallinson sees only one aspect of Conway's complex nature. A brilliant Oxford scholar and athlete, Conway returned from the Great War a changed man. When the situation demands it, he is the cool, competent leader admired by Mallinson, but at heart he is non-competitive, seeking satisfaction from his work rather than prestige. Shangri-La, with its philosophy of the middle way and avoidance of extremes, is tailored to his personal needs. When he learns that their presence there was brought about deliberately and that he has been singled out as the High Lama's successor, he is intrigued rather than dismayed. Nor does he seriously question the revelation that the High Lama was once a Capuchin friar who, as Father Perrault, came to Shangri-La in 1719. Many other guests, voluntary and otherwise, have reached advanced but active years: 'The Tibetans . . . are charming people . . . but I doubt if more than a few will pass their hundredth year. The Chinese . . . are better, but . . . have a high percentage of failures. Our best subjects are the Nordic and Latin races of Europe; perhaps the Americans would be equally adaptable . . .' There are uncanny echoes of another philosophy, an inverse Shangri-La, soon to be established in Europe in that year of 1933.

Some time later, the High Lama dies. Conway's destiny seems assured; it remains only for him to accept it. The outer world has not entirely lost its hold, however. Mallinson says that Lo-Tsen will go with him from Shangri-La and that the porters have been persuaded to take them. Will Conway escape too? A sense of responsibility for the immature Mallinson revives old habits of thought, shaking his belief in his dream-like refuge. He leaves Shangri-La.

The aftermath of his decision is reconstructed by a writer and Oxford contemporary of Conway's who finds him in a Catholic mission in Chung-Kiang in a state of amnesia. Later, the writer, Rutherford, learns that Conway arrived at the mission accompanied only by an incredibly aged Chinese woman, who died soon afterwards. Conway himself, when he recovers, will say nothing of what happened between Shangri-La and Chung-Kiang; he disappears again, telling Rutherford that he intends to head 'north-west'. Fade-out . . .

Did he find his dream-world again, his refuge from a civilization bent on self-destruction? The mechanics of Shangri-La, like the outwardly amiable philosophy of its ruthless rulers, may be somewhat suspect, but it remains an engaging and thoroughly British Utopia.

First edition   London: Macmillan, 1933
First US edition   New York: Morrow, 1933

46

C. L. MOORE
Northwest Smith

Before Jirel of Joiry matched swords with sorcery in medieval France, Northwest Smith had belted on his ray-gun and blasted off along the spaceways. Disparate as their worlds were, *Weird Tales* could accommodate them both. Eventually, their paths crossed in 'Quest of the Starstone' (1957). That momentous meeting also marked the first collaboration between Catherine L. Moore and husband Henry Kuttner. Unfortunately, it is not included in this collection, or in the companion volume, *Jirel of Joiry* (1977). Of the thirteen stories published, ten are here, beginning with 'Shambleau' (1933).

Specialization was a selling-point with the pulps. If your favourite reading was Western or Detective fiction, there were racks of magazines entirely devoted to them. Contemporary critics now complain that this practice, when applied to SF, put it into a literary ghetto and damned it by association with lurid covers and truss advertisements. This short-sighted view overlooks the fact that without the crude vigour of the pulps, today's mass market for SF and Fantasy would almost certainly not exist, and these same critics would be looking elsewhere for their meal-tickets.

Weird Tales, in its earlier years, followed a more flexible policy and provided an outlet for much unclassifiable fiction by refusing to categorize. Fantasies by Moore and Howard shared its pages with straight SF by Kline and Hamilton. All but one of the Northwest Smith stories appeared there, 'Song in a Minor Key' (1940), a brief coda to his wild career.

Leather-clad Smith, with his dark, scarred face and steel-pale eyes, roamed a Solar System unknown to modern planetologists. On Mars and Venus, ruined cities outnumbered living communities. Their builders, not content with decent extinction, frequently left active reminders of their unholy scientific creations to discomfort terrestrial adventurers. Still more disconcertingly, they could linger on in person. One such survivor was 'Shambleau'. The impact of this, her first published story, immediately made the name C. L. Moore one to remember.

It is not difficult to understand why the story has led a life independent of the series and been so frequently anthologized. Smith's mingled fascination and revulsion as he succumbs to the caressing crimson tentacles of the Martian vampire furnishes a feast for any amateur Freud. Death and sex walk hand in hand through C. L. Moore's fiction, but rarely with so intimate a grasp as here. It is almost as if she were unaware of the implications of her narrative.

Next to 'Shambleau', the most popular of Smith's exploits is probably 'Black Thirst' (1934). Like a fellow contributor to the magazine, Robert E.

Howard, she seemed to find the word 'black' irresistible. Appropriately set on Venus, it involves the immemorially old Minga Castle, supernaturally beautiful girls and the mysterious alien Alendar. Bred as the consorts of kings, the girls leave the castle only at the command of the Alendar, their ageless master. Until then, fearsome and nameless guardians hold them inviolate within its hoary walls.

So, when a Minga girl meets Smith in the open one starless Venusian night, his professional suspicions are aroused. Her patronizing invitation to enter the castle is greeted with ironic humour, revealing a 'deep-buried trace of breeding and birth'. Even so, he cannot resist the challenge. Step by step, he follows her through the curtained mysteries of the Alendar's stronghold, until the ultimate purpose of the alien is revealed. The claustrophobic oppression and growing tension are skilfully sustained, right up to the final, hideous confrontation.

Often, Smith is partnered by Yarol, a slim, sleek, cherubic-looking Venusian, as durable and insolvent as himself. For the most part, the duo are creatures of the inner planets; their most extended journey being to a Jovian satellite, in 'Yuala' (1936), where an extra-terrestrial Circe rules. The Earthman's weirder experiences tend to be solo passages, adventures in subjective worlds, where the perils are spiritual though clothed in seemingly physical forms. 'Scarlet Dream' (1934) draws him into a blood-hungry realm through the gateway within a scarlet shawl, found in a derelict spaceship. A rare visit to Earth leads to a trip by mental transference to a past age of the Moon, where cities of pearl and silver glimmer in the green glow of the primary. Martian police fliers hunt him into the shelter of 'The Tree of Life' (1936), and so into a space-time bubble enclosing a malign entity invoked by a long-dead king. If Brackett's Eric John Stark is the Conan of space, then Smith is its King Kull, a wanderer in dreams.

Female vampirism is a recurrent theme in C. L. Moore's fiction, whether of the physical, blood-sucking variety or the subtler psychic and sexual forms. The women whom he meets are usually evil and powerful, or the victims of evil. The victims do not always give in to their nemeses without a struggle —Vaudir, the girl in the Alendar's castle, displays courage at least as great as Smith's when faced with inevitable death. Of them all, it is the girl we never meet in 'Song in a Minor Key' who most deeply affects him. Because of the implied violence which ends their affair, he leaves Earth and its myriad Smiths and acquires that deceptively simple, marvellously evocative, Northwest.

As *Scarlet Dream*
First edition   New York: West Kingston (RI): Grant, 1981
Retitled *Northwest Smith*   New York: Ace, 1982

47

C. L. MOORE
Jirel of Joiry

Of all the categories of Fantasy, that which Fritz Leiber christened Swords and Sorcery seemed the most essentially masculine. Heroes were brawny and bold, heroines clinging, curvaceous and underclad. But it never was an exclusively male preserve. Back in 1934, when Conan the Cimmerian was rampaging through *Weird Tales*, his rule was already being challenged by Jirel of Joiry. Tall and red-haired, with lion-yellow eyes, she was the second of two enduring characters from the pen of C. L. Moore.

Possible accusations of Excalibur-envy did not deter Leigh Brackett from joining in with tales of heroic deeds on barbaric Mars and Venus. These forerunners of the now established female school of Swords and Sorcery had other things in common—both became Hollywood screenwriters, both married well-known SF writers, both collaborated with their spouses on numerous stories and novels. Brackett's stories differed in that the chief protagonist was usually a man. Misled by this and her uninformative first name, many readers assumed that the mind behind the feral, cold-eyed Eric John Stark could only be male. It was a compliment of a kind, if back-handed.

The five Jirel titles appeared in *Weird Tales* between 1934 and 1939. From the stony comforts of Castle Joiry in a romantic version of medieval France, the action usually moves rapidly to lands beyond, via interdimensional tunnels, strange doorways or enchanted windows. In 'Quest of the Starstone' (1937), which is omitted from this collection, she meets C. L. Moore's space-roving Northwest Smith. Regardless of his ray-gun and space-leathers, the sorcerous and science-fictional elements of their respective universes are largely interchangeable. 'Jirel Meets Magic' (1935) emphasizes the connection when the dauntless redhead explores a witch's castle and sees, through a crystal portal, a silvery object trailing fire as it hurtles across a sea of stars. Northwest Smith between planets?

C. L. Moore excels in the evocation of a pervasive, miasmic atmosphere of evil. This is achieved to a great degree by her descriptions of the distress and degradation evinced by its victims. Much of the horror of 'Black God's Kiss' and the sequel 'Black God's Shadow' (both 1934) arises from this sense of a deadly but unspecified menace. Jirel's motive in journeying to the nightmare land of the Black God reflects and so intensifies this effect. When Castle Joiry is stormed by scarred, steel-clad Guillame, its lady lives only for revenge. Or so she thinks.

Beneath the castle's uttermost depths, a spiral tunnel leads downwards to a nameless place. Once she and her religious adviser, Father Gervase, had followed its dizzying convolutions to the end. After a glimpse of what lay beyond, he had forbidden her to go further. She knows now that only there can she find a weapon sufficiently terrible for her purpose. Escaping from her cell, she goes down into the darkness.

Strange constellations hang in the black sky. Unseen, squirming things strike from the grass, snapping with vicious jaws, dying in splatters of foulness beneath her sword. Women flounder in the filth of Stygian swamps, naked and mindless. At the heart of the darkness waits the temple of the Black God. She presses her lips to the crouching, sexless image and a cold presence enters her heart. She has the weapon she seeks. Frantically she races to regain the tunnel before dawn breaks over the half-hidden landscape. With consummate craft, C. L. Moore makes the prospect of morning more terrifying than the dreadful night.

In a pretence of surrender, Jirel kisses Guillame. As the presence passes from her heart to his, she understands too late the real nature of her feelings for him. He dies, and in a fever of remorse she takes the spiral path again, to free his spirit from the Black God's grasp.

'Jirel Meets Magic' finds her in furious pursuit of Giraud, a wizard who has killed ten of her warriors. Recklessly, she follows him into the domain of the beautiful witch, Jarisme. Their enmity is instant and instinctive, but she defies the witch's powers and tracks her quarry to a mountain-top fortress, where inner doors open upon mind-wrenching vistas beyond this Earth. As so often in the series, her victory here depends less upon swordplay than upon sheer courage and the will to survive.

Survival can *be* the victory. Fatally wounded, she is snatched from the edge of death, into the weirdest world of all. Romne, 'The Dark Land' (1936), with its inverted, dissolving perspectives, exists in the imagination of its shape-changing ruler, Pav. Caught between overwhelming and incomprehensible warring powers, Jirel becomes little more than a pawn. Her concluding adventure in 'Hellsgarde' (1939), where the walking dead garrison the gates, is almost restful by comparison.

Conan the Cimmerian, for all his brawn, fell victim to the sequel-mongers, the literary version of Death by a Thousand Cuts. Long may Joiry's lady be preserved.

First edition   New York: Paperback Library, 1969

48

CHARLES G. FINNEY

The Circus of Dr Lao

Writers, of fantasy or mainstream fiction, are peculiarly fond of belabouring their hapless characters for being products of their environment. Social division in Britain and America's multiplicity of small towns provide the English-speaking author with innumerable targets. Ray Bradbury, an admirer of Finney's work, was so besotted with the small-town environment that he transplanted it to Mars in order to reveal its horrors. Finney was content to bring his Circus to the sticks to bemuse the hicks, an example which Bradbury later emulated.

After military service in China between 1927 and 1930, Finney returned to America, where he became a proof-reader on the *Arizona Daily Star* in Tucson. The two disparate experiments are neatly fused in his best-known novel. In the reactions of the citizens of Abalone, Arizona, to the Circus and its Chinese proprietor, one may, perhaps, see Finney's contemporaries listening uncomprehendingly to his tales of Oriental encounters.

Hollywood latched on to *Dr Lao* in 1963, with unhappy results. The film did, however, provide actor Tony Randall with a multiple role which portrayed the bewildering menagerie of mythological monsters as aspects of the enigmatic Doctor. There are clues enough in the narrative: Dr Lao is a veritable chimera himself, veering from pedantic lecturer to sober sage to caricature Chinese, while the manner in which beings of such diverse origins delivered themselves to China and so into the Doctor's hands is, at the least, improbable.

Mr Etaoin, proof-reader on the *Abalone (Arizona) Morning Tribune*, is the first to show curiosity over the advent of the Circus. Checking the extensive and extravagant advertisement placed with the *Tribune*, he is puzzled by the lack of a name. Circus-owners are not noted for personal reticence. One by one the citizens are hooked. The police are professionally suspicious; the railroad men wonder how the Circus arrived, for it did not come by rail; a widow wants her fortune told, having exhausted the local seers; a female teacher of English knows the meanings of 'pornographic' and 'hermaphroditic', although she doesn't seem startled by their appearances in a small-town newspaper. Sceptical or not, they are all present on Main Street when the promised parade begins.

Three dowdy wagons make up the parade. An elderly Chinaman drives the first, a bearded man the second, a man with a horned hat the third. Larry Kamper, back from Army service in Tientsin, isn't too sure that the horns are on a hat. But he's pretty sure that the beast pulling the wagon isn't a Unicorn.

And is there a Russian in that other wagon or a bear? The one being drawn by a Sphinx, that is, not the one hitched to a golden ass.

Improbabilities multiply. As in some film comedy where scores of manic policemen emerge from a minuscule hut, the three caravans give birth to a fieldful of capacious tents. The English teacher pays her two nickels to see the Satyr. The Satyr is greying and has a bald spot, but he is about to give the customer her two nickel's worth when Dr Loa enters to deliver a lecture. Apollonius of Tyana climaxes a display of magic by resuscitating a corpse. The corpse is not impressed. A Roc's egg hatches. Kate disapproves of the Medusa's unclad state and does not believe in her powers. Kate becomes a chunk of choice carnelian chalcedony. Mr Etaoin, for the first time, interviews a Sea-Serpent. On all of these fabulous beings lies the mark of age: they are shabby, wrinkled, shop-soiled, as if worn down by centuries of human incredulity.

The Circus begins. Into the triangular arena march the Unicorn, the Sphinx, the Chimera. Nymphs dance to the piping of the Satyr. The Medusa's crown of serpents writhes, a miniature counterpart of the sea-monster coiling before her. The march explodes into violence—Werewolf against Roc, Unicorn versus Chimera, the Serpent striking at Dr Lao. Before Apollonius can restore order, eleven members of the audience are gone beyond recall: the Medusa's blindfold has slipped. A Witches' Sabbath follows, attended by a cigarette-smoking, uncooperative Satan, who has his own notions of how it can be enlivened.

To forestall the boredom settling over the crowd, the Doctor brings on a spectacular finale, a re-enactment of a Virgin Sacrifice to the incredibly ancient god Yottle by the people of prehistoric Woldercan. The god falls, most of the people are saved, the performance ends and the Circus is over. Abalone returns to normal, its surface scarcely rippled. It has its own myths, born of the Machine Age, though it does not think of them as such.

Dr Lao is an odd and idiosyncratic novel, the high point of Finney's work. It would be interesting to know if the readers of the *Arizona Daily Star* took it to heart.

First edition   New York: Viking, 1935
First UK edition   London: Gray Walls Press, 1948

49
JOSEPH O'NEILL
Land under England

When the deadliest fantasy of our century began to be acted out in Middle Europe, the first tremors of the coming upheaval had already been recorded by writer's pens. Time and events relegated their warnings to the back-shelves of history. Some, cast in fictional form, lay dormant until changing public taste brought them back into favour. Among them was a novel by a senior civil servant of the Irish Free State, Joseph O'Neill.

Ironically, he wrote *Land under England* in the language of a foreign power. Ireland, no stranger to military, religious and political oppression, was an apt point from which to observe the darkness sweeping over Europe. The alien philosophy chipping at the foundations of British society is not named by his narrator-hero, Anthony Julian, until the closing pages; it is, of course, Fascism. In 1935, the term had a precise meaning, rather than being an all-purpose gibe to be flung at anything which displeased the flinger. That the hidden Land is held by a degenerate remnant of the Roman Empire makes the epithet doubly apposite.

The world beneath our feet has always fascinated fantasists who fought a tenacious rearguard action against the advance of scientific knowledge. In 1864, Jules Verne was already having to execute some fancy literary footwork in justifying the existence of a subterranean ocean; later, Edgar Rice Burroughs, never one for half-measures, portrayed a hollow Earth complete with inner moon. Superficially, O'Neill's vast cavern beneath Northumbria, with its towering fungi and outlandish fauna, is a playground for intrepid adventurers. In actuality, although its physical qualities are convincingly realized, the Land functions as a powerful metaphor.

For generations the Julian family lived beside that enduring relic of Roman Britain, Hadrian's Wall. At intervals throughout their history, Julian men have descended into a shadowy underworld via an entrance hidden among the crumbling stones. Only three have ever returned, giving unbelievable accounts of their experiences. Held to this ancient location by his father's obsession with the Julian tradition, Anthony and his parents are all that remains of the family at the outbreak of the First World War.

When his father returns from the war, Anthony, who had always wor-shipped this tall, handsome, outwardly charming man, finds him shockingly changed. It is as if the battlefield has stripped his personality to its core, a core of cold indifference. Not long afterwards, he disappears. Privately, his wife and son never doubt where he has gone. Years pass, in which Anthony, more practical than his father, achieves considerable success in industry, but he never ceases to search for the hidden way. Finally, he tumbles headlong into the underworld, as the earth gives way beneath him.

The hollow lands are huge beyond comprehension, a Martinien dream of looming peaks, cliff-girt waters and spider-thronged forests, lit by the flickering brilliance of a strange aurora. Surviving many hazards, Anthony is overjoyed when he finds a Roman-style galley and its oddly silent crew. His hopes of obtaining news of his father are quickly dashed. These men behave like zombies. The sole exception is their commander, who radiates an extraordinary aura of power. He attempts to invade and control Anthony's mind, without success. More frightening than the attack is the fact that he cannot comprehend why it is resented.

Out of his depth in this emotionless society, Anthony is sustained by the intensity of his quest. The subterraneans are quite willing, direct assault having failed, to try an alternative tack. Like the natives of the Country of the Blind encountering Nunez, they have his welfare at heart. Persuasion by example is the new approach. He is given a tour of their workshops, farms (where huge snakes are bred as cattle) and schools. There are no prisons. All material needs are simply but adequately met, on a communal basis. There is a brief incident eerily prophetic of coming events in the upper world, when he sees a corpse being fed into a furnace as fuel.

During this unavailing courtship, Anthony learns that his father did reach the underworld, but: 'There is no such man now as the man you call your father.' The metamorphosis is complete. Julian Senior has become one with the new Romans, immuring himself in a darkness of his own making, to shut out the surrounding night.

Failing to seduce Anthony by a display of their virtues, his captors exile him to the uninhabited mountains. As he stumbles through the blackness, frequently hallucinating, he begins to grasp the true nature of his relationship with his father. When the dark empire, unable to absorb him, finally puts him on the road to home, he has to push that relationship to the breaking-point.

Land under England succeeds as psychological study and weird odyssey. Underlying the acceptable anti-totalitarian message, however, are traces of condescension or even anti-intellectualism. Anthony thinks of his upper-world friends, including his mother, as being secure against Fascism's wiles because they are too 'stupid' to be led astray. It is a well-worn notion, but it comes oddly from a Permanent Secretary for Education.

First edition   London: Gollancz, 1935
First US edition   New York: Schuster, 1935

50
ROBERT E. HOWARD
Conan the Conqueror

Robert Ervin Howard committed suicide in 1936, ending a prolific career as an author spanning almost half of his thirty years. A small-town boy, a native of Cross Plains, Texas, his vivid imagination seized upon the history and mythology of the wider world and transmuted them into fantasy. He wrote for the pulp magazines, a voracious market. Hundreds of titles sported their lurid covers on the news-stands of the period, while their contents strove to match them in extravagance. Howard, from the first, revealed a natural talent for the sort of writing which hooked the reader from the opening paragraph and never let go.

Dozens of muscular characters shot, hacked and slugged their way through the fearsome perils spawned by his typewriter. For the most part, they were burly, reckless and possessed of a quixotic streak where pretty girls in distress were concerned. In foreign ports, in lost cities and Himalayan strongholds, in labyrinthine vice-dens, they outfaced fiendish crimelords and their swarming henchmen. Good rousing stuff, if occasionally reminiscent of Rohmer, say, or Mundy. But in the genre now labelled Heroic Fantasy, Howard truly came into his own, welding together various elements into a form which would not achieve its maximum popularity until thirty years after his death. And towering over all of the heroes created for this genre is Conan the Cimmerian, greatest warrior of the Hyborian Age.

Unlike many pulp heroes, Conan cannot readily be detached from his background. The Hyborian Age, falling between the destruction of Atlantis and the beginnings of recorded history, is as vigorous, colourful and improbable as the Cimmerian himself. Howard, dipping into the treasure-chest of Earth's past civilizations, selected the shiniest gems and combined them in a pattern which could exist only in his imagination. The counterparts of medieval Europe, Ancient Egypt, Assyria and many more share common frontiers; assegai clashes with broadsword, tulwar with battleaxe; wizards of deepest dye summon grisly creatures of the Underworld to further the ambitions of kings; a penniless adventurer can become an emperor or a princess a sorcerer's slave. Purists have balked at Howard's use of historical names for his mythical lands and characters, but they lose none of their exoticism by the practice, any more than do Leigh Brackett's Celtic-sounding Martians and Venusians. Conan, taken from this brawling, perilous setting, would be like an engine deprived of a governor; only the Hyborian Age can contain his furious energies.

Conqueror (in its original magazine format *The Hour of the Dragon*) is the more successful of Howard's two published novels. The other, *Almuric*, is a rather loosely constructed tale of adventure on a distant planet. He was essentially a short-story writer. Conan's progress from northern barbarian to thief, mercenary, adventurer, regicide and finally king is told in this form. When *Conqueror* opens, he has already crushed two rebellions and is about to face a third. Three nobles and a defrocked priest of Mitra plot to reanimate Xaltotun, a long-dead sorcerer from the vanished empire of Acheron. His ancient knowledge is needed to control a fabled magical stone, the Heart of Ahriman, which is to be used in usurping not merely one throne but two: those of Conan's Aquilonia and its deadliest rival, Nemedia. They succeed in reviving Xaltotun, but fail to foresee that he may have plans of his own.

The wizard soon sets to work. A plague strikes Nemedia, wiping out King Nimed and his sons. His younger brother, Tarascus, one of the plotters, ascends the throne and declares war on Aquilonia. Led into a trap by treacherous allies, the Aquilonian army is defeated and the sorcery of Xaltotun overpowers Conan. Instead of killing him, Xaltotun imprisons him, having other things in mind for the Cimmerian. With the help of Zenobia, a girl from Tarascus's seraglio, he escapes, after slaying a giant ape and severely wounding Tarascus. He is unaware that the Nemedian king has stolen the Heart of Ahriman, hoping to curb the growing power of Xaltotun, and has despatched a rider with orders to cast it into the sea.

Reaching the Aquilonian capital, Tarantia, Conan rescues the Countess Albiona from the headsman's axe, carving his way through nobility and soldiery alike. Given sanctuary by the priests of Asura, a sect he had protected from persecution, he learns of the power of the Heart of Ahriman and sets out to overtake Tarascus's messenger. Not without a certain relish, he reverts to the role of footloose adventurer, spattering his trail with the blood of ghouls, robber barons, giant serpents, and other Hyborian fauna. In the depths of a Stygian pyramid-necropolis, he has an amorous encounter with Princess Akivasha, a deathless vampire. He enquires of directions in the maze of corridors from an undead mummy. All of these incidents pale into triviality when Xaltotun unveils his masterplan, which is nothing less than to resurrect ancient Acheron and impose its evil magnificence upon the Cimmerian's world.

Since the upsurge of interest in Heroic Fantasy, many writers have been commissioned to add to the Conan canon. A few have caught something of the authentic feel of the Hyborian Age. But Conan and his times sprang full-grown from Robert E. Howard's embattled psyche. There can be no real substitute.

As *Conan the Conqueror; the Hyboran Age*
First edition   New York: Gnome Press, 1950
First UK edition   London: Boardman, 1954

51

H. P. LOVECRAFT
At The Mountains Of Madness

After the admirably-named Richard E. Byrd flew around the South Pole in 1929, Antarctic exploration ceased to be principally a question of survival. Vast areas of the last unconquered continent could be surveyed, albeit superficially, without the grinding labour endured by Scott and Amundsen. It remained, in essence, unknown and murderously hostile, an America-sized slab of ice thousands of feet thick through which poked frozen fingers of the underlying rock. Anything could be hidden there, even from the eyes of aviators.

Given a plausible means of moving their characters from A to B in hours rather than weeks, writers rose to the challenge. For Lovecraft it had a peculiarly personal element. His body was incapable of maintaining a normal temperature if the thermometer fell much below eighty degrees Fahrenheit. Outdoors in winter, sudden spells of acute cold could leave him helpless. The South Pole must have been his notion of the ultimate hell.

The Byrd expedition which founded Little America on the Ross Ice Shelf blazed a trail for fictional explorers, including Lovecraft's unfortunate scientists. Sponsored by that fount of dubious learning, Miskatonic University, their aim is to obtain evidence of Antarctica's tropical past by extracting core samples from the rocks. Much technical detail is included to establish an air of authenticity.

Lovecraft submitted the novel to *Weird Tales*—he scorned all other pulps—but it was rejected. In 1936, an agent sold it in abridged form to *Astounding*, an unlikely haven for a chapter of the Cthulhu Mythos. Maybe the background research paid off. Two years later, *Astounding* ran another monster-in-the-ice bloodcurdler, John W. Campbell's 'Who Goes There?'

The nature of the Miskatonic expedition changes when radio messages are recieved from an advance party describing a titanic mountain range, greater than the Himalayas. As their Dornier drones through the rarified air, the stupendous peaks reveal *outré* configurations conforming to no known geometry. Drilling at their landing-site opens up a palaeontologist's Aladdin's Cave, crammed with fossils covering whole geological epochs.

Among them are the remains of huge, vaguely crinoid creatures apparently pre-dating the most primitive of terrestrial organisms. Dissection of a specimen reveals a complex nervous system suggesting advanced intelligence and unguessable senses. Under the Antarctic sun, the leathery tissues begin to soften. And then, wouldn't you know it?, a storm severs radio communication with the main camp.

A relief party arrives at the site, only to find a shambles of smashed equipment and the surgically butchered bodies of the men. The disinterred creatures have gone, and the dissected specimen has been buried with every sign of respect, but not by human hands. Campbell was already a contributor to *Astounding* and it is impossible not to see in this incident a pointer to the malevolent tentacled alien of his classic short story. For Lovecraft's professors, this discovery is only an introduction to horror.

Anyone who qualifies as a faculty member at Miskatonic U is made of no common clay; curiosity drives them over the Martinien ramparts of the Mountains of Madness. Beyond them looms a 20,000-foot-high plateau, and scattered across it are the ruins of a colossal city. Familiarity with the pages of the abhorred *Necronomicon* evokes references to the evilly fabled plateau of Leng and lost pre-human lands. Undeterred, they land. Equipped with rope, camera, torches and (on the Theseus principle) a bag of torn paper, they venture into the Cyclopean labyrinth.

Lovecraft's determination to give credibility to the actions of his scientists involves a degree of precision not usually found in fantasy. As the explorers burrow deeper into the alien structures they measure and map, take photographs, record cryptic inscriptions. Their documentary zeal could be as incongruous as an YOU ARE HERE sign in the Emerald City; rather, it increases the mounting suspense and magnifies the impact of the cataclysmic climax.

It is a city of the Old Ones, beings from the stars who colonized Earth's primordial, lifeless oceans. In their laboratories they bred Shuggoths, huge amorphous masses whose substance could be shaped to various tasks by the thoughts of their creators. Depressingly for our environmental crusaders, the Old Ones were as heedless of pollution as any Victorian industrialist. Living cells leaked into the ambient seas, and the evolutionary rat-race was on.

Just how fundamental were Lovecraft's ethnic prejudices, it is difficult to say. Whenever chance brought him into extended contact with individuals not of Anglo-Saxon origin, he appears to have dealt with them courteously. It may be that in the mass they represented, for him, the uncontrollable universe beyond his front door. Whatever the basis of his fears, one can imagine him taking a gloomy pleasure in representing our forebears as laboratory sweepings.

The history of the Old Ones, cries the narrator, has not yet ended. If degraded humanity is to survive, better to let sleeping Shuggoths lie.

As *At the Mountains of Madness, and Other Novels*
First edition   Sauk City (Wisconsin): Arkham House, 1964
(first book publication of these stories in this arrangement)
First UK edition   London: Gollancz, 1966

52
WILLIAM SLOANE
To Walk the Night

There are authors who may not have written much but what they have written refuses to be forgotten. William Milligan Sloane, while in his early thirties, wrote two novels which hover on the borderline between sf and the occult, with a decided leaning towards the second category. One, *The Edge of Running Water*, is regarded as a classic. Before them, he had written two plays on supernatural themes. After them, for thirty-five years, there was silence, more or less, on the fiction front.

Which did not mean that he had lost contact. Writing was a secondary profession, a change of pace in the middle of a continuing career in publishing. In 1954 he edited two anthologies of sf, *Space, Space, Space* and *Stories for Tomorrow*. Whatever the impulse or influence which sparked off his burst of literary creativity, it was never repeated. Regrettably, because *Night* need not concede any points to its more celebrated stablemate. Both titles were included in *The Rim of the Morning* (1964); *Edge* had been filmed as *The Devil Commands* in 1941, as a Boris Karloff vehicle. *Night* had the potential for an occult thriller in the manner of Jacques Tourneur, but the chance has been lost; it commits the sin of placing some value upon human life and so has nothing to offer an industry trafficking in blood and bile.

It begins with a foreword in traditional style by the narrator, Berkeley 'Bark' Jones, doubting the wisdom of revealing the facts to the world. Jones has returned to the home of Lister, his foster-father, bearing the ashes of Lister's son, Jerry. He is afraid to tell the whole truth about Jerry's death, for his own and Lister's sake, but the older man's influence persuades him.

Two years before, while revisiting their old college, a mildly drunk Bark and Jerry decided to call in on LeNormand, the faculty's brilliant astronomer-mathematician. He had once published a highly controversial critique of Einstein's work, which was greatly admired by Jerry but outside the grasp of Bark. LeNormand retreated from the controversy, saying that it had become 'dangerous'. He never explained the nature of the threat.

When the two enter the observatory, he is in a chair facing the door, his body wreathed in white fire. For a second, he seems to be alive. They smother the flames with their coats and an extinguisher, but too late. During the police investigation, which reveals that the burns are of abnormal severity, they are startled to hear that the reclusive astronomer had been married for three months. A meeting with Selena, his widow, leaves Bark more puzzled than before, and worried about Jerry's reaction to her.

She has a remote, almost unhuman, beauty and a statuesque body, yet her clothes are dowdy and ill-fitting. Her precise and formal speech adds to the unsettling effect. Jerry doesn't share his friend's unease; he is intrigued and attracted by Selena, who seems to reciprocate his interest. His second mistake is to preserve the mathematical formulae upon which LeNormand had been working.

The enigma of Selena LeNormand grows with every fresh piece of information which Bark can uncover. Her reactions to everyday things show a naïvety at odds with her obvious intelligence. Under the tutelage of his mother, she learns how to dress and make-up to the best advantage. Meanwhile, the police continue doggedly to investigate the astronomer's death. No one who knew LeNormand had ever seen Selena until after the wedding. Two days before it, a family of tourists had stopped at a local filling-station. Their mentally retarded daughter had wandered off and disappeared. The only photographs the couple could provide for police identification were old and blurred, but there is a resemblance to Selena.

Bark is dismayed when Jerry and Selena marry. The couple go to stay in a desert house belonging to the Lister family. Against Selena's wishes, Jerry begins to work upon LeNormand's abandoned mathematical formulae. One day, Bark receives a telegram from him, asking him to come at once to the nearest town, Los Palos. Sloane's description of the vastness of the desert landscape, seen from the bleached and crumbling collection of frame buildings that is Los Palos, is as alien as a dream of another planet. It is a fitting curtain-raiser for the eerie and unforeseeable ending of Selena's story.

Someone's attempt to update a more recent edition of *Walk* by appending '1954' to the foreword and inserting an anachronistic reference to napalm is merely irritating. Any publisher (or author) who believes that his readers cannot appreciate a good story because it was written yesterday ought to be in a different profession.

First edition   New York: Farrar & Rinehart, 1937
First UK edition   London: Barker, 1938

53
SEABURY QUINN
Roads

Seabury Quinn was one of the mainstays of *Weird Tales* from the year of its inception. Though efforts are still being made to revive it, *Weird Tales* effectively died in 1954, after thirty-one years which have furnished material for whole racks of anthologies. Quinn contributed 145 stories during that period, and anyone under the impression that Jules de Grandin figured in at least 146 of them can be forgiven.

De Grandin, an expatriate Frenchman whose Frenchness was of the same order as the Belgianness of Hercule Poirot, was an investigator of the supernatural rather in the manner of Hodgson's Carnacki. The series, at first extremely popular, eventually went into a decline. A selection from it reappeared in paperback form in 1976/7. The contents represented only a fraction of Quinn's output. The hardcover edition (1948) of *Roads* credits him with over 500 published stories. It also refers to his parallel careers as an attorney and a journalist, delicately omitting to mention that they included editing a trade-paper for funeral directors. With such experience to draw upon, it's surprising that he didn't opt for writing a more down-to-earth type of crime fiction.

Roads is light-years away from de Grandin's fiend-plagued Harrisonville. There would have been few, if any, alternative markets to *Weird Tales* for this short novel about the legend of Santa Claus. Like the author, he was a product of America, in the form in which he is now known. Dutch settlers brought their tradition of St Nicholas to the New World, where their pronunciation of his name was gradually corrupted to Santa Claus. Behind this transformation lay a long history of fact, fancy and fallacy stretching back to the fourth century AD.

That Nicholas was a bishop in Asia Minor seems to be generally accepted; his life-story otherwise is an invitingly blank page. Persecution, torture, imprisonment and martyrdom have been his posthumously assigned lot. His remains were stolen from Asia Minor and reinterred in Italy. Children, sailors and pawnbrokers claim his protection, the last under his emblem of three balls. He saved three impecunious maidens from a life of sin by throwing bags of gold through their window at night, so beginning the tradition of surreptitious present-giving.

Quinn will have none of this. Shrugging off any hint of a Christian origin, he gives us as Santa a huge pagan ex-gladiator named Claus, in the service of King Herod. White-skinned, flaxen-haired Claus, described as 'a Northman', plans to return to his homeland 'to go a-Viking'. Quinn shares Robert E. Howard's vagueness about the dates of the Viking era; Herod had been dust for several centuries before the dragon-ships set sail. This fine disregard for history and hagiography is part of the novel's weird charm.

On the road out of Judea, Claus learns from a distraught mother that Herod, fearing the foretold birth of a new Jewish king, is slaughtering all infant males. Unwilling to believe that his one-time fellow soldiers are murdering children, he is forced to act when a patrol attacks a couple and their baby near where he is resting. Having killed the soldiers, he is amazed to hear a voice within his head, apparently coming from the baby. It says that the gods he worshipped are dead, but that he will live and be revered until: '. . . thy work for me is finished'.

Herod's soldiers overtake him before he can leave the country and he is forced to take refuge within the ranks of the Roman legions. Thirty years later he is Pontius Pilate's right-hand man and a Jewish prophet is about to be crucified. Delivering a merciful spear-thrust to the man on the cross, he hears the voice again, saying: '. . . thou shalt know . . . when I have need of thee.'

So far, Claus has followed in the footsteps of innumerable characters whose paths crossed those of Christ. It sometimes seems that the native population must have had to fight for elbow-room amid the influx of time-travellers, reformed charioteers and warriors who had seen the light, thronging the road to Calvary. But now the tale takes off on quite a different tack. Claus and his wife show no marks of ageing. They are immortal.

Quinn makes little of the difficulties and dangers this would entail in a world of witch-burners. Only when Claus begins to distribute gifts to the hungry in medieval Germany does he run foul of the Church. Travelling on, the couple meet a displaced tribe of the Little Folk, and together they establish a place of refuge in the far north. The story ends with Christian and pagan working for a common cause, the spreading of goodwill to the children of all nations. It's a great project, but it could use an influential sponsor. Perhaps if we all wrote a letter to Santa Claus?

First edition   New York: Conrad H. Ruppert, 1938
(pamphlet, highly limited edition)
First trade edition   Sauk City (Wisc): Arkham House, 1948

54
T. H. WHITE
The Once and Future King

The first three books of White's history of King Arthur were published in 1939–1940. Almost twenty years later, they reappeared, together with Book Four, as a single volume entitled *The Once and Future King*. During the interval, he had revised portions of the text and retitled Book Two, formerly *The Witch in the Wood*. He had also written a fifth book, *The Book of Merlyn*, which was not published until 1977, thirteen years after his death.

White's love-affair with the Middle Ages, as he saw them, is the mainspring of the series. It is equally plain that his medievalism is inseparable from his interest in natural history. His twin avocations produce some of their most evocative passages when the wizard Merlyn enables the young Arthur to assume the forms of birds, beasts and fishes as part of his education. Though the personalities of the creatures with whom Arthur converses are as basically human as Toad or Mole, the accounts of their habits and habitats are full of imaginative insights, giving us new views of familiar scenes. These experiences influence his attitudes and decisions throughout the rest of his life.

Anachronism is rampant in *The Once and Future King*, if anachronism can be said to exist in an alternative version of accepted history. White placed Arthur in a properly medieval setting *à la* Malory by reducing several post-Conquest monarchs to the status of mythical figures. Having rewritten history to his own satisfaction, he then began to illuminate Malory's sombre and convoluted tale, the basis of his narrative, with touches borrowed from later centuries. Merlyn derives much of his wizardly erudition from the fact that he lives backwards, travelling from some unspecified future point into the past. While this provides him with a fund of knowledge and experience denied to ordinary mortals, it can lead to absent-mindness—have certain events happened yet or are they still to come?

When teacher and pupil meet, Arthur is a boy, nicknamed Wart (to rhyme with Art), living in the castle of his guardian, Sir Ector. Sir Ector is an amiable, port-swilling feudal lord, who provides Wart with the same schooling as his own son, Kay. Kay, who will eventually be knighted, is aware that Wart does not know who his parents were and never allows the boy to forget his inferior social status. This, incidentally, contradicts White's later statement that Arthur was kind because 'he had never been unjustly treated'.

After Merlyn appoints himself tutor to both boys, it is Wart's turn to be privileged. His forays into the animal kingdom, a unique element of his education for kingship, are kept secret. Wart himself is unaware of their true purpose, and the fact that he is the unacknowledged son of Uther Pendragon.

Kay rides to be knighted, accompanied by Wart as his squire. Rather improbably, he neglects to take along his sword. White's characters are not always as breathtakingly dense as their medieval originals, but they do tend to trip over their own feet. Wart, sent to seek it, finds another blade embedded in a stone. Unaware of its significance, he pulls it free, and so becomes ruler of Britain. No longer will anyone address him by his nickname. He is now King Arthur, destined for renown and tragedy. His first reaction to the changed relationship between himself and his friends is dismay.

Soon he is beset by problems both personal and political. Queen Morgause of the Orkneys, daughter of Igraine of Cornwall and therefore Arthur's half-sister, seduces him by sorcerous means. She bears him a son, crook-shouldered Mordred, who could be seen as an alternative Richard the Third. 'Kind' Arthur tries to dispose of his bastard, Herod-style, by ordering the slaughter of every baby on the islands. The massacre fails. Mordred survives to become his father's nemesis.

On Merlyn's advice, Arthur plans to divert the random energies of his knights into constructive channels. Recalcitrant lords who harry their weaker neighbours are brought to heel. Ogres and monsters are hunted and slain. When these opportunities for fun are exhausted, a spiritual goal is substituted. The arduous quest for the Holy Grail begins, but proves to be too rarified a sport for all save the purest in heart. The third and final stage of his reformation is an attempt to create Justice through Law, forswearing recourse to armed force. It is a splendid dream, but it founders upon the all-too-human flaws of the dreamers. Mordred, perverting it to his own ends, uses the precariously balanced relationship between Lancelot, Guenever and Arthur as a weapon to strike at the people he hates and despises. The last battle begins.

And on that dying fall Arthur's story appeared to end. To have the machinery rewound by *The Book of Merlyn* is destructive of the established mood. A long debate between Arthur, Merlyn and a panel of animals about the general worthlessness of Man is rendered pointless by the anthropomorphic characterization of the animals. The real virtue of the book lies in what it tells us about that frustrated romantic Terence Hanbury White.

The Once and Future King (omnibus edition):   *First edition*   London: Collins, 1958, *First US edition*   New York: Putnams, 1958. *The Sword in the Stone: First edition*   London: Collins, 1938, *First US edition*   New York: Putnams, 1939. *The Witch in the Wood: First edition*   New York: Putnams, 1939, *First UK edition*   London: Collins, 1940. *The Ill-Made Knight: First edition*   New York: Putnams, 1940, *First UK edition*   London: Collins, 1941. *The Book of Merlyn: the unpublished conclusion to the once and future king: First edition*   Austin: University of Texas Press, 1977, *First UK edition*   London: Collins, 1978.

55
L. RON HUBBARD
Slaves of Sleep

If it sometimes seems that reports of the passing of Lafayette Ronald Hubbard are greatly exaggerated, it could be because his output of fiction has, if anything, increased. So much so that one book-dealer now lists certain titles as having been 'written while he was still alive'. No one who has followed, open-mouthed, his progress from pulp-writer to Scientology guru, trailing clouds of uncertainty, would be surprised to learn that the Other Side had been persuaded to grant him special terms. When some colourful personality strides to centre-stage in his books and dominates the mob, the degree of wishful thinking involved is minimal. Hubbard left that to his public.

As an sf and fantasy writer, he began at the top by making his first sale to *Astounding* in 1938. When John W. Campbell launched its companion title, *Unknown*, a year later, he was there with *Slaves of Sleep* and *The Ultimate Adventure*. Novels and shorter pieces poured from his typewriter. The period 1939–40 saw, in addition to the above, *Death's Deputy, Fear, The Indigestible Triton* and *Typewriter in the Sky*. To prevent readers of *Astounding* from forgetting him, he wrote the long-remembered *Final Blackout*.

Enid Blyton, chronicler of the mishaps of Noddy, took in her stride the prospect of completing a 50,000-word novel between Monday and Friday. Hubbard, in that respect, was a kindred spirit. Campbell, himself a talented author, was an eyewitness of his typewriter technique. Like a marathon runner limbering up, Hubbard would begin the day by going back two pages, so that when the new section of the story was reached he was hitting his full, phenomenal speed.

In a highly entertaining interview in Charles Platt's *Dream Makers* (1987), Hubbard described how Street and Smith insisted, when taking over *Astounding*, that his stories should be published regardless of Campbell's wishes. There were occasional short stories in later years which suggested that their edict had never been revoked. Speed had its penalties, and the energy which characterized his best work didn't always atone for repetitive plotting and lack of substance. Two Hubbards ran in harness—the painter of Technicolored dreamscapes, in which wimps could become flamboyant adventurers, and a more sombre artist who drew super-competent but doomed heroes pitted against entrenched evil and corruption.

Two examples of the latter, *Final Blackout* and *To the Stars*, expressed views which, within the sf field at their respective times, were controversial. Hubbard's real fireworks were yet to come, and the sparks are still flying. Dianetics, forerunner of Scientology, was ushered into the spotlight and detonated in the pages of the *Explorer's Journal* in 1950. It must be assumed that most of the people who rushed to take the cure were unaware of his fiction, with its strong wish-fulfilment element and emphasis upon the superior individual.

Magical talismans, ensorcelled gems and errant supernatural beings stood in for Dianetics as a means of awakening Hubbard's heroes to their full potential. His choice of an *Arabian Nights* framework for several of his *Unknown* novels is extremely apt. Jan Palmer, the affluent, ineffectual central character of *Slaves of Sleep*, is cursed by an Ifrit and simultaneously implicated in a murder. Imprisoned, he finds that his dreams have become another life, in which he occupies the body of carefree, roistering Tiger. Tiger's world is shared by many of Jan's mundane acquaintances, whose dream-selves are slaves of the ruling Genii. As might be expected, they include the girl he desires but is unable to attain.

The Genii, equipped with headlamp eyes, foghorn voices and formidable fangs, are the kind of over-the-top villains required by Hubbard's highly coloured but oddly convincing mock-Arabia. Intelligence is not their forte, but with magical powers, who needs it? For Jan, who cannot even deal with his own relatives, they make overwhelming foes before his twin personalities begin to merge. As an amalgam of Tiger and Jan, he takes on the baddies of both worlds. Swords clash, sails billow (ex-navy man Hubbard is in his element here), writhing serpents guard an unassailable temple filled with equally supple dancing-girls, Ifrits bellow and fume, and buckles are swashed to great effect. Like Hollywood's sand-and-sequins epics of the 1950s, it is entertainment pure and simple, but it has a swagger and panache which they lacked. Shasta Publications put it into hard covers in 1948, and Lancer Books into paperback in 1967.

A tardy sequel, *Masters of Sleep* (1950), replaced the magical ring used by Jan in *Slaves* with a fabulous diamond. Objects of power, which can be lost, stolen, found and lost again *ad infinitum*, are useful devices for moving a narrative along. The hero of an earlier Hubbard *Unknown* novel, *The Ultimate Adventure*, broke the rules for this type of fantasy by taking a more prosaic object of power, a hand-gun, into his dream-world. Unlike Harold Shea, he was allowed to shoot his way out of trouble. Too great a reliance upon such gimmicks can kill suspense, but the weakness of *Masters* lay elsewhere. Hubbard had fallen victim to the H. G. Wells syndrome, and was using his fiction to Spread The Word. And the Word was Dianetics.

Fantasy's greatest showman has gone, but, to quote one of his *Astounding* titles, *The End Is Not Yet*.

First edition   Chicago: Shasta, 1948

56
FRANK S. STUART
Caravan for China

Books had a bad war. When not being blitzed, they were liable to be pulped by enthusiastic salvage collectors. So perished such titles as *The Grimpton Bride*, which combined bat-winged fiends with a Hunnish plot to nobble London's fire-fighters by dosing their water supplies with petrol. Ephemerality was part of their charm, but there were others deserving of a second chance. Among them were Frank Stanley Stuart's historical fantasies, *Caravan for China* and *Elephant in Jet*.

The second, which has the unusual setting of India in the time of Alexander the Great, has disappeared, unless it lurks in some collector's library. *Caravan* is also concerned with Asia, though it begins in Rome during the reign of Tiberius. Stuart puts twentieth-century speech into the mouths of his Ancient World characters. Racy, flippant and cynical, their dialogue deliberately emphasizes the parallels between the corruption of Imperial Rome and that of post-Munich Europe. It is a risky device, particularly in the Chinese episodes, but it keeps the narrative moving at a sprightly pace.

China and the West were aware of each other's influence much as astronomers before Tombaugh were aware of Pluto. What if, Stuart speculates, some daring individual decided to cross the gulf between the empires? The pioneer is Pallas, a socially mobile trader who has already made the greater leap from slave status to independence. While he assembles a fantastic caravan, his sophisticated brother, Felix, charms Tiberius into giving it his Imperial blessing. The historical model for Pallas never saw China, which did not prevent him from becoming a multimillionaire.

As escort to the caravan, he enlists a company of mercenaries commanded by a gigantic Greek ex-gladiator, Black Simon. Simon's childhood sweetheart, Helen, was sold into slavery when Rome crushed her rebellious kinfolk. His obsessive search for her would be a standing joke to those in the know, were it not for his penchant for breaking necks. Felix, who bought her, owes his continued existence to the fact that she immediately escaped from him.

Rather improbably, Pallas has learned through his many contacts that she is in the Chinese Emperor's palace. He hooks Simon with this lure. Should the reports prove unreliable, he has hired the crookbacked, devious and hard-drinking mercenary Narcissus to protect his own neck. Charmian, Felix's mistress, insists on joining the group, with the aim of curing Simon of his fixation.

The epic journey begins with a stormy Mediterranean crossing and a galley-slave's revolt. Simon overpowers the leader, a huge Chinaman called

Aurum, and by sparing his life gains a deadly and devoted shadow. Action and intrigue take precedence over bodice-ripping; sensuality is reserved for the torrents of silks, spices, gold and gems, silver and aphrodisiacs spilling from the storehouses of India into the bales burdening 1,000 camels. Stuart sees these treasures through the eyes of his characters, whose known world is bordered by mystery and monstrous possibilities. An elephant looms like a giant from some alien mythology, treading reality underfoot.

China exceeds even the golden dreams of Pallas. Blinded by their inturned fantasies of riches and revenge, the Westerners fail to appreciate that they are part of another, Chinese, dream. The Emperor wants their knowledge, particularly Simon's military expertise, and will not release Helen. Trapped in the heart of a civilization which regards them as useful but dangerous barbarians, the merchant adventurers stake lives and fortunes upon a desperate stratagem. With the help of the Emperor's dissident nephew, Simon negotiates the pitfalls of the Palace to rescue Helen, only to be betrayed. Believing that Helen has fled to his nephew's stronghold, the Emperor imprisons Simon and allows the caravan to depart.

Simon awakes to horror. Madness is a quality prized and exploited by the Chinese. A madman designed the Palace defences; a demented artist painted the interior of the ten-foot sphere in which he is incarcerated. The caravan is winding away into the immensities of the Gobi. Only Aurum remains. The most testing battles of Simon's life are still to come, physical, mental and spiritual. Clues to the latter have been planted at several points and the outcome will be no great surprise. Physically, the return journey must rank as the longest rearguard action ever, strewing white, brown and yellow corpses across the monster-haunted mountains.

Stuart wrote so vividly of battle that it is rather disconcerting to learn that he was a conscientious objector. Once a Fleet Street journalist, he passed the greater part of his life in rural Wiltshire. His wartime service was spent in agriculture and his most popular books were works of natural history. Born into a generation which twice saw Europe devastated before they reached middle-age, he died under the shadow of the hydrogen bomb, believing peace to be a lost cause. The empire-rulers of today have yet to prove him wrong.

First edition   London: Paul, 1939
First US edition   New York: Doubleday, 1940

57
L. RON HUBBARD
Fear

Ron Hubbard made his début in *Unknown* with swashbuckling adventures laid in a mythical Middle East of afrits, magical jewels and dancing girls. They were fast, funny and improbable in the extreme. Then, just when readers thought they knew what to expect of him, he hit them with *Fear*.

Jim Lowry doesn't quite fit into either of the two principal categories of Hubbardian heroes. Though well travelled in the earth's wild places, he is no raffish Tiger, carving himself a niche in dream-land kingdoms; though a Professor, he is no grim-jawed scientist-soldier, sacrificing himself and others for an ideal. In effect, he *is* the story, the setting and the chief protagonist rolled up in one.

Fear, according to the individual reader's point of view, is a story of supernatural persecution summed up by 'Hubris clobbered by Nemesis' or a purely subjective fantasy for which the supernatural agencies form a framing device. Professors, for all Hubbard's assumption of a similar role in the realm of mental health, do not usually get a good press in his fiction. Lowry is one of his more sympathetic specimens, but is handed the rawest deal of all.

A prefacing Author's Note warns the reader that, whatever the apparently random nature of the narrative may indicate, it is logically worked out. A second reading, unless you're so well versed in symbolism and dream-psychology that you can figure it out the first time around, shows the truth of this. Hubbard's interest in this field clearly predated his presentation of Dianetics to a wrong-thinking world by many years. His youthful travels, which gave him the experience required to qualify for membership of the Explorer's Club, lend an authentic flavour to Lowry's ethnological field-trips. An unlikely side-effect was that Dianetics got its first airing in the Club journal.

Lowry returns to Atworthy College from Yucatan in good spirits, apart from a slight touch of malaria. The doctor warns him, half-seriously, that his newspaper article on superstition may have offended college president Jebson by mentioning Atworthy. A summons to Jebson's office does not worry him unduly, until he realizes the depth of the president's anger. Back in 1940 on this side of the Atlantic, Jebson's reaction to what he interprets as an oblique attack upon Christianity might have been regarded as overdone. The rise of religious fundamentalism now makes it a deal more plausible. The argument descends to the personal when Jebson rakes up Lowry's expulsion, as a student, on a charge of theft. His reinstatement after the real thief was discovered has never erased a feeling of irrational guilt and the remark cuts deep. Jebson turns the knife by firing him.

Dazed, he heads for home and his wife, Mary. Passing the house of a boy-hood friend, Tommy Williams, he calls in. Tommy, also an academic, is a good-looking bachelor (Lowry calls him pretty) and a witty defender of demons and all matters occult, a natural foil for Lowry's outward ruggedness and rationality. As he prepares to leave Tommy's house again, he notices the time is 2.45 p.m. His next awareness is of standing in a darkening street, minus his hat. The time is 6.45 p.m. *Fear* is the story of his search for the four lost hours.

As he walks up to his home, he thinks that he hears Mary shouting: 'Jim! Oh, my God! Jim!' He bursts into the house, but cannot find her. Then she comes in, saying that she had been out looking for him. They talk and he reminds her that Tommy once proposed to her, but she asks him not to be jealous again. When he goes to bed, he notices that his jacket has somehow become torn and marked.

Restless, he rises again and decides to take a walk. He begins to descend the steps to the street and all semblance of reality vanishes. The steps go down, and keep on going down. Alarmed, he looks back, but there is nothing behind him but darkness. Far above, Mary is standing on the porch. She is shouting, telling him that he has forgotten his hat. The darkness closes over his head and there is nowhere to go but into the earth.

Flickering intervals of normality fade into nightmares of running, climbing, falling. Always behind him is a black-clad figure carrying a noose. Mary and Tommy's faces change almost imperceptibly into sly, mocking masks. And then there comes the last walk down the stairs, all the way down to the lost four hours.

Fear is not quite like anything else which appeared in *Unknown* during its brief but influential life. Hubbard wrote many other stories, which have, deservedly, been often reprinted, but never another quite like *Fear*. As a case-study or as a pure fantasy, it is as dark as they come.

As *Fear; an Outstanding Psychological Science Fiction Novel*
First edition   New York: Galaxy, 1957

58
JACK WILLIAMSON
Darker Than You Think

A tall, slow-talking man from Arizona, Williamson is the James Stewart of sf. Raised in territory which is still dream-country for most of his readers, he travelled by covered wagon, knew the harshness of life in New Mexico when Apache renegades still roamed and typed his early stories by the light of an oil-lamp. Romantic as this Western life may have seemed to outsiders, it ran a poor second for him to the wilder worlds depicted in Gernsback's newly founded *Amazing*. While Williamson wore denims and rode dusty trails, his imagination roved the starry heavens in search of adventure.

Since the acceptance of *The Metal Man* in 1928, he has racked up an impressive total composed of novels, long and short stories, non-fiction and literary criticism. At first strongly influenced by Merritt, he soon found his own distinctive voice. Though the bulk of his work is sf, he is also known for some notable fantasies, of which *Darker Than You Think* is an outstanding example. Originally published in *Unknown* in 1940, it reappeared in an expanded, much lengthier hardback version from Fantasy Press in 1948. The action had been brought forward into the post-Hiroshima period, but the changes involved were mostly superficial.

The opening scene, which runs for fifty-seven pages, takes place at the airport of a small American city, Clarendon. Will Barbee, reporter for the *Clarendon Star*, is covering the arrival of two 'planes, one carrying a corrupt politician, ex-Colonel Walraven, the other a team of scientists returning from Ala-shan, in the Gobi Desert. He is approached by April Bell, a fascinating green-eyed redhead, who works for the rival paper, the *Clarendon Call*. She quizzes him about the scientists and their expedition. Barbee's suspicion of women and rival reporters fades before her charms and he tells all.

Lamarck Mondrick, founder of the Humane Research Foundation, has devoted decades of work in anthropology, archaeology, religion and superstition to an undisclosed end. Together with his associates, Quain, Spivak and Chittum, he has brought back a mysterious box from a prehistoric burial-ground in the Gobi. Whatever it is, it is the climax of his efforts; the four men are ready to defend it, quite literally, with their lives. Barbee is doubly affected by this secrecy, for he had been part of Mondrick's team several years ago, before being inexplicably rejected. Mondrick attempts to explain the meaning of their discoveries to the clustered reporters, but collapses and dies.

Later, Barbee makes a dinner-date with April as she leaves to file her story. When she has gone, he looks for a black kitten she had been carrying in a basket. It is in a trash can, garrotted. A jade pin, carved into a wolf's head, is driven into its heart. Quain had said that Mondrick was allergic to cat's fur.

Barbee is caught in an ever more complex web of fear and fascination, as the evidence against the redhead mounts along with his desire for her. His drinking, already heavy, increases.

Then, one night, she calls to him telepathically. He has a mental picture of her as a white wolf. Half-asleep, he succumbs to her instructions and is suddenly free of his human form. He is a huge, grey wolf, running free in the sleeping city. April persuades him to enter Quain's home, but some force emanating from the sealed box drives them off. Barbee accepts April's explanation that they are *Homo lycanthropus* and that 'normal' humanity is their deadliest enemy; Mondrick's expedition brought back a long-buried weapon with which *Homo sapiens* had once defeated them. The battle is on—the scientists and the weapon must be destroyed, to make way for the lycanthropes' leader, the Child of Night.

Williamson works hard to establish the credibility of *Lycanthropus* and, within the limits of scientific knowledge *circa* 1948, succeeds. He is less successful with Barbee, whose inability to grasp the fact that *he* is the awaited leader, as he progresses from wolf to serpent to sabretooth tiger to pterodactyl, borders on the moronic. The human characters are, in general, awkwardly drawn, their desperation and exhaustion reiterated to the point of caricature. Williamson is much happier when April and Barbee are ranging the night in animal form; the writing is vivid and joyous in these sequences. Red-haired April, naked on Barbee's back as, with tiger's fangs or pterodactyl's claws, he rends his enemies, is the novel's enduring image.

In expanding the necessarily short *Unknown* version, Williamson has gone too far in the opposite direction; the narrative would benefit from being shorn of a few thousand words. But at the core of the book is an idea so ingenious and unsettling that it is easily capable of sustaining the reader's interest. It is an eminently visual story and would be even more effective on the screen.

First edition   Reading (PA): Fantasy Press, 1948
First UK edition   London: Sphere, 1976

[1941]

59
H. P. LOVECRAFT
The Case of Charles Dexter Ward

Relationships between cities and the writers they have nurtured can be fraught. London has never shaken off the Dickensian image compounded of gaslight, cobbles and fog. It doesn't do justice to the agglomeration of third-rate skyscrapers, cut-price Trump Towers and huckster's booths at the dingy heart of the modern capital, but the tourists, bless them, love it. For many Sassenachs, and perhaps a few Scots, Glasgow is still *No Mean City*. Providence, Rhode Island, had only one widely known chronicler, and for him Dickens belonged to a generation of upstart newcomers. Lovecraft felt that little that was good had happened in his beloved Providence within the past two centuries.

As expressed on paper, this attitude applied to the world outside of Providence and very probably to the limits of the observable universe. Britain was a bright spot in the moral murk because of its historical associations and Lovecraft's partly English ancestry. Lesser breeds, which means just about everyone, tended to be squint-eyed, pock-marked, ill-complexioned persons who spoke a debased patois, and at the lowest level were not wholly human in origin. They crowded together in squalid streets and conducted unspeakable religious rites. They had little choice in this, because the gods of Lovecraft's universe *were* unspeakable. Christianity and other orthodoxies got short shrift. Nobody ever waved a crucifix at Nyarlathotep twice.

While the past had all the best architecture, manners and spelling, if his fondness for archaisms is any guide, Lovecraft did not depict it as a time of sweetness and enlightenment. Rather, it was the past as a mental landscape into which one could retreat or as a dream of childhood that was attractive. It is young Charles Dexter Ward's passion for the antique which involves him with an evil influence emanating from the seventeenth century. Ward's explorations of his native Providence are lovingly described; the clustered spires of its churches seem to float on a golden sea of evening light.

Following up an obvious alteration in a book of town records, Ward discovers that one of his ancestors was the mysterious Joseph Curwen. Just enough evidence survives to suggest that information about Curwen has been deliberately effaced and that the reason for the cover-up is no ordinary scandal.

Fleeing from Salem lest his alchemical experiments have him branded as a witch, Curwen arrived in Providence and went into the shipping business. There were aspects of his activities which began to make his associates suspect that he wasn't the solid, sober citizen he appeared to be. Foremost among them were his constant traffic in drugs and other chemical substances and his partiality for graveyards. To this list was added, as the years passed, his unchanging physical appearance. People began to shun his society. In an attempt to regain public esteem, he married the daughter of one of his sea-captains and established her in a fine, newly built mansion.

He continued to prosper and his dealings became ever more bizarre. Particularly strange was his commerce with traders from across the sea. For Lovecraft, the sea was a source of evil. Ports were inlets for abominations and the antecedents of those who lived and worked within their environs scarcely bore investigation. Matters reached such a pitch that the affrighted citizenry banded together in traditional style and marched upon Curwen's Pawtuxet farm, around which the rumours of his monstrous practices had gathered. A terrible battle ensued and nameless things fled and were slaughtered.

Curwen's widow reverted to her maiden name of Tillinghast and retreated, with her son, to her father's house. The farm mouldered into ruin. When Ward begins to pry into the unholy story, he begins at Curwen's town mansion, now dilapidated and inhabited by a Negro family. He uncovers a portrait of his ancestor, painted on a wall and concealed under layers of house-paint. The features are identical to those of Ward. Behind the portrait is a recess holding Curwen's private journal. From this point on, Ward is doomed in a particularly horrible way.

History repeats itself. Ward acquires a knowledge of occult and historical lore beyond the scope of the most assiduous antiquarian. He travels abroad, conferring with men learned in obscure and cryptic areas of human endeavour. Growing alarm about his mental state is reinforced by puzzling changes in his physique observed by his family physician, Dr Willett. The doctor is drawn into investigating the terrible secret behind Ward's trans-formation. This time, there will be no mass attack with swords and muskets. The entity known as Charles Dexter Ward is to be fought with his own weapons.

Willett's solitary odyssey through the Stygian pits beneath the ruins of the Pawtuxet farm is one of Lovecraft's finest evocations of sheer terror. Even his inability to resist a jibe at T. S. Eliot's *The Waste Land* doesn't impair the mood. There were times when the Sage of Providence could make readers squirm with embarrassment rather than fright, but when he was good, he was *evil*.

First edition, in *Beyond the Wall of Sleep*   Sauk City (Wisc): Arkham House, 1943
First US edition (and first separate edition)   London: Gollancz, 1951 (for 1952) (text reportedly defective)
First separate US edition   New York: Belmont, 1965

60
FLETCHER PRATT and
L. SPRAGUE DE CAMP
Land of Unreason

This novel originally appeared in a shorter version in the magazine *Unknown* in 1941. It was an outstanding story, even for that late lamented publication, and the best ever to bear the Pratt and de Camp byline. If it does not exactly hold up the mirror to Nature, it does reflect, in a contemporary glass, *A Midsummer Night's Dream*. The glass in question is filled with Scotch.

Fletcher Pratt, an authority on the American Civil War, and de Camp, patents adviser turned author, shared an interest in history and a sense of the absurd. Their twinned talents produced for *Unknown* the Harold Shea series, the first of which can be seen as setting-up exercises for *Land of Unreason*. Harold Shea, a psychologist, devises a 'syllogismobile' to transport himself into worlds of romance and myth. Applying modern logic to the problems presented by the Eddas, *Orlando Furioso* and *The Faerie Queene* among others, he has many wild and woolly adventures before returning to good old American apple-pie. Fred Barber's excursion into Oberon's kingdom is involuntary; for him there is no formula guaranteeing escape.

Red-haired Barber, a vice-consul at the American Embassy before his country entered the Second World War, is wounded in the head during an air-raid. Sent north to recuperate, he lodges with a Yorkshire family, the Gurtons. On Midsummer's Eve, as bombers illuminate the night over nearby towns, he drinks the milk Mrs Gurton left for the fairies, leaving in exchange a slug of Scotch. He awakes in Faerie, conveyed there by a drunken elf.

Matters there are in no better shape than in the world he left. The realm, from Titania and Oberon downwards, is hexed. Barber, by royal request, applies his diplomatic craft to the situation, though still suspecting it to be an hallucination resulting from his injury. He discovers that he has the ability, unknown to his hosts, to tell when someone is lying. Another and less immediately welcome gift follows—he begins to develop wings. Equipped thus, and with a wand given him by Titania, he sets out on a mission to the Kobold Hills. The Kobold smiths can handle iron, a metal deadly to Faerie folk. Oberon suspects them of being behind the plague of ill-shaping disrupting his realm. Barber, being mortal (but of mixed mortal and Faerie blood, as he learns with a shock) need not fear iron. How to find the Kobold Hills is another problem; directions in his new environment tend to be vague, and doubly so when affected by malicious magicking.

Employing a Bertrand Russell paradox to defeat an obstructive elemental, Barber reaches *the* forest and meets Malacea, an attractive though faintly transparent tree-sprite. She agrees to help him reach his objective, but instead

129

steals his wand. He is pursued by a homicidal plum tree, until a repentant Malacea tells him how to nobble it.

Rather illogically, he goes to considerable trouble to do so before leaving *the* forest, while making no attempt to recover the wand. A flurry of jive-talking sand-devils, who now serve only to date the story, help him to cross a desert to the foot of the Kobold Hills. To the accompaniment of hammers beating in three-four time and bierkeller choruses, he enters the metalsmith's caverns. It takes little knowledge of modern history to identify the real-life counterparts of the Kobolds, with their ponderous humour and disregard of diplomatic niceties. Just as things turn nasty, Barber uses a Kobold sword to touch a metal plate inscribed: 'Of places three/The one you see/Fyrst touched shall bee.' The result is literally explosive. Rapidly leaving the suddenly deserted caverns, he meets another mortal, an American farmer.

During his time with the farmer, even more alarming bodily changes take place. His incipient wings disappear; his eyes begin to swivel independently; his feet expand. He develops a taste for flies caught on the wing. Swimming in a woodland pool, he meets a beautiful redhead, Cola, who reminds him of a past girlfriend. But when they leave the water, he is a frog and she a vole. Cola will not believe his tale of being a mortal messenger from Oberon, thinking it a froggy delusion. He enters Hirudia, another easily identifiable analogue of a totalitarian state, precipitating a fierce battle. Touching an engraved mirror, he resumes his human shape and is forced to desert Cola and other underwater allies.

Now his wings and fiery beard are fully grown. He has become the prophesied saviour of Faerie, the Redbeard. In an ice-shrouded castle, the Princes of the Ice work their evil against Oberon's subjects. Barber must enter the castle and, in defeating the Princes, both find himself and lose himself.

Looking back over the past few decades, we should never have left him to the fairies.

First edition   New York: Henry Holt, 1942
First UK edition   London: Stacey, 1974

61
FRITZ LEIBER
Conjure Wife

Most Fantasy authors and artists would look out of place within the worlds of their imaginations. At best they could serve as spear-carriers, drawers of water or nameless victims. Fritz Leiber would be prominent among the adaptable minority. Inheritor of his actor father's tall, lean physique, impressive features and artistic talent, he was to find his outlet in the written word rather than the theatre.

Science-fantasy, crime, an 'official' Tarzan novel, big-city Gothics and less classifiable works have brought fame and enough awards to equip an Oscar ceremony. He was among the first to recognize that the glass caverns and industrial caldera of the modern metropolis breed their own monsters. Over the years he has developed the theme with increasing subtlety, from *You're All Alone* (1950) to *Our Lady of Darkness* (1976), and beyond. A forerunner of these urban horrors is his *Unknown* novel, *Conjure Wife*, which admits witchcraft to the mock-medieval cloisters of Hempnell College.

For those who share the alleged male belief that women possess supernatural powers, Leiber's basic premise will ring bells—the premise being that all women are, literally, witches. It works within the sheltered confines of a college; it sounds a deal less plausible in the paddyfields and sweatshops. What females lack, apparently, is the masculine ability to systematize their knowledge and direct it for maximum effect. Accept this and the rest goes down smoothly.

Successful young professor Norman Saylor finds the world a very satisfying place. Already attracting attention for his studies of primitive rituals and superstitions, he hopes to quit his sociology classes soon for better things. Only now, as the novel opens, has he paused to wonder at the ease with which he and his wife, Tansy, non-conformists both, have fitted into the college's rigid social structure. When the answer comes, it is unacceptable. Tansy has been shielding him from faculty snipers with protective spells. There is considerable irony in the fact that the subject-matter of his studies has invaded his domestic sanctum, but he is no mood to appreciate it. In a subsequent paperback edition, a little witchcraft on someone's part has frayed Saylor's youthfulness at the edges. His marriage date, 1929, remains unchanged, but an inserted reference to the nuclear threat jerks events forward into the Cold War era.

Every foible and failing of Leiber's sharply drawn characters is magnified by the claustrophobic academic environment. The situation transferred remarkably well to a British college in the Independent Artists film *Night of the Eagle* (1961), losing none of its essential tension. Released under at least two titles, one of them being *Burn, Witch, Burn*, which is also the title of a famous Merritt fantasy, the film transformed the novel's sorcerously animated stone dragon into a gigantic eagle which pursued Saylor in a terrifying chase sequence. The late Peter Wyngarde convincingly played the harried professor, while sporting an excruciatingly fashionable line in suits. Had it been made a decade earlier, it might have slotted neatly into Hollywood's paranoia period, between *The Thing from Another World* (1950) and *The Invasion of the Body Snatchers* (1956).

After a verbal and physical battle with a suddenly alien Tansy, Saylor imagines he has won by the use of logic and common sense. The discovery, afterwards, that his wife has only pretended to submit is doubly disturbing. And then inexplicable things begin to happen. Long-buried enmities break through into the daylight. His prospects of promotion recede. Instead of being a fascinated but detached student of the myth-making activities of the human race, he is down among the believers, fighting for his own and Tansy's lives and sanity. Forced to accept the power of witchcraft, he applies scientific methodology to its rituals, striving to drag it hissing and squirming into the light of reason.

Leiber skilfully adds the elements of a mystery story to his supernatural struggle. The powers of his deadliest opponent include the ability to transfer personalities, or souls, from body to body. Who, at the critical moment, is who, and who is to be saved or destroyed? The traditional denouement in the presence of all suspects gains a new and grisly twist.

Witch-figures proliferate in Leiber's fiction. He has a predilection for dark ladies whose attentions are ultimately deadly. On the other hand, he has been selling stories since 1939, so has obviously learned a few counter-spells of a more than adequate kind.

First edition, in *Witches Three*   New York: Twayne, 1952
First separate edition   New York: Twayne, 1953
First UK edition   Harmondsworth: Penguin, 1969

62

A. E. VAN VOGT
The Book of Ptath

Literary Golden Ages are movable feasts, their location in time usually coinciding with the reader's adolescence. When, as with sf and fantasy, the appeal of the literature is reinforced by its presentation in a colourful magazine format, first impressions can go deep. In so far as a general consensus exists, the first Golden Age coincided with the Second World War. Evidence is still plentifully present. Names which came to prominence during those paper-starved years continue to appear on the multitudinous new and reprinted titles filling bookstore shelves. Yet, even among these founders of the modern school, there was one who was unique. Other writers wrote about the future. A. E. van Vogt wrote *from* the future.

Systems designed to move us into that future, by promoting mental and physical development, were his forte. He was an early supporter of Dianetics, the forerunner of Scientology. A system for writing fiction sparked off his literary career. Non-Aristotelian logic, hypnotism, the Bates exercises for improving eyesight—all were put to amazing uses. Though his first sf story sold to *Astounding*, no less, the impression remains that his beloved systems were no more than a veneer of pseudo-rationality laid over wild, dark, labyrinthine dreams. The madness, so to speak, had taken the method for its mouthpiece.

For an author whose particular gift it was to evoke magic from scientific fact and speculation, the switch to fantasy must have been as natural as breathing. *Unknown*, the short-lived companion of *Astounding*, used many of the senior title's contributors. Van Vogt's method seemed to work equally well there; *The Book of Ptath* ran in *Unknown* in 1943.

An alternative title is *200,000,000 A.D.*, a round figure if ever there was one. After the passage of this typically Van Vogtian splurge of zeros, the slow waltz of the continents has obliterated any resemblance to the maps of today. Three great powers occupy the new lands: Gonwonlane, Nushirvan and Accadistran. Their combined populations total almost 80 billion people, a figure calculated to make twentieth-century demographers break out in a cold sweat. This seething mass remains a row of ciphers, for the physical implications of such numbers are never explored. How the future states contrive to feed them is not touched upon, nor is there a satisfactory explanation for the medieval level of weapons and transport. When the hero, Holroyd, observes that the Moon is now so close to the Earth that its apparent diameter is ten *feet*, that is the sole reference to this astonishing fact. It remains a stage prop, influencing nothing. Ptath's world, in short, must be accepted as one accepts a vivid dream.

The significance of these future billions, as with those of Asimov's Galactic Empire, lies in their very numbers. Only such a vast aggregation of worshippers can generate the God-power which is the source of Ptath's strength and being. To renew his human qualities, he has submerged his dominant personality within the mass of humanity, travelling into the distant past to take on a succession of identities. In this state, he becomes vulnerable to the scheming of one of his two wives, golden Ineznia. She recalls him while he is still occupying the body of Holroyd, an American officer on war service. Thus divided in mind, she reasons, his protective 'spells' should be more easily negated and his power broken. His other wife, dark Lônee, she holds captive in the God-king's citadel.

Ptath-Holroyd's arrival in Gonwonlane is a classic example of a favourite van Vogt motif, the displaced and bewildered superman. Conscious only of his own existence, he must determine the nature and meaning of the world around him in relation to himself. Anything which obstructs him or causes pain is an enemy. Completely ignorant (the term 'blank', in reference to mental states, constantly recurs in Van Vogt's fiction) of social rules, he blunders into a battle with mounted warriors and finds that he is impervious to spear and arrow wounds, an advantage appreciated by his Holroyd component in later episodes. A more telling test comes with his dawning awareness of the plot against him, as the soldier's persona grapples with the scale and strangeness of the coming war. The outcome can be summed up in a phrase familiar to Holroyd: there are no atheists in fox-holes.

If Gods can be improved by doing a stretch among the common herd, would it work for secular leaders too? Perhaps van Vogt could set his still-fertile imagination to work on a system . . .

First edition   Reading (PA): Fantasy Press, 1947

63
HENRY KUTTNER
The Dark World
The Valley of the Flame

An experience known to long-time magazine readers is that of discovering that two or more of their favourite authors are actually aspects of the same person. When publications were plentiful and payments low, a prolific output was required to sustain a moderate income. As a result, pseudonyms abounded. Speed and adaptability brought in the cheques, while inflicting an anonymity which could be compounded by the use of publisher's house-names allotted in turn to a string of contributors. Adaptability was Kuttner's forte, and his multiplicity of bylines was increased by numerous story collaborations between himself and his wife, C. L. Moore. Which of them wrote what will probably never be known with certitude. In an informal interview reported in the sf and Fantasy news magazine *Locus*, she is said to have claimed sole authorship of *The Dark World*.

Merritt was a potent influence upon the generation of writers which included Kuttner. *The Dark World* owes much to *The Dwellers in the Mirage*; to use a favourite euphemism of film students, it is his homage to the master. It is a measure of his talent that it has become a minor classic in its own right. Some find it preferable to the original.

The Dark World of the title is an alternate Earth which follows its own peculiar scheme of evolution. We are shown very little of it, but it seems thinly populated and unindustrialized. Though the two worlds are on steadily diverging paths, there is still sufficient resemblance between them for the duplication of personalities to occur. On Earth, Edward Bond is a wartime flyer; his counterpart is the ruthless Ganelon, a member of the Dark World's ruling Coven. Above the Coven is Llyr, in a region withdrawn from normal time and space, whose hunger for human sacrifices is the price the Coven must pay for their power.

Ganelon has been given false memories of a life as Edward Bond and then exiled to Earth by the white witch, Freydis. Her magic produces an equal and opposite reaction which draws Bond to the Dark World. Experienced in the methods of modern warfare, his knowledge and daring adds a new ferocity to the Robin Hood style campaigns of Freydis and her forest-based rebels. Already shaken by the increasing inaccessibility of Llyr, the Coven contrive to snatch back Ganelon, displacing Bond to Earth.

Still struggling with the pseudo-personality of Bond, Ganelon is slow to grasp that he has been brought back as a sacrifice to Llyr. When he does, the total destruction of the other Coven members becomes his consuming purpose. Looking at them in the light of Earthly science, he rationalizes their supernatural attributes in terms of radiation-induced mutations; when the worlds were more intimately linked, they were the source of the myths of the vampire, the werewolf, Medusa. In 1946, with post-Hiroshima fever raging through the magazines, nuclear power had been transformed in one blinding instant from Aladdin's Lamp to Pandora's Box.

He presents himself to the rebels as Edward Bond, newly returned from Earth. With their help, he will destroy the Coven and even omnipotent Llyr. Only Freydis is aware of his secret, but she needs his peculiar knowledge and talents. The tangle of allegiances is resolved in a weirdly logical climax which adds an extra dimension to Merritt's original.

Kuttner devised one of the most amazing of lost cultures for *The Valley of the Flame*, secluded in a vast meteoric crater in the Amazon rainforest. The Flame is life run wild, the alien reality behind the legend of Curupuri, spirit of the forest. Its influence touches Brian Raft and Dan Craddock, downriver in their medical research station. There has been some needless and rather slipshod updating here. In 1946, the action was placed in the near future: '. . . ten years since the end of World War Two . . .' The revised version substitutes 'forty' for 'ten', making a reference to Raft's expedition to Tibet seem an unlikely event in view of Chinese policies. Not that this is Kuttner's doing. He died in 1958.

Craddock disappears upriver with a mysterious visitor, Pereira, whose physiology is only superficially human. Raft tracks them through a cavernous underworld of hideous monstrosities in the land of the Flame, Paititi. Within the aura of the Flame, life moves with abnormal rapidity. Under its spell, Raft sees rivers flow like molasses and avalanches tumble in slow-motion. Here, Pereira represents the norm. His ancestors, artificially evolved as the result of Craddock's past tampering with the Flame, were jaguars.

The equivalent of millions of years of Paititian evolution have been compressed into three decades of Craddock's life, a dizzying vision of flesh and bone flowing and changing faster than the eye can follow. Now the fires of life are sinking and he must return to save his dying Eden. Kuttner speculates fascinatingly upon the mores and psychology of a feline civilization, though skating too lightly over the anatomical differences between man and cat. In this respect, Raft is luckier than the hero of Hollywood's *Island of Lost Souls*. He gets his panther girl. Popular fiction too had evolved.

The Dark World
First edition   New York: Ace, 1965
First UK edition   London: Mayflower, 1966

The Valley of the Flame
First edition   New York: Ace, 1964

64
MERVYN PEAKE
Titus Groan/Gormenghast/Titus Alone

Mervyn Peake died in 1968 of a disease which gradually, over a period of years, robbed him of his ability to draw. So ended the career, at fifty-seven, of a writer and artist whose work remains comparatively little known, despite major exhibitions and a television adaptation of his novel *Mr Pye*. The *Titus Groan* trilogy lacks the easy accessibility of, say, *The Lord of the Rings*, though there was a time when both seemed of equally specialized appeal. It did attract, and continues to hold, the fiercely partisan regard of many other artists and authors.

Part of the origin of Peake's singular vision must lie in his childhood circumstances. The son of a missionary doctor, he was born in Kuling, in southern China. From there, his family moved north to Tientsin, where the young Mervyn spent his early schooldays on an Occidental island set in an Oriental sea. Though his parents were British, he came to England, at the age of twelve, as if to a foreign country. Already, he had shown for some years an extraordinary commitment to the act of drawing, which was never to leave him. The handwritten drafts of his novels are annotated with a gallery of grotesques, as if the text had sprouted heads, figures, faces. Words beget images, which in turn beget words.

Maeve, his wife, was also a painter. Their house, in London's Drayton Gardens, provided an incongrously relaxed setting for the strange and phantasmagorical products of their twin talents. Among the many pictures hung an eerie, enigmatic figure which he had painted for her as a surprise Christmas gift while she was attending Midnight Mass. It fell to Maeve to fend off the vultures who descended upon this treasure-house after the news of Mervyn's death. Few things so enhance an artist's reputation as evidence of his mortality.

Titus Groan, the first volume of the trilogy, was a child of the Phoney War period. As Peake, like so many others, marked time while awaiting call-up, he began writing the novel which was to accompany him through all the rigours of Army routine. He was not an ideal soldier. In 1943, despairing of Peake the trained killer, the Army released him to become a war artist. During the next few years he began to write *Gormenghast* and illustrated, among many other things, *Alice's Adventures in Wonderland* and *The Rime of the Ancient Mariner*.

Like Peake, the young Earl of Groan spends his childhood in an enclave. Gormenghast, the family castle, is a vast and rambling structure, a country in stone, a way of life, a state of mind. Tradition is all. Titus is the seventy-seventh Earl, succeeding to the title when his father is eaten by owls. If Peake had needed a model for the infant Titus, nature provided one when Maeve gave birth to their first child, Sebastian, at the time of the novel's conception. Both grew up in a world where custom had ceased to guarantee security. Peake the war artist saw, by the black light of Belsen, a future which even his pen could not adequately depicit. To take Titus from the stifling shelter of his ancestral home, in *Titus Alone*, and have him reject it in favour of a hostile and arbitrary outer world seems to fly in the face of reality. Yet for his creator it was the only possible decision.

The looming walls of Gormenghast enclose a host of wittily drawn individuals. Comparison with Dickens is inevitable, for however monstrous Peake's creatures may be, their core of authentic humanity makes their farcical humour and tragedy of absorbing importance to the reader. Perhaps the most telling example of his ability to tap boyhood memories is his loving caricature of the teaching staff, complete to the last ingrained fragment of chalk. Running it a close second is the Hall of Bright Carvings episode, in which craftsmen from the surrounding villages submit wood-carvings to the judgement of the Earl: 'The competition . . . was bitter and rabid. The air . . . was turgid with contempt and jealousy. The craftsmen stood about like beggars . . . . uncouth and prematurely aged. All radiance gone.' Any self-employed artist will recognize the scene.

Many an accomplished novelist might blanch at the prospect of stage-managing so many idiosyncratic characters, but Peake pursues their labyrinthine interrelationships with an intoxicating energy. Fuchsia, the infant Earl's older sister, could have strayed backwards through time from the 1960s, with her long, wild hair, vivid yet sullen face, shapeless, colourful clothes and love of art as sensation. The kitchen-boy, Steerpike, dark counterpart of Titus, gnaws at the structure of his ossified society like a rat in the wall. Between Earl and kitchen-boy, rebels at opposing poles, the teeming life of Gormenghast loves, hates, suffers and rejoices.

The gates are open. There's always room for one more. Enter.

Titus Groan
First edition   London: Eyre & Spottiswoode, 1946
First US edition   New York: Reynal, 1946

Gormenghast
First edition   London: Eyre & Spottiswoode, 1950
First US edition   New York: Weybright, 1967

Titus Alone
First edition   London: Eyre & Spottiswoode, 1959
First US edition   New York: Weybright, 1967

65
MAURICE RICHARDSON
The Exploits of Engelbrecht

Damon Runyon Gothic is an unduly neglected sub-genre of fantasy. Its sole practitioner is not mentioned in otherwise excellent works of reference such as the *Encyclopedia of Horror and the Supernatural*, while *Trillion Year Spree* quotes him only as a reviewer of Stoker's *Dracula*. To those familiar with his style, the single quoted sentence needs no byline. Twelve words long, it contains eight adjectives, two of them hyphenated. This is the Richardson whose essay in *Lilliput Magazine* on *Melmoth the Wanderer* must have drawn a flock of new readers to Maturin's masterwork. Richardson, under his fiction-writer's hat, was something else.

And so was *Lilliput*. Though only one of a number of digest-sized magazines born in the shadow of the Second World War, its roster of contributors was unmatched. A far from comprehensive list could include Shaw, Wells, Mervyn Peake, Arthur C. Clarke, Patrick Campbell and a schoolboy called Gerard Hoffnung, who ought not to have been reading it. Like its more light-weight competitors, such as *London Opinion* and the original *Men Only*, it featured morale-building pin-ups and nudes. Patrick Campbell's comment that the post-war examples featured poses which 'would rupture an Algerian acrobat' was possibly inspired by athletic dancer-actress Pamela Green, who was on the way to achieving the status of a minor cult-figure. In reality, the nudes were innocuous by current standards. The prime attraction of *Lilliput* was the variety and quality of the fiction and articles, often accompanied by artwork on fantastic themes. Unhappily, the declining market for unspecia-lized magazines proved fatal. After a quarter-century of varying fortunes, *Lilliput* became a collector's item.

In the issue dated June 1946 appeared the first of the exploits of Engelbrecht, the Dwarf Surrealist Boxer. He was the rough diamond of the Surrealist Sportsman's Club, some of whose clientele could have given your average Thing a nasty turn. His most memorable bouts found him wildly overmatched, in the manner of Popeye but without the spinach. Surrealist Boxers customarily fought against clocks and assorted amusement machines, but the Dwarf took on all comers, from Apparitions to Zombies.

Written in a style which lightly parodies Runyon's racy idiom while remaining unmistakably Richardson's, the series ranges over all of Time, Space and the bits in between. The illustrators included Ronald Searle and Gerard Hoffnung, but the artist who stamped his mark upon it was James Boswell. His artwork embellished the book version, first published in 1950. It was a brave venture, for the time. The boom in sf and Fantasy was as yet not even a dream. Twenty-seven years were to pass before it was reprinted. It still awaits the attention a more ambitious format might attract.

Membership of the Club involves Engelbrecht in a wide variety of sports, which usually end in a brawl. Making his debut in *The Big Witch Shoot*, he has a tussle with a downed Witch and is dropped from a great height before returning, muddy and triumphant, to Nightmare Abbey. His attitude to the Noble Art is practical yet romantic. When his manager, Lizard Bayliss, matches him against a formidable Grandfather Clock, his first question is: 'What'd he take to lie down?' On being told that the bribe would be more than he could afford, and that he ought to bet on the Clock and take a dive, he retorts: 'If I can't frame, I fight.'

Betting in the Surrealist arena is peculiarly hazardous. Time, not money, is the currency, and a loser is apt to end up white-haired and trembling. Engelbrecht has to overcome induced senility and the machinations of the Club's notorious fixer, Chippy de Zoete, in addition to his brass-weighted opponent. Staged on a wasteland 'between two parallel canals that don't even meet at infinity,' the fight literally brings Time to a stop.

The Day We Played Mars puts the entire human race into the field to play Surrealist Rugby against formidable extra-terrestrial opposition. Salvador Dali plays fullback and the pitch is on the Moon. Things are looking bad for humanity until Marx and Engels play the old Trojan Horse trick by concealing the Dwarf inside the ball. Culture occasionally prevails over muddied oafishness, though Opera and the Drama are attended by perils unknown to patrons of the South Bank. Plant Theatre productions demand, at the very least, endurance. The New Forest's *King Lear*, with a cast of oaks, has been on stage for 5,000 years and the curtain is not yet. Some of the more susceptible members of the audience are rooted to the spot. Chippy de Zoete, taking bets on the chances of *The Dog's Opera* lasting beyond the opening night, improves the odds by introducing the entire population of The Good Samaritan Cats' Home into the proceedings in mid-performance.

Golf, wrestling, chess, cricket, racing and even politics get the Richardson treatment, an indescribable mélange of mythology, Gothic horror, nuclear warfare and plain low-life. Don't wait for some enlightened publisher to resurrect the Dwarf—start digging for him now.

First edition   London: Phoenix House, 1950

66
T. H. WHITE
Mistress Masham's Repose

Appearing midway between the first and final versions of White's Arthurian sequence, *Mistress Masham's Repose* is usually categorized as a children's fantasy. In this genre, however, adult readers know that such distinctions can be ignored to advantage. White speaks to all ages, even though his heroine, Maria, is ten years old.

Familiarity with Swift's *Gulliver's Travels* will help in appreciating the background to White's story, but it is not essential. For that matter, few children are likely to be capable of grasping the literary jokes and historical allusions strewn throughout the text, often arising from the activities of Maria's friend and tenant, the Professor. White brings off the feat of sustaining a running gag involving the Professor's efforts to define the meaning of the Latin word *Tripharium* and making it funny. His own view of the modern world cannot have been improved by five years of war, and the impractical pedant serves as a mouthpiece for his disaffection.

The Repose of the title is one of those neo-classical structures once beloved of the lords of country estates, a miniature temple pillared and domed, standing upon an island. Mistress Masham has long since departed the scene. The last of her line, Maria rattles around in the enormous spaces of the family mansion, Malplaquet, together with her Governess, Miss Brown, and the cook, Mrs Noakes. Mrs Noakes, being of the lower orders, is naturally incapable of forming a coherent sentence but is doggedly loyal. The post-war social revolution obviously still had some way to go.

Malplaquet's population is more numerous than its young mistress could possibly suspect. Evading the awful Miss Brown in the near-wilderness of the grounds, Maria invades the briary island of the Repose. She finds a baby in a walnut shell. Alive and one inch long. A sharp pain in her ankle apprises her of the presence of the mother, armed with a harpoon. To Maria, unfamiliar with *Gulliver's Travels*, the woman's cry of 'Quinba Flestrina' is no clue. Annoyed and intrigued, she carries mother and child off to her room.

The Professor soon identifies the newly discovered tenants as Lilliputians and conjectures that they were taken from their homeland by Capt John Biddel, who had been instrumental in returning Gulliver to England. Luckily, among his overflowing library is the only copy extant of *A General Description of Lilliput with a Brief Vocabulary*, which he loans to her. He also points out that though tiny, they are people, not toys. They must be allowed to pursue their own ways. As she sets out to repair her damaged relationship with the islanders, her Governess and the local Vicar are plotting to profit from her inheritance. Though Maria is unaware of their schemes, she is determined to keep her new friends secret from them. Hungry for love, she had been in danger of exploiting them for emotional reasons. The Governess and the Vicar would have more sinister motives.

Bit by bit, however, the secret comes to light. Gifts from the Lilliputians to Maria excite the cupidity of her guardians, who can only suppose that she has located a hoard of treasure somewhere in Malplaquet's mouldering magnificence. Thwarted by her silence, Miss Brown sends her to bed without any supper. The islanders daringly scale the walls to bring her reassurance and a meal—three roast oxen, two barrels of wine and four dozen loaves.

The Governess's ears are sharp. She bursts into the room, expecting she knows not what, and finds an undreamed-of prize. After a desperate struggle she captures one Lilliputian and takes him to the Vicarage to display him to her accomplice. But Gradgnag, a kind of miniature Allan Quartermain, rescues the prisoner. White's description of the perils of the Malplaquet gardens, vast as prairies to Gradgnag and swarming with feral beasts and birds, makes of his safari a small epic.

So eager are Miss Brown and the Vicar to find the home of the highly marketable Lilliputians that they resort to the novel tactic of kindness to weaken Maria's resistance. She makes the most of this. Knowing that they will trail her in the hope of being led to their goal, she walks their legs off. The strain of assumed benevolence proves too great and her guardians resolve upon firmer measures, beginning with the dungeons. Mrs Noakes, unable to oppose them effectively, appeals to the Professor.

The Professor is wrestling with two consuming problems, the meaning of *Tripharium* and the mysterious disappearance (or so it seems) of his *Du Cange*, a dictionary of medieval Latin. It takes some time to divert him from this double quest. The Professor is a marvellous creation, at times almost too painfully real. When he becomes aware of Maria's peril, the authorities whose help he solicits are rather less able than himself.

In a tense, thrilling and farcical finale, the aroused Lilliputians storm the inner landscapes of Malplaquet to the rescue. Villainy is confounded, Maria comes into her rightful inheritance and the Professor is presented with a *Medieval Latin Word List* (Baxter and Johnson, 10s 6d), which tells him all about *Tripharium*.

Anyone similarly curious will find the definition on page 220 of the New Windmill Edition of *Mistress Masham's Repose*.

First edition   New York: Putnams, 1946
First UK edition   London: Jonathan Cape, 1947

67
FRITZ LEIBER
Adept's Gambit

Street and Smith's *Unknown* ran from 1939 to 1943, establishing in that brief span a new attitude to Fantasy. Horror had not been banished; instead, it had to share equal billing with humour. This untraditional policy invited a kind of fiction for which no market had hitherto existed and brought with it a crop of new bylines. Among them was Fritz Leiber, Jnr.

The tall, silver-haired Leiber of today, looking like one of the more distinguished sorcerers from his fabulous city of Lankhmar, is nobody's notion of a Junior. In 1939, things were different. The famous Fritz Leiber was his father, a stage and film actor. For a while, Leiber Junior had a show-business career too, until it was eclipsed by his true vocation, writing. Father and son now share a flickering immortality on the television screen when it is doing what Nature intended it for: reviving old black-and-white films.

His first submission to *Unknown*, and his first published story, starred those clown princes of Swords and Sorcery, Fafhrd and the Gray Mouser. 'Two Sought Adventure', a.k.a. 'The Jewels in the Forest', was followed in 1940 by 'The Howling Tower', the forerunners of volumes of exotic adventures. The language of the series has, over the years, tended towards over-elaboration, so that digressions and descriptions curl about the characters like the scrolls of a medieval manuscript, retarding the flow of the narrative. *Adept's Gambit* strikes a balance between these and the shorter, starker mood-pieces, but the order in which the stories were written is less straightforward than this would suggest. For anyone who believes that fiction springs, Athene-like, fullblown from the author's forehead, Leiber's account in *Amra* of the genesis of Fafhrd and the Mouser will be a revelation.

In the beginning was Harry Fischer, a widely read and imaginative young man, destined for an outwardly prosaic life as a packaging designer. Fantasies flourished in the letters between himself and Leiber as they picked up on each other's invented worlds and characters, not all of them heroic. It was Fischer who produced, seemingly out of thin air, the swart, elusive Mouser and the towering, barbaric Fafhrd. A stereoscopically vivid vignette limned them against Lankhmar's torch-lit streets, their past and future already wreathed in mystery. When Gnome Press published the hardcover collection, *Two Sought Adventure* (1957), Leiber added the intriguing stroke: '. . . they were two long-sundered matching fragments of a greater hero.'

The saga grew and ramified. Within three years it included early versions or portions of *The Lords of Quarmall, The Tale of the Grain Ships* and *Adept's Gambit*. For the first time, Leiber tried to sell a story, to *Weird Tales*. Though the magazine had a fairly flexible editorial policy, it rejected *Adept's Gambit*, and several other adventures of the disreputable duo. Not until it had passed through much rewriting was it published by Arkham House in 1947 as part of *Night's Black Agents*.

Today, the reluctance of *Weird Tales* seems almost incomprehensible. The opening scenes, set in ancient Tyre at the time of King Antiochus, are a dazzling blend of wit, casual erudition and slapstick. We have Leiber's word for the shortlived existence of a version which flirted with Lovecraft's pantheon of Elder Gods, supernatural foes of such stupefying humourlessness that the peregrinatory pair might well have been slain by terminal boredom. Certainly, Nyarlathotep would not have appreciated a curse which transformed one's girlfriend, when kissed, into a sow or a snail. Driven to desperation, Fafhrd and the Mouser go to consult one of their tutelary deities, Ningauble of the Seven Eyes.

Compared to the verbal fencing between the adventurers and the sly, enigmatic Ningauble, most Swords and Sorcery dialogue is at best serviceable, at worst mere babble. *Adept's Gambit* itself never quite rises to such heights again and suffers from rather too much exposition towards the end. Despatched upon a half-comprehended mission, impelled by obscure threats should they fail, the two set out, accompanied by the mysterious Ahura, one of Leiber's many dark ladies. By the time that the complete series was published, by Ace Books, Leiber had rationalized the link between our mundane Earth and their bubble-world of Nehwon; in 1947 the period setting was presented without explanation.

To her frustrated companions, the presence of the alluring Ahura is a constant reminder of paradise lost. Admonitory messages from Ningauble, delivered in various unlikely ways, only aggravate the tension. At the moment when it snaps, the Mouser and his nimble blade, Scalpel, clash with the unhumanly fast and untiring Adept, risen from a place of dust and spiders. His uncanny resemblance to Ahura intensifies the horror of their whirling dance of death. As its conclusion, the quest might be assumed to have ended. Fafhrd and the Mouser, wise in the ways of their idiosyncratic Gods, know that there are always riddles beyond secrets beyond mysteries. They saddle their horses, load up their camel, and carry on.

Packaging designers are probably worthy citizens, even if their products are too often expensive, obstructive and infuriating. Good fantasy writers are a rarer breed. The industry could well have spared us Harry Fischer, though his bank manager would doubtless disagree.

First edition, in *Night's Black Agents*   Sauk City (Wisconsin):
Arkham House, 1947
First UK edition   London: Spearman, 1975

144

68
FLETCHER PRATT
The Well of the Unicorn

Except in the memories of American Civil War buffs, Fletcher Pratt's name is probably known chiefly in association with that of Sprague de Camp. Time and the vagaries of publishing have accorded his two Swords and Sorcery novels, *The Well of the Unicorn* and *The Blue Star* (1952), less recognition than they deserve.

The Well had an unfortunate start. It was fine for a Huxley or a Stapledon to publish sf under his own name because, coming from so elevated a source, it couldn't be sf, could it? Lesser-known writers with established reputations as historians must not be allowed to appear between hardcovers with works of Fantasy, whatever they got up to in magazines when respectable publishers' backs were turned. So Fletcher Pratt, at William Sloane, Inc's request, became George U. Fletcher. Just in case the whole thing proved too much for the book-buying public, they added an explanatory foreword to the author's preface. The book flopped.

An historian's discipline underlies the world of the *Well*. Rafael Palacios's maps, some of the finest ever to grace a fantasy, show lands which are more than just names to play with. Scandinavia is the obvious model for Dalarna, recalling Pratt's fondness for the Icelandic Eddas; it is dominated by the Vulkings, who sound like the Vikings but are more nearly comparable to the Romans. Airar Alvarson, heir to his father's estate, is dispossessed for debt by the Vulkings and by page 2 is a homeless wanderer. He has something of a gift for magic, but enough sense not to try it against an armed party. Along the road, a talking owl guides him to the house of a fulltime magician, Meliboe, who offers him gold in return for performing an errand.

Before very long he is swept up in a plot to overthrow the Vulking oppressors. Yet his dislike of the conquerors doesn't blind him to the fact that all governments are imperfect and that the Vulkings' ways do have something to recommend them. Throughout the book, there is a running debate upon the degrees of individual choice permissible under any system which must handle the affairs of an entire nation. Airar, as he gains experience and rises to the command of a body of warriors, has to test his own answers upon the field of war, where faulty reasoning is punishable by defeat or death.

The Well of the title illustrates the peril of seeking answers outside of oneself. There are four tales of the Well at appropriate points in the narrative; each tells of how a solution was sought by drinking of its waters and how the solution came about to the detriment of the drinkers. Airar again learns that no satisfaction can be gained by recourse to magic, even that of professionals such as Meliboe.

Comparisons have been drawn between the *Well* and *The Worm Ouroboros*; Sprague de Camp is positive that Pratt was strongly influenced by Eddison's novel. Both authors were well versed in the Norse myths, though their styles and temperaments were very different. Pratt could never have countenanced the granting of the Demonlords' wish for eternally recurring conflict as an antidote to boredom. He could not ignore the fact that war, even in imaginary lands, was 'horror and pain and the death of friends'. His grasp of military strategy and tactics was firmer than Eddison's. Battles need not be less exciting for being knowledgeably planned and executed. Another and minor influence, to which he admitted in his preface, was that of Dunsany. He took the events of Dunsany's 'King Argimenes and the Unknown Warrior' and wove them into the ancient history of Airar's Dalarna. For good measure he added on an incident based upon a real-life misadventure of L. Ron Hubbard.

William Sloane, Inc went out of business, but the *Well* reappeared as a paperback and established a wider reputation. Twayne Publishers, Inc put out a three-novel anthology in 1952 which included *The Blue Star*. Pratt continued his debates upon life, the universe and everything in a world dreamed of by three men during an evening's drinking, so breaking the unwritten rule about opening a story with a conversation in a bar.

It has to be said that *The Blue Star* is more of a talking-piece than a tale of action. The Star is a gem with magical powers; witchcraft and revolution are the moving forces. Oddly, in both *Well* and *The Blue Star* there is a religion indistinguishable from Christianity, though it is never referred to as such. Pratt was a Christian Scientist. His fantasies are not for those who ask no more than the vigorous action and primary colours of the Howard school, nor are there any retirement pensions beyond the Grey Havens for his walking wounded. His characters grow as they go, and when they stop growing, they stop. Finis.

First edition   New York: William Sloane, 1948
First UK edition   London: Futura, 1977

69

FRITZ LEIBER
You're All Alone

Red-rimmed, the eyes of an enormous hound blaze from the cover of *Fantastic Adventures*. In the dripping jaws of the massive green and purple head, a redheaded girl stares in horror at her captor. Shreds of dress cling to rounded limbs, caged in the hound's curving fangs. The vivid red background is devoid of detail. Everything superfluous has been stripped away in order to sock the browsing buyer between the eyes. They don't do them like that no more but when they did, Robert Gibson Jones was among the best.

With pulp magazines, the packaging could be considerably more lurid than the contents. *You're All Alone* lives up to its cover in every way, and more. Leiber does here what *Our Lady of Darkness* did for San Francisco, only on a larger scale. It could well be the ultimate expression of big-city paranoia, justifying the darkest fears of every tenant of bedsitter-land. They really are out to get you, on the streets.

Leiber spent his first five decades in Chicago, studying physiology and psychology at university, working as an editor when the Depression killed any prospect of a fulltime acting career and only gradually edging into authorship. His familiarity with the capital of the Mid-West adds an extra frisson to a narrative already humming with tension. No illustrator could improve upon his superbly staged scenes in the cavernous public library, hemmed in between walls of dead knowledge in a dead city. Carr Mackay is one of the urban automata, clerking in an employment bureau, kept on a short leash by his contriving girlfriend Marcia, never breaking step. Until a frightened girl walks into his office and tells him who really runs the world.

Being a clerk rather than your average private-eye, he is rattled. Only a few people, she tells Mackay, are truly alive, and he is now one of them. So is the statuesque blonde waiting menacingly in the doorway. The presence of the girl, Jane Gregg, has awakened him. Like her, he is no longer part of the machine. As she leaves, the blonde slaps her, viciously. She walks on. No one else seems to notice. Suddenly the office routine becomes something eerie and alien. An interviewee sits at Mackay's unoccupied desk, talking to empty air. Another clerk introduces him to a non-existent girl.

Mackay tries to rationalize these events, in the face of ever-increasing evidence of wrongness. His disbelief, as so often in this kind of situation, goes on beyond the bounds of credibility before he is persuaded to accept the truth. The world is a vast machine of which human beings are merely components, going through predestined actions, speaking predestined words. Here and there individuals awake, become aware of the machine and break away. When they do, their associates continue to behave as if they were still present, holding one-sided conversations, serving never-eaten meals, making love. Humanity becomes a toy for the few, an endless source of perverted pleasure.

An aware person can sometimes awaken others simply by being present at the right moment, though more often it is done deliberately for selfish motives. Jane, knowing that a gang of such people suspect that she is aware, is desperately pretending to be part of the machine. The slap was meant to test her reactions; registering shock would have been a fatal giveaway. She warns Mackay to keep up his daily routine and to avoid getting involved with her. He ignores her advice. Soon they are fellow-fugitives, pursued by the gang and their gigantic hound. Leiber adds a mythological touch by having one of the blonde's henchmen lose a hand to the beast, echoing the fate of Tyr when he bound the wolf Fenrir.

There are dangers for all who break free. The machine is no less powerful for being blind and there is no place in the pattern for independent pieces. On the roads the awakened drive at their own risk, for to the automata they do not exist. One of the most hair-raising episodes has Mackay involved in a Keystone Kops race through traffic-laden streets, driven by a drunken friend of Jane Gregg. As if one band of sadists wasn't enough, Mackay stumbles upon a sinister black-clad quartet ghoulishly at work in a department store, as if a hit-squad had wandered into Collier's 'Evening Primrose'. The discovery that they terrify his original pursuers too is cold comfort.

You're All Alone makes a perfunctory nod towards optimism at the close, without conviction. After the nail-biting suspense, hair's-breadth escapes and hysterical humour, it is the city which stays in the memory. Cold, harshly lit, impersonal, cramming its millions together in meaningless intimacy, it no longer needs an encircling wall. Jane and Mackay don't plan to leave. Even the awakened can't survive anywhere else.

First edition, in *The Sinful Ones* (bound with another title)   New York: Universal Giant, 1953
First separate edition, as *You're All Alone*   New York: Ace, 1972

70
JACK VANCE
The Dying Earth

In 1961 *Amra*, that durable and erudite organ catering to lovers of Heroic
Fantasy, featured a review by mathematician Robert Briney of *The Dying
Earth*. It ended with a plea to his readers to let him know if they found a spare
copy. His own, published in 1950, was on the verge of disintegration. At that
time, the disappearance into limbo of books by much more famous authors
than Vance was common enough. On this occasion, someone Out There
must have been listening. By 1962, Lancer Books had republished his first and
most sought-after title.

Unlike many writers who began their careers in the pulp magazines,
Vance's first collection was of previously unpublished stories. Three of them
relate the interwoven adventures of characters inhabiting Ancient Earth and
an adjoining world of magic. In the other three, although some of these characters recur, the strongest link is the setting and the overwhelming presence
of the past. A huge red sun smoulders in Earth's dark-blue sky, painting her
worn contours with rich and sombre light. Scattered human communities, the
dwindling descendants of her swarming billions, dot the vast spaces where
ruins predominate. Strange and ferocious entities haunt the forests, preying
upon travellers unequipped with protective spells.

Parallels for this vision of the far future are not difficult to find. Clark
Ashton Smith's tales of Zothique and other exotic lands come first to mind. A
thinly peopled world thick with the dust of countless civilizations, the prevalence of sorcery, fell creatures lurking in wild and lonely places, a gift for the
placing of uncommon words to maximum effect—all find their echoes in *The
Dying Earth*. Smith, an acclaimed poet, was besotted with the archaic and *outré*
elements of language, while his love of the macabre far outstripped that of
Vance, particularly in his disregard for the welfare of his characters. In his
latter-day world, power to manipulate the environment resides chiefly in the
hands of necromancers. Michael Moorcock's *Dancers at the End of Time*, conversely, subscribes to Arthur C. Clarke's dictum that any sufficiently
advanced technology would be indistinguishable from magic. Vance blends
both viewpoints in the sixth story, *Guyal of Sfere*, an eerie and witty account of
a demonic invader repelled by science rather than incantations. When, in *Ulan
Dhor*, he introduces a stock 'city of the future' replete with airboats and anti-
gravity elevators, the effect is to weaken the *fin-de-siècle* mood.

One of the several joys of Vance's work is his talent for devising evocative
names, and in *The Dying Earth* it serves him well. The catalogue of spells
available to his wizards provokes wonder and amusement, without ever
lapsing into the cute or the twee. There is magic in the very sound of them:

the Omnipotent Sphere, the Excellent Prismatic Spray, Phandaal's Gyrator, the Call to the Violent Cloud. Only four spells can be memorized at one time, save by the most accomplished magicians, and once used they must be relearned.

Pandelume, reputedly the greatest master of the Art, dwells in a world of his own, Embelyon, where the eponymous hero of *Turjan of Miir* must seek him out. Turjan's attempts to grow an artificial human being in his laboratory having failed, he resorts in desperation to Pandelume, aware that the wizard drives a hard bargain. Once in Embelyon, he discovers that the master too can make mistakes. Pandelume's creation, the beautiful T'sais, has a mental flaw which causes her to see all things as vile and ugly, including herself. Turjan becomes the master's assistant, but T'sais slays his first perfect creation, gentle Floriel. Conscious of T'sais's inner torment, he cannot bring himself to exact revenge. Instead, he devises her flawless twin, T'sain. When the two women meet, T'sais sees her vat-sister as a mockery of her own imagined ugliness, until T'sain persuades her to accept a different view of herself. She leaves Embelyon to seek new experiences upon Earth.

In *Mazirian the Magician*, T'sain rescues Turjan from an evil wizard, at great cost to herself. Meanwhile, T'sais has learned that Earth has ugliness of a degree undreamed of in Embelyon. In *T'sais*, rather equivocally equipped with a 'warm, quivering' living rapier, she meets and despatches sundry ill-intentioned males, including the handsome, hazel-eyed psychopath Liane. Apparently slain, he nevertheless reappears in *Liane the Wayfarer*, only to meet a Dunsanyesque fate at the hands of Chun, an entity who earns his sobriquet, 'The Unavoidable'.

Vance returned to the elegiac landscapes of his dying Earth in 1966 for *The Eyes of the Overworld*, a picaresque novel. A number of short stories followed. Author Michael Shea wrote a sequel to *Overworld*, *A Quest for Simbilis* (1974), but the success of the 1950 original could not be duplicated by either the master or the pupil.

As with so many tales of Humanity's twilight, the source can be traced to the view from the Time Machine, with the ruined Eden of the Eloi superimposed upon the haunted shadowlands of the last sunset. Wells, wisely, quit the saddle after that first enthralling trip and handed over the controls to his imitators.

First edition   New York: Hillman, 1950
First UK edition   London: Mayflower, 1972

71

JOHN DICKSON CARR
The Devil in Velvet

The murder mystery still retains a close affinity to the ancestral Gothic romance, not least in sharing an element of improbability. If anything, the older form is the more plausible by virtue of its improbabilities being largely supernatural, while the murder mystery strives to convince us that the behaviour of its characters reflects our everyday experience, however *outré* the nature of the crime. Only a handful of hardy souls dare to re-combine the two genres. John Dickson Carr is one of them. As a final flourish, he throws in a historian's picture of Restoration London, stenches and all.

Of British and American parentage, he is recognized in both countries as a master of the puzzle story. The supreme example of this fascinatingly artificial mode of homicide is the locked room mystery, of which he was an exponent and an expositor, the latter through the mouth of the redoubtable Dr Gideon Fell in *The Hollow Man*. Here, the question is less whodunnit than how it was done. Victims are customarily found murdered in rooms where the exits are locked *from the inside*. 'Room' can be an elastic term—Sexton Blake, the people's Sherlock, once accounted for a corpse found in a sealed and sunken bathysphere with a knife between its shoulderblades. In *The Devil in Velvet* the murder has taken, or will take, place in that least accessible of locations, the past.

No lightning-bolt or time-machine transports Professor Nicholas Fenton, Cambridge history don and war veteran (the year is 1925), into the seventeenth century. His chosen method is a deal with the Devil, for the usual fee. Military strategy was his business on the Western Front and he has faith in his ability to outmanoeuvre the Father of Lies. What he cannot admit to himself is that he is only partly motivated by a historian's obsession with the time of Charles the Second. Underlying it is the fact that he has fallen in love with the portrait of Lydia Fenton, wife of his namesake Nick Fenton. She lived and died in the house which he now occupies and a document survives which indicates that she was poisoned. Armed with foreknowledge and modern medical lore, he hopes to change history by saving her.

Lydia's husband was a hard-living nobleman with a murderous temper and the swordsmanship to back it up. The Devil's plan is nothing less than to transfer Nicholas Fenton's personality into Nick's body. Such transfers, he hints, have been arranged before, leaving the reader's imagination to work upon the idea. What will become of the Professor's body, we never learn. Nor does Carr seem interested in the yet more horrible crime the change entails, the imprisonment of Nick Fenton within his own brain and the usurpation of his wife, life and identity. His fitful attempts to regain control are shown only from the unpitying viewpoint of Nicholas. Carr, skilled in misdirecting the reader's attention, as are all good crime novelists, knew that he could not afford to evoke sympathy for the unfortunate if unloveable Nick.

Fenton's quixotic yet self-centred mission hits unforeseen snags almost immediately. Nick was thirty years the younger and his domestic affairs reflected the uninhibited age to which he belonged. To find Nick's mistress, Meg York, residing in the house is startling enough, but what really bewilders Fenton is her uncanny resemblance to Mary, the daughter of a college friend. He had always regarded Mary as a child, but Nick's unsubdued libido takes a different view. And Mary knew of the pact with the Devil.

There are suspects and clues and tangled motives to be sorted out, enough to satisfy any amateur detective. The star of the show, however, is Restoration London. Carr brings to life a city where the wealthy and the titled parade in peacock finery through streets which are open sewers, under a black drizzle of soot from crowding chimneys. Severed heads stare sightlessly down upon the passing pageant; not the heads of felons, but those of unidentified corpses, displayed in the hope that someone will recognize them. Without the aid of the internal combustion engine, it is still a noisy city, clattering, crashing, creaking, a city where lethal steel is part of a gentleman's everyday wear. Crime is rampant in the streets and alleys, political intrigue festers in the rooms above. Not infrequently, the two form alliances. Historian Nicholas, passionately partisan, makes an enemy of the powerful Lord Shaftesbury and needs his superior swordplay and tactical knowledge in order to survive. They are not enough to defeat His Satanic Majesty. The Devil has the last, grisly, laugh. Which is no more than his due, for he furnished the vital clue to the mystery of Lydia's death.

With admirable restraint, Carr gives a single taste of his phonetic reconstruction of seventeenth-century speech, and then leaves the rest to the reader's own discretion. The result should be required reading for writers of historical epics and Heroic Fantasy.

First edition   New York: Harpers, 1951
First UK edition   London: Hamilton, 1951

72
L. SPRAGUE DE CAMP
The Tritonian Ring

Until Tolkien unwittingly conferred respectability upon it, Swords and Sorcery was the lunatic fringe of fantasy. If an Oxford academic was an unlikely master of the genre, Lyon Sprague de Camp appeared equally unlikely as its promoter. Tall, ramrod-straight and sober of mien, holder of degrees in engineering and an expert in patent law, he was outwardly the personification of orthodoxy. That impression doesn't survive even the briefest examination of his fiction.

In 1939 he brightened up the Dark Ages with *Lest Darkness Fall*, written for *Unknown*. Still highly regarded, the novel describes the efforts of a stranded time-traveller to introduce printing and personal hygiene to sixth-century Europe. It was an impressive demonstration of the scholar and the humorist working together, backing the adventures of fallible hero Martin Padway with historical and technical detail. A meeting in the same year with historian and sf writer Fletcher Pratt led to their collaboration on the Harold Shea series. These forays into myth, legend and romance wittily exploited the inconveniences of the heroic life. 1949 brought the first of de Camp's *Viagens Interplanetarias* stories, which rationalized that blend of space-travel and swordplay beloved by the fans of Edgar Rice Burroughs.

All of this was a prelude to the day in 1950 when Fletcher Pratt handed him the Gnome Press edition of *Conan the Conqueror*. For some reason, de Camp had never encountered the Cimmerian in the pages of *Weird Tales*. Now he devoured the Conan canon, which, being then entirely the work of Robert E. Howard, required a very short shelf. It was a momentous meeting. From it followed the uncovering of unpublished Howard material and, for better or for worse, the continuation of Conan's adventures by other hands. And in the Winter 1951 issue of *Two Complete Science-Adventure Books* (as snappy a title as ever graced a news-stand), finally, there was de Camp's own Swords and Sorcery epic, *The Tritonian Ring*.

Given the difference in training and temperament, it could be expected that his invented prehistoric world would have a greater internal consistency than Howard's Hyborian Age. Centred upon the area which would become the Mediterranean Sea, it includes an Atlantic continent called Pusad and several inhabited islands. The dominant power is the Tartessian Empire, with a capital located in what is now southern Spain but was then part of a land-mass embracing northern Africa, the site of Atlantis. A map would have helped; even the Owlswick Press illustrated edition (1977) does not feature one, though their magazine *Amra* did so in 1975, adapted from de Camp's original.

It is an age of metal and magic, in which the Gods are a real, if fading, force. Iron, traditionally feared by supernatural beings, has been found in meteoric form. Scarce as it is, it represents a threat to the Gods. No human mind can receive their messages in its presence. They hold a council of war. It is decided that Vakar of Lorsk, heir to the Pusadian throne, must take the iron Ring of the Tritons from its wearer, King Ximenes. Vakar himself is a Godly problem, being as psychically 'deaf' as if he already wore the Ring. The God's commands have to be conveyed through the Pusadian court wizard, Ryn.

Vakar, eager to see the world, sets out to travel incognito with one servant, Fual the thief. His elder brother, Prince Kuros, is pleased to see him go. Under Pusadian law, the crown goes to the younger son. If he lives. Being the novel's hero, Vakar is basically a Mr Nice Guy, but de Camp never forgets that he is a prince, with a prince's outlook and expectations. Compelled to conceal his royal status for safety's sake, he finds the world to be a place of hard knocks, where a hasty temper can be fatal.

The quest has a full quota of wizardry, murderous monarchs, swordplay by sea and land, passionate ladies (not all of them what they seem) and assorted monsters. It also allows de Camp to poke his usual fun at the loonier aspects of social and political systems. The story culminates in a satisfyingly blood-thirsty battle which pits Vakar's iron sword against sorcerous invaders of Lorsk.

De Camp continued to chronicle the affairs of his Bronze Age world in short stories for twenty years or more after *The Tritonian Ring*. Regrettably, there were no more novels.

As *The Tritonian Ring, and Other Pusadian Tales*
First edition   New York: Twayne, 1953
First UK edition   London: Sphere, 1978

73
POUL ANDERSON
Three Hearts and Three Lions

In 1953 Poul Anderson demonstrated his versatility by producing two novels which are still regarded as outstanding in their respective genres of sf and Heroic Fantasy, *Brain Wave* and *Three Hearts and Three Lions*. Revised and expanded, the latter appeared in book form in 1961, the alterations provoking some controversy among Anderson enthusiasts. It is the earlier version, from *The Magazine of Fantasy and Science Fiction*, which is considered here.

The legend of Denmark's greatest folk-hero, Holger Danske, was tailor-made for Anderson. Of Danish descent, a student of medieval Romance and a translator of the Norse sagas, he has a deep and informed love of the subject. Here, and in *The Broken Sword* (1954), he virtually re-created the lands of Faerie; his cool and subtle Elf-lords and ladies, moving with unhuman grace through their world of blue twilight, are memorable figures. Their remoteness forms an effective foil for the turbulence, warmth and humour of the relationships between the human characters. So seductive is their alien style that many readers have argued that the hero, a product of twentieth-century society, would naturally have chosen to take their side rather than that of the peasantry.

Holger Carlsen, for all his technological background, is only superficially a modern man. Though he could have continued to pursue his engineering studies in the safe haven of America, Hitler's onslaught upon Europe draws him, irresistibly, back to Denmark. Joining the Danish Resistance, he is wounded while helping an important refugee to escape to the Allies. He awakes in a dense and hoary forest, unlike anything in contemporary Europe. Nearby grazes Papillon, a huge warhorse. On its back are the weapons, armour and clothing of a knight, while from the saddle hangs a shield emblazoned with a design featuring three hearts and three lions.

Holger, an indifferent horseman, becomes an expert once mounted upon Papillon. Some part of him too knows instinctively how to handle lance, sword and shield. His bewilderment and scepticism rapidly crumble under the accumulating evidence for this improbable world's reality. The lions and bears which roam the forest seem all too real. So does Mother Gerd, who inhabits a tumbledown cottage among the trees and who obligingly summons up a demon in response to his request for information.

The news it brings is not reassuring. Holger must seek the help of Duke Alfric, the Elf-lord, whose realm borders the marches where the cottage stands. Hugi, a dwarf, acts as his guide. Finding Holger more sociable than the usual run of knights, Hugi introduces him to a swan-may, Alianora, to obtain her counsel. She tells him that a Saracen noble is searching for a knight bearing the insignia of three hearts and three lions.

On the dusky frontier of Faerie, Holger has his first taste of Alfric's powers. After a fast and furious battle, he unhorses an opponent clad in plate armour, only to discover that the armour is empty. Anderson the writer cannot resist speculating, through Holger the engineer, upon Elvish technology. If the mere touch of iron sears their flesh, which metals and alloys do they use in its place? Is their magical manipulation of matter a highly developed form of ESP? One of the highlights of a story filled with action comes when, having fought his way out of an Elven trap, he is pursued by a dragon. Swords and armour will not prevent himself, or his friends, from being barbecued. But in order to emit such heat, the beast's internal temperature must be even greater. The engineer applies basic professional skills to the problem and thaumaturgy yields, painfully, to thermodynamics.

The importance of Holger, or his alter ego, becomes ever more apparent. One way or another, many people want to put him out of circulation. Morgan le Fay, the greatest sorceress of this world of magic, almost seduces him into returning with her to her island retreat. Alianora, who has a host of acquaintances, human and otherwise, persuades wizard-of-all-trades Martinus Trismegistus to change the appearance of Holger and the equally distinctive Papillon. In their new guise, they meet the mysterious Saracen, Carahue. Carahue knows much about the man whom Holger once was and is not entirely deceived by the efforts of Trismegistus. Holger likes him but dare not trust him. Nevertheless, he allows the Saracen to accompany them.

Now the decisive battle between Law and Chaos looms. Allegiances must be declared and masks discarded. Holger rides to the ruined church of St Grimmin's, where the blade Cortana sleeps beneath the altar-stone. When he wields Cortana, his true self will be made known. Behind them storms the Wild Hunt, the dogs of Chaos, shrieking down the sky.

Something of the timelessness of Faerie must have got into Poul Anderson's typewriter, for anyone dissatisfied with Holger's involuntary and unexplained return to the twentieth century had to wait until 1974 and *Midsummer Tempest* for the sequel. There was also a book of illustrations, by the author, depicting scenes and characters from *Three Hearts and Three Lions*. But it would probably tax the powers of Duke Alfric to find a copy of that today.

First edition   Garden City (NY): Doubleday, 1961
First UK edition   London: Sphere, 1974

74
LEIGH BRACKETT
The Sword Of Rhiannon

She was the girl in the gingham dress who came from Kinsman, Ohio, and made good in Hollywood. The frontier overtones of the name, Kinsman, were prophetic. Screenwriter Brackett soon came to be associated with the films of Howard Hawks, her scripts enlivening some of the later Westerns of another portrayer of rugged individualism, John Wayne. Some day, perhaps, the even more rugged protagonists of her inter-planetary adventures will be given screen-time and, with luck, an equally talented screenwriter.

Before her Hollywood fame began, she was already selling to the science-fiction pulps of the 1940s, although her first published book was a crime novel. If the byline 'Leigh Brackett' was generally assumed to be that of a man, readers would scarcely be blamed for their error. Her fiction had the qualities usually regarded as masculine: full of action and colour, told with economy but rich in exotic atmosphere, it was acted out by some of the toughest characters, male and female, ever to rove the wilder corners of the Solar System. Sadly, she had little opportunity to exercise her talent for fantasy on the screen before her death in 1978. Her husband, veteran sf writer Edmond Hamilton, had died in the preceding year.

Though she was a more sophisticated storyteller than Edgar Rice Burroughs, his influence is evident in much of her work, and she never hesitated to acknowledge it. The Solar System, in magazines such as *Planet Stories*, consisted chiefly of Earth, Mars and Venus, and there was an un-written agreement regarding the nature of the latter two. Mars was inhabited but dying, criss-crossed by great canals which ran through perilous wilder-nesses linking ruined cities of incalculable antiquity. Venus, hidden by eternal clouds, was wet, misty, lushly fertile, barbaric. This version was still accept-able, even in the austere pages of *Astounding SF*, in the mid-forties. When Bertram Chandler's story 'Special Knowledge', appeared later in book form, the action had been transferred to another planetary system. Leigh Brackett's best-known character, Eric John Stark, was to undergo a similar journey in the *Skaith* series, a process which revealed just how much he owed to his original setting.

Stark was the ultimate Brackett hero: mean, moody and muscular, of Earthly stock but raised on Mercury by humanoid aliens. An amalgam of Conan, Tarzan, and Northwest Smith without being precisely like any of them, he lived on the wrong side of Earth's laws, following his own savage code of honour. Matt Carse, the hero of *The Sword Of Rhiannon*, had a less exotic upbringing but is cut from the same cloth. Few Earthmen ventured into the wild hinterlands of Mars, or the timeless streets and alleys of the Low

Canal cities, but Carse has been accepted by the Martian society of thieves as one of their own. Once a respected archaeologist, he has changed his motives rather than his objectives.

Like all Martians, Carse knows of the Quiru, godlike beings of Mars' remote past, and their legendary betrayer, Rhiannon the Cursed One. (Brackett's habit of drawing upon Earth's past history for the names of her extraterrestrials displeases some readers, but it works within the context of her fate-laden narratives.) When he enters Rhiannon's long-lost tomb, Carse is thrown back through time, bearing the Cursed One's sword. More than this—Rhiannon, imprisoned in the tomb, has usurped a part of his mind. Together in one body, they emerge to face a world alien to both; far in the future for Rhiannon, a million years gone for Carse.

This is the Mars of the Sea Kings, of fertile lands and rolling oceans, and of Caer Dhu, stronghold of the Dhuvians, the Serpent Folk. Rhiannon taught the secrets of Quiru science to the Dhuvians, and for this he was punished by his kin, before they passed from the face of the planet. Now Carse must play a fiendishly complex game, for Rhiannon's name is spoken with loathing in this age. Yet he carries Rhiannon within him, and only the outcast demi-god can withstand the Serpent Folk. Taken as a slave by the soldiers of Sark, a powerful nation in league with Caer Dhu, he rebels and captures the beautiful, arrogant Ywain, daughter of the king of Sark. With the help of the defiant Sea Kings, he may be able to outwit the Dhuvians and defeat her people. But the winged Sky Folk and the aquatic Swimmers, enemies of Sark, sense the dark presence of Rhiannon and distrust him, as do some among the Sea Kings' people.

Can Carse trust Rhiannon? Or has the Cursed One deeper secrets than he can fathom? And will Carse ever be able to regain the Mars he loves, the ruined, mysterious world to which he gave his allegiance? Read on. . . .

With Brackett, you always will.

First edition   New York: Ace, 1953
First UK edition   London: Boardman, 1956

75

POUL ANDERSON

The Broken Sword

Nuclear warfare, whatever its critics may say, was good for business in the post-Hiroshima sf magazines. From Henry Kuttner's reconstructed world of telepathic mutants to the frighteningly plausible Armageddon-in-a-crate of Chan Davis, the Bomb boomed. In 1947, intoxicated with Apocalypse, *Astounding SF* featured a modest example, 'Tomorrow's Children', under the combined bylines of F. N. Waldrop and Poul Anderson. For Anderson it was a first sale, but it was prefaced by a verse which already indicated the future tenor of his work:

> On the world's loom
> Weave the Norns doom
> Nor may they guide it
> nor change

Relativity and Ragnarök were to be guiding stars of a prolific and successful career. Following upon a burst of creative energy which saw three novels achieve magazine serialization in 1953, including *Three Hearts and Three Lions*, came the hardcover edition of *The Broken Sword*. Inspired by the Norse sagas, it is still one of the starkest and most uncompromising stories of the Heroic Fantasy genre.

As the influence of the White Christ spreads throughout Europe and Britain, the older gods retreat, leaving their worshippers torn between allegiances. Some, like Orm the Strong, played it both ways for political reasons. Pagan or Christian, they are destined to be manipulated by powers beyond their comprehension, their religious and personal ties twisted to further the purposes of the gods.

The scientific aspect of Anderson's imagination induces him, in a foreword, to attempt to justify his description of British winters severe enough to split tree stems. As he is dealing with a world in which magic is common currency, and mankind shares land and sea with a host of supernatural beings, to balk at the meteorology would be to strain at gnats. Also, he cannot resist rationalizing the aversion of Faerie's people to iron and exploring the alternatives developed by Elvish metallurgy. This is amusing and interesting, but raises the question of why their technology has advanced no further. The answer, presumably, is that continued development would have rendered the Elves invincible and made inter-species conflict impossible. No conflict, no story.

Orm the Strong carries with him from Jutland to his new steading in Britain all of the beliefs of his forefathers. With Viking ruthlessness, he slaughters the men of an English family and seizes their land for himself. This act sets in motion the forces which will bring destruction upon his kin. The slain man's mother is a witch and lives now only to wreak vengeance upon his murderers, though it means selling her soul.

Orm marries Aelfrida, daughter of an English ealdorman, and grudgingly accepts the faith of the White Christ. When their first child, a son, is due, the witch informs the elf-earl Imric. Ever eager to abduct a human child, Imric begets an identical changeling upon the imprisoned daughter of Ilrede Troll-king, his greatest foe. The exchange of babies succeeds, but the Elves' jubilation is chilled by the arrival of a messenger of the Aesir, bearing a broken sword as the foster-child's naming gift. Behind all Aesir gifts lies a hidden motive.

Skafloc Elf's-foster and Valgard the Changeling grow to manhood in ignorance of each other's existence. Valgard is cold, moody, distanced from his human siblings. Skafloc, raised in the magical blue dusk of Faerie, knows of no human kin and needs none. Seduced by the false, sorcerous beauty of the witch, Valgard is tricked into slaying his 'brothers'. Becoming an outlaw and a berserker, aware now of his unhuman origins, he delivers Orm's daughters, Asgerd and Freda, to the trolls and allies himself with Ilrede. In the first great battle of the coming Elf–Troll war, Skafloc rescues Freda and clashes bloodily with Valgard. Ignorant of their blood-tie, Freda and Skafloc fall in love, and the witch's vengeance approaches its culmination.

The war goes ill for the Elves. Aided by myriad lesser nations, the Trolls storm all but the greatest of the Elf strongholds. Skafloc, gaunt and desperate, recovers the broken blade. After a weird and perilous odyssey, he delivers it to the giant Bolverk, in whose smithy it is reforged and made whole again. Even on the verge of extinction, the Elves shrink from its unknown powers, but Skafloc ignores their fears. He returns to the struggle, carrying with him his doom and the fate of Faerie. Freda bears his son, whose life is forfeit to the Aesir. Child and sword are destined to play crucial roles in future events, completing a great design of which Skafloc's saga is only the beginning.

What was the greater design? What was the sword's ultimate purpose? The tale of the great black blade has been taken up by other writers, most notably by Michael Moorcock, who freely acknowledged Anderson's influence upon the Elric series.

The end, it is to be hoped, is not yet.

First edition   New York: Abelard-Schuman, 1954
First UK edition   London: Sphere, 1973

76
J. R. R. TOLKIEN
The Lord Of The Rings

Once upon a time there was a Hobbit . . ..

Now there are millions of them. Or so, sometimes, it seems. For *The Hobbit* spawned a sequel so massive as to dwarf its parent. And the sequel generated theses, quiz-books, pseudo-scholarly studies of its pseudo-history, an incomplete animated film, and more bad artwork than any book since The Book. And a flood of heroic fantasy novels followed.

The sequel, *The Lord Of The Rings*, no longer appears so massive in terms of actual wordage. Three decades on, nothing less than a quartet will serve to give new entrants to the genre sufficient elbow-room. But few of these literary constructions cast so long a shadow, or stand upon so solid a foundation, as Tolkien's Middle-Earth. A Professor of Anglo-Saxon at Oxford, Tolkien drew upon his language studies to create Elvish and other imaginary tongues. As a consequence, his world of Middle-Earth grew, over many years, to accommodate them. *The Lord Of The Rings* now tops a vast substructure of invented history, myth and legend, of which its tumultous events form only a small part.

Readers looking for a Conan or a Jirel will be disappointed. There are no irresistible warriors, male or female, in Tolkien's saga. Its strength lies in its embracing sweep, a combination of the panoramic view with a wealth of homely detail. Power, wisdom and authority rest largely in the hands of the older generations, and in Middle-Earth 'older' can be old indeed, for the Elves are virtually immortal. Aragorn, the half-elven hero, and the Hobbit, Frodo, are entering their sixth decade, although their long lifespans make them physically 'younger' in our terms. It may be significant that when *The Lord Of The Rings* appeared in 1954–55 Professor Tolkien was sixty-three.

Hobbits are unique to Tolkien's version of Middle-Earth. Seldom over four feet tall, they resemble human children in many ways. Gregarious among their own kind, they are content to live upon the borders of the kingdoms of Men. Being unwarlike and skilled in the arts of concealment, they are little-known even in the times of The War Of The Ring, and have faded entirely from the knowledge of latter-day humanity. The War brought them brief fame, of an unwelcome kind, and peril. Bilbo, Frodo's guardian, the Hobbit of *The Hobbit*, returned from distant lands with a ring won from a strange being who lived in darkness under a mountain. Many years later, Sauron, master of evil, seeks an ancient Ring of Power; Bilbo, unwittingly, possesses it.

Gandalf, the crotchety, much-travelled wizard of *The Hobbit*, persuades Bilbo to yield the Ring to Frodo. He does so, with reluctance. The Ring confers power upon its wearer, in proportion to his ability to use it, but in the end it will dominate him, however versed in sorcery he may be. Frodo, at Gandalf's urgent request, sets out with three friends, Merry, Pippin and Sam, to destroy it in the fires of Orodruin, in Sauron's land, where it was forged. Already, Sauron's Black Riders are scouring The Shire, Frodo's homeland. Only with the aid of Aragorn, the mysterious Ranger of the wilderness, do the Hobbits reach Rivendell, house of the Elves.

Until the entry of Aragorn, the novel reads much like a continuation in style of *The Hobbit*, and it is this juvenile quality which has deterred many readers from continuing. After this point the colours darken, the landscapes broaden, and the history of the Ring is revealed as an ancient and evil story. Aragorn is acknowledged as the heir to the greatest kingdom of the West, bearer of the broken sword Narsil; he becomes one of the Nine Companions, chosen from Men, Elves, Dwarves and Hobbits, who must carry the Ring to Orodruin. Great dangers beset them, but the most insidious threat comes from within—the power of the Ring to arouse jealousy and dissension. There is no more potent example of its fascination than Bilbo's old opponent, Gollum. Throughout the long journey of the Nine he is never far behind, seeking to regain what he calls his 'Precious'. In the end, it is by the manner of their response to the Ring that the principal characters stand or fall.

So short a summary conveys no real impression of the diversity of Tolkien's Middle-Earth, the wealth of human and non-human races populating its varied landscapes, or the equally rich past which shaped it. Over all of the swift-moving narrative hangs the knowledge of history as an unending process. Things must change and pass away, come victory or defeat. Tolkien, a young veteran of the First World War, must have learned this bitter lesson early in life.

The Fellowship of the Ring
First edition   London: Unwin, 1954
First US edition   Boston: Mifflin, 1954

The Two Towers
First edition   London: Unwin, 1954
First US edition   Boston: Mifflin, 1955

The Return of the King
First edition   London: Unwin, 1955
First US edition   Boston: Mifflin, 1956

77
HENRY TREECE
The Golden Strangers

Invasion threats were old news to RAF Intelligence Officer Henry Treece, serving during the dismal days following Dunkirk. The difference on this occasion was that the threats looked like being realized within his own lifetime. They were no longer events in the unwritten histories of pre-literate peoples, reconstructed by archaeologists and given life through his poetic vision. To live through a time when only a narrow sea divided us from the new barbarians must lend insight to the work of any imaginative writer.

The poet, without ceasing to be a poet, became a novelist. *The Dark Island* (1952) was the first in a series of novels covering the Roman conquest and colonization of Britain, ending with the revolt of Boudicca of the Iceni in *Red Queen, White Queen* (1958). Chronologically, *The Golden Strangers* predates them. To the Romans, the Britain it describes would have been as remote as the world's beginning. When the ancestors of Garroch of the Barley People crossed to the newly sundered island, the Channel was a treacherous graveyard of submerged forests, a province of the drowned lands from which amber rises to litter the Baltic coasts. With them they brought their fears, dreams and magic.

Garroch begins as the son of the village chief and undergoes bloody and agonizing ordeals before becoming chief in his turn. His mental world expands beyond anything the Old Man, his father, could have imagined; through suffering and battle he makes allies and friends. The most engaging of these is the tall, red-haired Asa Wolf, of the forest-dwelling Hunters. He is a Cro-Magnon, from a people older by far than Garroch's line. Asa's blood-brother relationship with the small, dark chieftain of the Barley People is one of the few rays of light illuminating a dark wilderness of violence and superstition.

Cutting into the interwoven lives of Hunters and Farmers alike come the Golden Strangers. They wear coloured linen and helmets of metal. Shining copper knives and swords hang at their leather belts. On boats and rafts laden with their horses, cattle, dogs and families, they cross the Channel. Four millennia or so later they would be labelled as Indo-Europeans, warlike worshippers of the Sky God and enemies of the Mother Goddess.

In Garroch's youth, a small party of the Strangers had been guests in the hut of the Old Man. They boasted of the superior magic of their shaman and threatened one of his people with a copper knife. Their shaman died as readily as the rest after drinking poisoned beer and their blood fed the furrows of the barley fields. Blind to the implications of the tall men's metal technology, the villagers throw away the weapons with the bodies.

Garroch's defiance of the invaders is born partly of ignorance. As with primitive cultures the world over when faced by incoming waves of heavily armed settlers, he has no conception of the real nature of the threat they represent or of the pressures which are driving them on. When the Sky God's magic proves stronger than his own, he has to fall back upon naked courage. He overcomes their leader and takes his shining sword.

To his amazement the leader's niece, Isca, surrenders herself and her followers to his authority. The Golden Strangers accept his rule and go with him to the village on the chalk hill. He is the king of two tribes, but crowned heads rest no more securely in the Neolithic Age than in the days of Shakespeare.

Early Atomic Man cannot hope to reconstruct the outlook of the men of the flint-using Barley People. We are too conscious of the universe which contains us; Garroch's chalk-hill village has become a sphere hurtling through limitless vacuum, upon which 4,000 million individuals cling to life beneath a fragile film of air. Why the realization of this doesn't make us all fall flat, dig our fingernails into the earth and scream is one of the mysteries of the human psyche. Henry Treece has been more adept than most at fitting into the skins of these long-gone Britons and showing us how their island may have looked. But all such visions must remain fantasies, based upon the evidence of archaeology, the drawing of comparisons with known primitive societies and an ability to shed habits of thought inculcated by a civilization increasingly divorced from the natural world.

Treece wrote several books for children, set in various historical periods, including three linked Viking adventures. He was too honest to write down to a young audience and in consequence, as with all of the really good juvenile novels, they can be enjoyed almost as well by adults. For some reason his three adult novels on Greek mythological themes remained in print while the superior Romano-Celtic series fell into obscurity. Savoy Books revived the latter in 1980 and added an essay by Treece, 'Notes on Perception and Vision', a personal and powerful statement about the act of literary creation. He wrote it in May 1966; in June he died.

First edition London: Bodley Head, 1956
First US edition, as *The Invaders* New York: Random House, 1957

78

HENRY TREECE
The Great Captains

As if to compensate for the paucity of contemporary documentation, British history *circa* AD 400–600 has inspired countless reams of fiction and speculative scholarship. In consequence, the handful of identifiable figures who walked its misty landscapes have become giants, expanding to fill the available space. Their function is now little short of religious. Looming over them all, silhouetted against the red twilight of a dying empire, is Arthur of the Britons, the Once and Future King.

Arthur casts a shadow across the centuries, and yet in some ways he is as insubstantial as smoke. A hero-figure and an abstraction, a woad-streaked barbarian and the principle of Justice incarnate, a mail-clad medieval monarch and the last heir of Rome. Treece has chosen a man made for his time, a physical giant whose hands bear the callouses of plough-handles and sword-hilts.

Some critics have seen Treece's Artos the Bear as a crude savage, ruling a ramshackle collection of superstitious tribesmen. Such criticism seems to demand that the magical elements be overt, that there be wands, warlocks and rune-carved swords. They overlook the dark magic inherent in the earth and air of Britain as portrayed here, the forces which drive the characters headlong to their fates. As the last Roman ship stands out to sea, the darkness is closing in, the stage being set for the entrance of a Captain greater than kings.

From the shore, two men watch the departing ship. The eyes of young Medrawt see the Saxon pirates waiting in ambush for it. Grey-haired Ambrosius, Count of Britain, can barely see the broken edge of the cliff at his feet. This union of age and youth, Roman aristocrat and street-bred pleb, exists in a state of perpetual tension. Picked from the gutter by Ambrosius to be his lieutenant, Medrawt has proved too unstable for the role, too hungry for the authority symbolized by the Count's jewelled sword. Ambrosius, almost blind, has no alternative now but to rely upon him. Medrawt fears and resents the old man as an embodiment of the almost supernatural power of the distant Caesars.

While Ambrosius sleeps in the ruins of a deserted city, Medrawt is visited by the spirit of a druid, Merdinn. In the only 'magical' scene in the novel, Merdinn tempts him with a vision of treasure sufficient to hire an army to defeat the Christ and restore the old religion. Now Medrawt is burdened by a new fear—if he became Count of Britain, must he defend the Cross against the heathen invaders or resurrect the ancient gods? For a while this problem is forgotten when the two Romans meet the son of Uther Pendragon, Artos the Bear.

As part of his punishment for having lain with his half-sister, Gwenhwyfar, Artos has been forbidden to carry a sword. At a drunken feast in Uther's hall, he takes the great blade which Ambrosius was about to present to Medrawt. Enraged beyond fear, Medrawt demands its return, whereupon Artos drives it deep into an oak-log, challenging him to free it. He fails. Artos withdraws the sword and his men hail him as Count of Britain. Ambrosius is dimly aware of what has happened; Uther is acutely aware that his own rule has been undermined. Surrounded by cheering, jeering warriors, Artos can still find words of consolation for Medrawt.

The Cymry cavalry commanded by Artos ride to Caerwent to attend a council of war being held by the Kings of the West. Medrawt rides with them, his craving for recognition having led him to undergo a bloody initiation ritual at the shaky hands of Uther. At the council, the senile and immensely wealthy King Constantine of Dumnonia, in a moment of inspiration, declares Artos to be the *Dux bellorum* who will lead the disputatious kings to war. Artos, casting a round shield upon the ground, demonstrates that there can be no place of pre-eminence at such a 'table'. All are seated equally.

His rise to legendary status has begun. In a series of hard-fought battles, the Cymry scatter the Jutes and Saxons. Medrawt's cruelty to prisoners earns the hatred of the Saxon prince, Cissa, who later exacts a terrible revenge. Artos acquires Lystra, a beautiful Byzantine refugee ('a Gwenhwyfar from home' as *Time*'s reviewer memorably described her) and consummates their meeting on the hard bed of Stonehenge.

As he becomes more and more the Captain of Battles, the personal casualties mount. He rides down and kills his half-sister and their child during the confusion of the taking of Caerwent. Lystra, who has betrayed him with Medrawt, is sentenced to die in the arena in the old Roman tradition. Medrawt is badly wounded while trying to kill Artos. Fleeing for sanctuary to Dumnonia, he falls into the hands of Cissa.

In a chilling epilogue the two inseparable enemies, reunited in old age, enact a tottering parody of their youthful rivalry. New invaders are at the gates and Artos has no heir to preserve the brief peace which his efforts have brought upon the land. For those who come after him, the dream must suffice.

First edition   London: Bodley Head, 1956
First US edition   New York: Random House, 1956

[1959]

79
SHIRLEY JACKSON
The Haunting of Hill House

Ghosts, generally speaking, are at their best in short stories. In the more rambling structure of the novel, they can evaporate, leaving the reader's attention to wander down narrative byways, dispiritedly. Shirley Jackson ranked highly among those authors who could handle the supernatural in long or short form. She had a particular flair for depicting haunted houses in which the very bricks and mortar are imbued with malice, a malice which infiltrates, insidiously, into the cracks in the human psyche.

Disabling complaints with a possible psychological basis, such as asthma or migraine, are often the lot of writers of Fantasy. Asthma and depression periodically affected her until her death, at forty-five, of a heart attack. The fact that her uncompleted last novel involved a woman of forty-four was doubtless seen to be more than a coincidence by some of her more extreme fans. It is not an attitude she would have shared. Her ability to summon up irrational fears was allied to a certain scepticism and a saving sense of humour.

From the first, the men and women caught in her webs of terror were not simply horror-fodder. Beginning in 1937 with the short story 'Janice', she drew sharply realized individuals with their own histories, hopes and obsessions. Dr Montague and his three volunteer assistants, recruited to investigate the evidence for the malign reputation of Hill House, find that success may depend upon mutual toleration. Eleanor Vance, selected because she was once a possible cause of poltergeist phenomena, has escaped from home after years of tending her ailing mother, now deceased. For her, the project is a call to adventure. Artistic Theodora, gifted with ESP, has left her shop and well-appointed apartment at the prompting of some inner vision. Luke Sanderson, due some day to inherit Hill House, has been detailed by his older relatives to count the spoons while the strangers are around.

As Eleanor drives to the House, she rewrites her past, selecting a cottage here, a piece of favourite china there, as they catch her fancy in passing. Dr Montague has asked them all not to pause at the nearby village of Hillsdale, but she disobeys. Drinking coffee in a squalid diner, she discovers that the waitress, a local girl, has never heard of Hill House. When she arrives at the gates, the caretaker extracts the maximum of satisfaction from delaying her. His wife, the cook, has seen prospective tenants come and go; her conversation has become codified until it resembles a protective incantation in which one misplaced word would admit the forces of evil. Neither of them will stay after dark, preferring unlovely Hillsdale.

The exterior of the House matches the mood of the staff. A detailed survey of the interior reveals subtle wrongnesses in the proportions. Walls meet at strange angles. Doors, unless stopped with weights, close of their own accord. Before the entrance to the nursery lies an area of abnormal, numbing cold, perceptible to their flesh but not to the Doctor's instruments. Dr Montague directs everyone to make observations and keep notes, but there is little mention of these activities later. Shirley Jackson is more concerned with the developing conflicts and alliances within the group. When two self-styled psychic investigators, the Doctor's wife and her friend Albert, arrive equipped with planchette and preformed opinions, she pillories them mercilessly.

Mrs Montague has firm ideas about the conduct of the House's tenants, corporeal or otherwise. Plainly, she would like to reorganize the Other Side too, if that were possible. As the forces imprisoned within the structure begin to manifest themselves in manic and terrifying outbursts, she and Albert remain sublimely unaware of them. Eleanor Vance, by contrast, moves at their centre. Eleven years of nursing a fretful invalid have left her friendless, unloved and unloving. She is rootless, an emotional vacancy open for occupation. Hill House moves in, gradually but irresistibly.

Women as victims, understandably enough, were the focal points of Shirley Jackson's stories, even where the supernatural was not involved. Bringing up a family of four while sustaining a fulltime writing career might have seemed sufficiently fulfilling for anyone, male or female, but the several illnesses which plagued her could have been, according to modern medical thinking, the outward expression of psychological disturbances. She certainly disturbed subscribers to the *New Yorker* with her short story 'The Lottery'. Though it was only one of several she had contributed, it hit tender spots the others had not reached. It cost the magazine numerous readers, but the publicity was priceless. Like any adept of the genre, she was able to draw upon her inner turmoil to strike chords in areas of the psyche usually concealed.

An unfailing recipe for inducing sleep, even in a haunted house, says Dr Montague to his bewildered band, is to read Richardson's *Pamela*. After reading Shirley Jackson, nobody sleeps.

First edition   New York: Viking, 1959
First UK edition   London: Joseph, 1960

80
MICHAEL MOORCOCK
Stormbringer

Among the hordes of perishable paper heroes pouring from the world's presses every year, a handful cling to life with a tenacity which can confound their creators. To be asked to repeat past successes can be irritating to a writer seeking to develop, even though it helps to meet the electricity bill. If the hero has been killed off, the problem is compounded. If his entire world was destroyed at the same time, the outlook is bleak. For Holmes, one bound set him free of Reichenbach; Elric had to contend with Ragnarök.

Stormbringer, first published in *Science Fantasy* in 1963–4, was the intended finale of the Elric series. Written to meet the growing demand for Sword and Sorcery fiction, the stories were far removed from the hearty muscularity of the Howard school. Elric, tall, slim, bone-white, scarlet-eyed and black-clad, is a Demon Lover in the Gothic mould. Self-exiled Emperor of dying Melnibone, empire of sorcerers, he roams the lands of men, bearing the black runesword Stormbringer. Women are fascinated by him and usually come to grief as a result; he is a walking revenge fantasy, bringing destruction upon lovers, kin and homeland.

The Lords of Law and Chaos are the ruling forces in Elric's universe. His race, the Melniboneans, predate humanity, though sharing most of their physical characteristics. Sorcery is part of their heritage, for the element of Chaos is predominant in their natures. Events on other planes of existence are moving towards a great conflict between Law and Chaos, which will decide the fate of the world; the reverberations of this supernatural struggle have already destroyed Melnibonean dominance of the new human kingdoms. Their empire has shrunk until it is encompassed by the shores of the Dragon Isle, ruled by many-towered Imryrr. Betrayed by Elric, Imryrr falls, and Melnibone's warriors scatter abroad, often as hired mercenaries.

Elric, marked out from his kind by his albinoism, is further alienated by his longing for some sense of purpose in the universe. He is led to commit the ultimate betrayal by becoming an instrument of Law, perversely using the Chaos entity, Stormbringer, to that end. The relationship between sorcerer and sentient sword is vampiric and ambivalent—Stormbringer channels energy into Elric's deficient veins, but it is energy drawn from the souls of its victims, which include the people he loves and respects. In the end, he becomes one more helpless prisoner within the great black blade. His world has died, but a new world of Law has been born because of his actions.

The novel begins with Elric, temporarily free of his dependence upon Stormbringer, finding contentment with his human bride, Zarozinia. Agents of Chaos abduct Zarozinia, demanding as ransom the surrender of the rune-blade and its sister-sword, Mournblade. Forced to resume the hated relationship, Elric joins with his cousin, Dyvim Slorm, and obtains Mournblade from its guardians. Outwitting the Chaos forces, they rescue Zarozinia while retaining the blades. She returns to her family, while Elric and his old friend, Moonglum, ride against the wizard-king, Jagreen Lern. An ally of Chaos, Jagreen Lern has already won the first great battle of the war. Elric and Moonglum enter his citadel and banish three Dukes of Chaos, but Stormbringer vanishes and they are taken prisoner.

Rapidly, the scope of the struggle expands. A fleet of gigantic golden battlecraft, crewed by dead men, smashes the navies of Elric's allies. Jagreen Lern's armies overrun the land. The power of Chaos becomes hideously manifest as flesh and rock and water melt and merge in a boiling, bubbling maelstrom. The golden ships, which can travel on land, destroy Zarozinia's home city. Elric, Moonglum and Dyvim Slorm, together with Rackhir the Red Archer, steal the Chaos Shield, fashioned by an exiled God, Mordaga. Under its protection, Elric storms the golden flagship, where Zarozinia is imprisoned. Her body has been transformed into that of a serpent by Jagreen Lern and she impales herself upon Stormbringer, giving her soul to Elric. The three friends retreat to their last refuge, the Dragon Isle.

From this point onwards, the action moves into what could be described as an Apocalyptic-Surrealist mode. The three surviving Earthly representatives of Law lead the dragon-horde of Melnibone in a last assault upon the stronghold of Chaos. Sky, sea and land have become a swirling, fragmenting mass of multihued matter. Human emotions—fear, love, hatred—are visible and tangible, mingled with blood and tissue. Across this nightmare fly the dragons, searing the monstrous minions of Chaos with their corrosive, fiery venom. The Horn of Fate is sounded and the Lords of Law pierce the black skies with their blinding spears of light. The final battle begins, which only Gods can win. And Stormbringer claims its last victim.

It is a scenario which only a young writer would have the gall to tackle. Fortunately, he also had the talent.

First edition London: Herbert Jenkins, 1965
First US edition New York: Lancer, 1967

81

JANE GASKELL
The Serpent Atlan The City
Some Summer Lands

In July 1965, a *Sunday Times* reviewer said of *Atlan*: 'Stirring stuff, but too much of it'. Little did he know. Two more volumes were to follow, stuffed with battle, rape, gossip and wild coincidence. When the series was republished, *The Serpent* fissioned into two fat paperbacks, one under the original title, the second as *The Dragon*. All five presented Heroic Fantasy told in the first-person female, if not feminist.

Included in that review was *The Fabulous Heroine*, the story of a girl on the make in a magazine publisher's office. Both novels were by Jane Gaskell. An amateur writer at fourteen, she was a published novelist two years later with *Strange Evil*, in 1957. When the living fantasy of Swinging London blossomed around her, she blossomed with it. Something of the scabious splendour of those years seeps into her 'translation' of the diaries of Cija, Empress of Atlan, and her daughter, Seka.

She possesses to an outstanding degree that vital element in a writer's make-up, the ability to daydream constructively. The opening of *The Serpent* finds adolescent Cija in a classic fairy-tale situation. Daughter of a Dictatress whose family claim descent from the Gods, she has spent her childhood immured in a castle, because of a prophecy foretelling national ruin should she enter the world before reaching maturity. Men, she has been told, are extinct. Then, one fateful day, she sees from her tower a huge, extremely ugly woman who hails her in an extraordinarily deep voice.

It is the beginning of the end of her seclusion. At her mother's command, she is despatched to the headquarters of the army which has occupied their land, with instructions to seduce and assassinate the leader. Men, it appears, are still very much alive. Her proposed victim proves to be both strange and familiar. Familiar, because he is the 'woman' seen from her tower. Strange, because upon closer acquaintance his skin is composed of fine blue serpentine scales. He is Zerd, a hybrid, his mother a female of the supposedly subhuman blue race.

An inept assassin, Cija becomes one among a crowd of hostages taken to ensure the good behaviour of their various homelands. Whirled off on campaign with the conquerors, she finds military life to be a succession of rugs whisked from under her feet, as her status changes bewilderingly from inviolate goddess to hostage, prisoner to fugitive, assassin to wife. Her one constant ally is Ums, a savage black riding-bird modelled on the prehistoric flightless Diatryma; his spooky death-scene is the most affecting in the entire saga. Throughout her breathless peregrinations, come pregnancy, storm or dirty dishes, she never neglects her diary.

Gory battles rage over hill and plain, but they are no bitterer than those fought in tents and bedrooms, where sex and status intertwine. Obsessively pursued by her half-brother, who fathers her son; intermittently bedded by Zerd, father of her blue-skinned daughter; protected by every opportunist male, human or otherwise, Cija proves to be a survivor in a world she never made. Pterodactyls flap, volcanoes smoulder, earthquakes heave, but she scribbles on.

Atlan, the fabled island-continent, is the glittering prize of this antediluvian Earth. Across the dividing seas, the mainland powers are plotting her overthrow. Until now, her scientific defences have proved impregnable and in consequence she has neglected the arts of warfare. Her principal defence, a barrier of vacuum encircling the continent at sea-level, is a wildly implausible concept. Apart from its ability to asphyxiate unwary invaders and seabirds, the authoress ignores the numerous implications of this device. Cija, as usual on the run and aware that the vacuum is about to be breached (!), crosses to Atlan via a secret submarine tunnel of glass.

Her bid to warn the islanders is wasted. Fate, in the snakeskinned shape of her husband, overtakes her when Atlan's leaders petition him to become their resident protector. Reunited with Zerd, she becomes Empress of Atlan. Her brush with Imperial splendour is destined to be brief. With Jane Gaskell, this is just another day in the life of Cija, prostitute, cross-dressing kitchen skivvy, goddess and apeman's mate. When the fighting breaks out, as it always does, she escapes with the aid of a friendly homunculus patched together from members of her retinue by the resident Frankenstein.

Returning by devious paths to the tower of her childhood, she is abducted by a tribe of giant apes. Exercising her talent for meaningful relationships with the less-than-human, she soon out-integrates Tarzan by becoming pregnant. The affair ends unhappily, especially for the father, but life must go on.

A decade separates *Some Summer Lands* from the rest of the series, and the diary is now that of Cija's daughter, Seka. Though the tone is perhaps more thoughtful, and some of the ideas are explored at greater length, there is still a full measure of adventure and bizarre incident.

Too much? Never! Stirring stuff, all of it.

The Serpent: First edition   London: Hodder & Stoughton, 1963,
First US edition   in two volumes as *The Serpent*   New York:
St Martin's, 1977; and *The Dragon*   New York: St Martin's, 1977.
Atlan: First edition   London: Hodder, 1965, *First US
edition*   New York: St Martin's, 1978. *The City: First
edition*   London: Hodder, 1966,*First US edition*   New York:
St Martin's, 1978. *Some Summer Lands: First edition*   London:
Hodder, 1977, *First US edition*   New York: St Martin's, 1979.

82

J. G. BALLARD
The Crystal World

As it recedes from the sullen waters of the Grand Union Canal, Ladbroke Grove casts off its shabbiness layer by layer until, sweeping up and over an imposing hill, it conjoins with tree-lined Holland Park Avenue. On the wrong side of the hill, *New Worlds SF* was reborn in 1964, under the editorship of Michael Moorcock. But London, with increasing momentum, was beginning to Swing. The wrong side of almost anywhere was becoming the stylish place to be. For some of sf's more perturbed spirits, style was synonymous with Ladbroke Grove. As *New Worlds* grew in notoriety, a colony of British and American contributors flourished briefly in nearby Portland Road.

J. G. Ballard, though not a colonist, probably did more than any other *New Worlds* writer, save Norman Spinrad, to raise the hackles of lovers of traditional sf. Fittingly, the first Moorcock-edited issue featured his serialized novel *The Crystal World*. Though nominally sf, its rationale is no more scientific than that of his first book, *The Wind from Nowhere* (1962). As fantasy, it is almost hypnotically fascinating, transfixing the imagination with a succession of increasingly bizarre images. The effect is like that of being trapped in a Hall of Mirrors with the Ancient Mariner.

A recurring figure in Ballard's fiction is the regressive man. Not for him the tight-lipped coffee-swilling (in sf, all things are possible) sessions in the lab as annihilation looms over the horizon. Most memorably incarnated as Kerans of *The Drowned World* (1962), regressive man adjusts his psychic pressure to match that of his changing environment and is last seen on his way to some unimaginable rendezvous, severing all merely human ties as he goes. To readers accustomed to identifying with resourceful extroverts, this Oriental mood of resignation was distasteful. Their response echoed Bertram Chandler's verdict on Stapledon's doomed, passive Spirit of Man: '. . . very beautiful. But I'd prefer something with more guts.'

Well, you pays your money. And a lot of buyers were more than willing to go along for the ride, wherever it led. It leads, always, to the region designated by Ballard as Inner Space. Here, like some Surrealist Capability Brown, he constructs the landscapes which reflect and ensnare the psyches of his alienated characters. Most dazzling of all his traps is the prismatic forest of *The Crystal World*, where jewelled saurians crash through the surfaces of crystallized rivers and trapped birds vibrate in webs of light strung between frozen trees.

It is a vision which cries out for filming, as do so many of his narratives. Not, however, until he tackled directly his wartime experiences as a civilian prisoner of the Japanese did Hollywood show a positive interest. It may be that they too saw no box-office potential in the regressive man. Success for *Empire of the Sun* may yet bring these inner landscapes to the screen.

The Crystal World opens with its doctor-hero, Edward Sanders, aboard a steamer approaching Port Matarre, in the Cameroon Republic. From the first page, mystery and a brooding unease pervade the narrative. A darkness lies over the African forest that seems to drain the tropical sunlight of its power. There is an unexplained delay in allowing the ship to dock. Ashore, the military are busy, but the nature of their activities is not immediately clear. All that Sanders can discover, as he seeks his friends, who run a leper clinic, is that entry to the forest is being discouraged.

Aware that his motives for trying to find Suzanne and Max Clair are ambiguous, coloured by the affair he once had with Suzanne, Sanders persists with his search. He sees the answer to the mystery of the forest when shown some curious artifacts, as he thinks them to be, in the local market, but does not recognize it. Orchids, twigs, leaves, apparently carved with incredible fidelity to life, are encased in crystal. He has a one-night stand with a journalist, Louise Peret, who reminds him of Suzanne. From their bedroom, he watches the Echo satellite transit the night sky and wonders at its vastly increased brilliance.

All of the enigmas and oblique references come together when Sanders is able to journey upriver. The trip ends in a forest of glass. Trees, grass, the water itself, are crystallizing. Sealed in faceted, glittering sheaths, the vegetation reflects myriad rainbowed images. Animals, birds and, finally, men are encased in iridescent armour. It is no local phenomenon. Other areas of the globe report similar effects. And from the world's observatories come accounts of entire galaxies succumbing to this leprosy of light.

As the multiple probabilities of matter crystallize into rigidity, Sanders and his acquaintances pursue their private obsessions like demented spiders in a bottle. Glittering immortality advances upon them, remorselessly reducing their area of choice. The Universe has been written off in myriad ways before Ballard, but seldom with such style.

First edition   London: Jonathan Cape, 1966
First US edition   New York: Farrar, 1966

83
JAMES BLISH
Black Easter/
The Day After Judgement

The late James Blish dedicated this book to the memory of C. S. Lewis, author of many notable fantasies upon religious themes. While the author of *The Screwtape Letters* would have appreciated its humour, he might not have approved of the ultimate punchline, logical though it is. Published as two novels, it was considered a unity by Blish, and the concluding part of a trilogy which included *A Case of Conscience* and *Dr Mirabilis*. Underlying all three is Man's quest for knowledge, with its spiritual and temporal consequences.

The events of *Black Easter*, rather puzzlingly, take place in a world whose technology is little different to that of 1967. There is an ill-fated Governor of California named Rogan, an obvious joke. Yet this is a society which includes professional practitioners of black magic, who operate openly and in some style, commanding high fees for the services of their associated demons. Heaven and Hell have become, in effect, business rivals competing in a limited market, and Hell's stock is in the ascendant. Blish fails to provide a convincing bridge to link this near-future scenario with our own time. It must simply be accepted; to regard it as, say, a parallel world would be to remove the sting.

Dr Baines of Consolidated Warfare Services has found the scope for his talents circumscribed by the nuclear option. As a merchant of death genuinely in love with his trade, he is artistically frustrated by the lack of really large wars. With his assistant, Jack Ginsberg, he goes to Positano to consult the world's greatest magician and specialist in murder, Theron Ware. As a test of Ware's abilities, he requests the deaths of Rogan and a famous scientist, hinting that there will be a greater assignment to follow. Meanwhile, the Catholic order of White Monks has learned that Hell expects monstrous consequences to arise from the meeting of Ware and Baines. They contact sundry Angels, fallen and otherwise, but are disturbed by their air of confusion. Finally, Father Domenico is appointed as their observer at Ware's conjurations, which is permitted by the terms of a Covenant.

With the preliminary murders accomplished, Baines hands the magician the big one. He wishes to have the principal demons of Hell set loose upon Earth for a day, to see what use they make of their opportunities. Ware is intrigued by this unprecedented demand upon his powers. Father Domenico is horrified. The monk says that his order must be allowed to stand by as an emergency reserve, in case the experiment goes beyond Ware's control. The magician agrees. He can summon only those demons with whom he has pacts, but this horrific legion proves to be more than enough. The djinni, once out of the bottle, cannot be replaced. Now Father Domenico learns the cause of the Angels' uncharacteristic behaviour. Heaven is in shock. God is dead.

With the globe reeling under myriad demonic caprices, including the odd nuclear holocaust, the quartet of Ware, Baines, Ginsberg and Domenico stand amid the ruins of Positano picking up scattered news bulletins on a transistor radio. As the second half of the novel opens, the tone becomes reminiscent of Dr Strangelove, inducing a slight feeling of dislocation. Down below Denver, or where Denver once stood, Strategic Air Command have builded better than they knew; Hell's first strike has resulted in minor scrapes and a lot of dust. High Command survives in the shape of General McKnight and his advisers, RAND Corporation man Buelg and Czech-born physicist Satvje. There is a non-human fourth, the SAC computer, but it appears to have gone haywire.

Having assessed the global situation in terms of their professional death-jargon, the human trio are thrown by the computer's announcement of a huge enemy installation in Death Valley, California. The notion that some unspecified foe has invaded and occupied American soil, and at appalling speed, has to be verified. High-altitude reconnaissance shows a circular con-struction of red-hot iron, turreted and moated. At its gates, gigantic figures look up at the aircraft. Satvje identifies three of them as the serpent-haired Furies. The moat is the River Styx. The circular structure within is Hell's fortress, Dis.

There is only one textbook adequate to the occasion and it happens to be already stored in the computer's memory-banks, along with the entire Library of Congress. Dante's *Divine Comedy* becomes a manual for battle. A nuclear missile lobbed into Dis does no discernible damage, but neither does it pro-voke any retaliation. The situation, in fact, has become strangely static after the first, devastating onslaught from Hell. As the world licks its wounds, Baines and his fellows are drawn irresistibly, by various paths, to the iron city.

Entering unopposed at the brazen gates, they make their way to the throne of Satan to receive a revelation. God is dead—long live God! Humanity has been given another chance, and another Deity. Satan is learning what it means to be Chief, rather than the leader of the Opposition. The outcome, as always, will be up to the voters.

As *Black Easter; or Faust Aleph-Null*
First edition   Garden City (NY): Doubleday, 1968
First UK edition   London: Faber, 1969

The Day After Judgement
First edition   Garden City (NY): Doubleday, 1971
First UK edition   London: Faber, 1972

84
IRA LEVIN
Rosemary's Baby

When the author of *A Kiss before Dying* switched from crime to fantasy, he created a new subdivision of the genre. Malign entities had stalked midnight metropolitan streets since the advent of Stoker's *Dracula*, if not before, but as hated and hunted outsiders. Levin introduced the urbane urban menace, cosily integrated with the routine of coffee mornings and commuting. In 1972, he gave a science-fictional twist to the notion with *The Stepford Wives*, the ultimate solution to the seven-year itch.

Hollywood put *Rosemary's Baby* on the screen almost before the ink was dry, in an adaptation so faithful that it is difficult now to visualize the characters apart from the cast, even when the physical descriptions don't match. Directed by Roman Polanski, the film generated a classic publicity image, the solitary pram abandoned in a wasteland. Few of the imitators who followed in Polanski's wake showed a like restraint.

Levin deftly sets the scene, building up in convincing detail the life of a newly married couple in New York, while undermining it with odd, disquieting touches. Rosemary and Guy Woodhouse, from Omaha and Baltimore respectively, find the apartment of their dreams in the fashionable Victorian Bramford Building. Guy, a struggling self-obsessed actor, likes it for its nearness to the principal theatres. Rosemary sees it as a future nursery.

The first faint note of unease sounds as they tour the apartment with the building's supervisor. When they move a heavy piece of furniture standing before a cupboard, they find that the cupboard holds freshly laundered towels and was obviously in use. Yet the deceased tenant, an elderly woman, plainly could not have put the furniture there. On a desk, Rosemary finds part of an unfinished letter which ends: 'I can no longer associate myself . . .' She and Guy have dinner with an English writer, Hutch, who befriended Rosemary when she arrived in New York as a depressed exile from her disapproving family back in Omaha. Hutch has been studying the history of the Bramford and he does not like it.

Briefly, it has not been a happy house. In its Victorian past, it sheltered the Trench sisters, who varied their diet with the occasional boiled child, and one Adrian Marcato, who claimed to practise witchcraft and was attacked by a mob in the lobby. These and later events earned it the name of the 'Black Bramford'. Time and the housing shortage of the Second World War restored its fortunes. Hutch advises his young friends to move. They refuse. Of course.

In an adjacent apartment lives an elderly couple, Minnie and Roman Castevet, together with Terry, a girl they have unofficially adopted. Terry tells Rosemary that the previous tenant of the apartment died shortly after having a dispute with the Castevets. Soon, Terry dies too, plunging from a seventh-floor window. Later, Minnie invites the couple to dinner. She is a terrible cook, but Guy is flattered by Roman's seemingly knowledgeable comments upon his acting ability.

The friendship ripens. An actor who had obtained a role coveted by Guy goes blind and Guy takes it over. Rosemary is surprised and pleased by Guy's suggestion that they should start a family; he had previously argued that his career wasn't yet secure enough. They celebrate with a meal which includes an odd-tasting chocolate mousse contributed by Minnie. As they eat, television is covering the Pope's visit to New York.

Another spiritual eminence visits the Big Apple that night, in a more personal capacity. Drugged by the mousse, Rosemary experiences a wild sexual fantasy in which she and Guy fornicate amid a strangely dressed gathering which includes the Castevets. There is a terrifying instant of awareness when she *knows* that it is not Guy but a scaly, yellow-eyed being grunting above her shackled body. Next morning it seems like a vivid nightmare—but her skin is cruelly scored with scratches.

She is pregnant. From here on, the grip of her all-too-friendly neighbours tightens, aided by Guy. She goes to an obstetrician recommended by Minnie and Roman, Dr Saperstein. The pregnancy becomes crucifyingly painful, but the doctor tells her not to worry. Her friends outside the Castevets's circle, including Hutch, are alarmed by her appearance. Visiting her, Hutch expresses some of his feelings in the presence of Roman. Some time afterwards, Hutch is taken to hospital, in a medically inexplicable coma. Guy's career advances by leaps and bounds.

A message from Hutch just before he dies puts Rosemary on the road to the incredible truth. The Castevets are the leaders of a coven, with Guy as their willing tool. In return for theatrical stardom, he has tricked Rosemary into becoming the vessel for Satan's child.

The baby is born. With desperate courage, Rosemary defies the coven and tries to kill her yellow-eyed son. But mother-love, in a final sardonic twist, triumphs.

One wonders what sort of welcome he'll get, back home in Omaha.

First edition   New York: Random House, 1967
First UK edition   London: Michael Joseph, 1967

85
URSULA K. LE GUIN
A Wizard of Earthsea

In Fantasy, the boundary between childhood and maturity can often become blurred. Stories written for children often examine adult problems in the guise of odysseys through imaginary lands or conflicts with extra-terrestrials. As the handling of them requires more than the average degree of sensitivity, what results can have something of value to say to all generations. Ursula K. Le Guin put herself into this category with the completion of a trilogy comprised of *A Wizard of Earthsea, The Tombs of Atuan* (1971) and *The Farthest Shore* (1972), published as one volume entitled *Earthsea* in 1977.

The circumstances of her early life made her choice of subject-matter almost inevitable. Her father was an anthropologist, her mother a writer. At university she took a Master's degree in Romance languages. Stimulated by these scientific and literary influences, she wrote novels which were fantasy only by virtue of their setting, a fictional version of Europe. Until she rediscovered sf and found that it had broken new ground since her childhood, none of her stories had been published.

Rocannon's World (1966) marked the beginning of the Hainish series, in which humanity originates upon the planet Hain and spreads throughout the stars. Rocannon, a space-faring ethnologist, carries a traveller's manual which sounds uncannily like an early edition of *The Hitch-Hiker's Guide to the Galaxy*. The Hainish concept combined a unifying background with a diversity of locales into which she could pour her accumulated experience and studies. Her reputation grew with each new novel or short story; she has seven times received the sf community's highest awards.

The *Earthsea* trilogy, by contrast, is confined to the planet of that name. A multiplicity of cultures is made possible by the fragmented geography of Earthsea, an oceanic world studded with a myriad islands. There may be larger landmasses, but they are unknown to the people among whom the hero, Ged, is raised. On Earthsea, magic works. Gont, Ged's native island, is famous for the number of wizards it has produced. But the boy Ged, then called Duny, herds goats and helps in his father's smithy, doing neither with enthusiasm.

His aunt, the village witch-woman, finds that he has a talent for magic-working and teaches him everything within her powers. Then the yellow-haired warriors of the Kargad Empire, whose longships are laying waste to the islands, land on Gont. Ged saves the village by summoning up a mist in which the Kargs can be slain from ambush and becomes famous throughout the land. While allowing that writers must put limitations on their magicians' abilities so as to preserve the possibilities for conflict, there appears to be a major inconsistency here. For Kargad to pursue a career of conquest by purely physical means, in a world of wizards, would seem at the least perilous; that Gont, a breeding-ground of the species, has only a precocious goat-herd to defend it sounds improbable.

The incident brings a great magician, Ogion, from a nearby town to see Ged. Where was Ogion when the heat was on? He takes Ged as an apprentice. An enchantress tricks the boy into researching forbidden lore and the shadowy thing he inadvertently arouses has to be exorcised by Ogion. The incident is an omen. Ogion gives him the choice of remaining on Gont or of learning his art at the college of high wizardry on Roke Island. Ged chooses Roke.

His enormous potential as a mage is quickly established and appreciated. The details of his training and the house rules of wizardry are presented with great conviction. One of the basic principles of magic is the importance of names; to know the real name of something is to have a means of exerting power over it. Real names, in consequence, are disclosed only to those who can be trusted implicitly.

Ged is once again tempted into breaking the rules, this time with catastrophic results. In attempting to bring back a woman a thousand years dead, he draws to himself a faceless black entity which tries to absorb him into itself. Only the combined efforts of the greatest mages of Roke save him from destruction, but they cannot send it back to its dark otherworld.

Ged is scarred physically and mentally by his ordeal. Worse than his injuries is the knowledge that the thing is loose in the world, hungering for his soul. He accepts the post of resident wizard on the island of Low Torning and serves the community well, defeating a family of dragons which threatens them. His Nemesis is not to be avoided, however. After many terrible trials he is driven to seek the advice of his mentor, Ogion. From him he receives the only, inescapable, answer.

With bookshop racks tottering under tales of polystyrene princesses and battery-powered swordsmen, the tough, clear vision of a Le Guin is the sort of magic the genre needs.

First edition   Berkeley (CA): Parnassus Press, 1968
First UK edition   London: Heinemann, 1973

86
KINGSLEY AMIS
The Green Man

Kingsley Amis established his reputation with a series of novels mordantly recording the manners and mores of Britain's New Elizabethan society. Less appreciated was his interest in sf and Fantasy. When the two were combined, the result made most contemporary examples of the horror story seem thinly textured stuff.

Maurice Allington, middle-aged owner of a Hertfordshire inn, The Green Man, is a skin into which Amis fits comfortably. Mine Host is a role which sits less easily upon Allington. A misanthropic hypochondriac, remarried after his first wife's death, father of a thirteen-year-old girl and well on the road to alcoholism, he finds even his own company unbearable. As he and his wife, Joyce, drift apart, he plans to seduce his doctor's wife, Diana. He receives a sharpish nudge from Time's chariot when his father, a resident at the inn, collapses and dies. The loss distresses him, without deflecting him from his pursuit.

That night, sedated by sex, drink and tranquillizers, Maurice's customary hypnogogic edge-of-sleep visions end with a new, sinister image, that of a manlike figure composed of twigs, stems and leaves. A Green Man.

Among the inn's reputed ghosts, the most notorious is Dr Underhill, a seventeenth-century scholar. Gossip credited him with two murders, in which the victims were literally torn apart by some unknown agency. Though he is buried in a nearby graveyard, the service was conducted by clergy from another parish, for the local rector refused the task. His ghost is said to stand at the window of what is now the inn's dining-room, looking across to the woods. By coincidence, perhaps, they are the woods where Maurice keeps his strenuous rendezvous with Diana. But something else is stirring down in the forest, sending the lovers hurrying away. Back at The Green Man, in the busy dining-room, Maurice sees Dr Underhill, standing at the window.

Well aware of his heavy drinking, Joyce, his son, Nick, and daughter-in-law, Lucy, discount his descriptions of ghostly sightings. Driven by some obscure impulse, Maurice resolves to make as thorough an investigation of the Doctor as records allow. With the help of Nick's former tutor, he consults the library of All Saints', Cambridge. The librarian is a typical Amis creation, fighting a tenacious rearguard action against seekers of knowledge, until out-manoeuvred by the tutor.

The Underhill diary is a shocker. Using drugs, liquor and induced halluci-nations to terrify and subdue two girls of twelve and fourteen years of age, the Doctor then repeatedly violated them. These revelations deeply affect

Maurice, father of adolescent Amy, though they are only the lesser part of Underhill's dabblings in the supernatural. Other passages obscurely refer to tree-worship and a hidden something which will make its finder 'Master of Himself'.

The paths of Maurice and the Doctor are now irrevocably entangled. After another session with Diana, he persuades her to help him dig up Underhill's coffin, on the pretext that it contains valuable objects. He also gets her consent to participating in a threesome with himself and Joyce, his current fantasy. Before either of these projects is realized, he has a series of alarming experiences. Alone in his upstairs room, he is suddenly aware of silence. The sunlit world beyond the side window has become a soundless scene. From the front window, the view is of a moonlit landscape of the seventeenth century. He hears voices and sees a woman walk off into the night. Following her comes a monstrous Golem of bark and twigs and rotting leaves. Presently there is a far-off screaming.

Sound and sunlight return, all round. Amy hurries in to ask if he had heard screams. His relief at this confirmation of the actuality of his visions is short-lived. He is soon driven to screaming himself, by the apparition of a tiny, brilliantly feathered bird which flies *through* his hand as if through thin air. Shakily shrugging off this apparent attack of the DT's, he joins Diana in the graveyard to exhume Underhill's bones. The coffin also holds a metal box containing papers and a repulsive silver figurine. It is Diana's turn to scream when she glimpses a huge, deformed shape watching them from the road.

Maurice is startled to find a message for himself in Underhill's buried papers, suggesting a meeting. He goes ahead with the threesome, even so. It proves to be a twosome. Deflated, he retreats to his room, finding God waiting for him. They have an enlightening, if acerbic, conversation. Rounding off a fraught day, he goes to meet the Doctor, who assails him with strange, erotic hallucinations. Almost too late, Maurice realizes that they are meant to distract him from Underhill's true intent. The Green Man still walks, and Amy is thirteen years old.

Afterwards, Maurice reflects upon God's assurance that the afterlife will be unlike anything that he can imagine. Does this mean that he will lose his identity? If so, it is a happy ending, of a sort.

First edition   London: Jonathan Cape, 1969
First US edition   New York: Harcourt, 1970

[1969]

87
GORDON HONEYCOMBE
Neither the Sea nor the Sand

Television news presenters rarely exhibit more than a token involvement with the content of their stories, and Gordon Honeycombe is no exception. Lurking behind that controlled facade, nevertheless, is a fiendish imagination which finds its outlet at the typewriter. It has brought him success as a playwright and novelist, but breakfast-time viewers have not been deprived of his presence on the small screen, as yet.

Neither the Sea nor the Sand, regarded by some as his most powerful novel, was no overnight creation. By his own account, it had a gestation period of twenty years, beginning during his studies at Oxford in the 1950s. Already an amateur writer—a novel, two musicals (!)—he was inspired by the horror films of the time to attempt a screenplay. This, apart from establishing the theme of a love which endures beyond the grave, came to nothing. The theme retained its grip upon his imagination. During a trip to the island of Jersey in 1963, it began to take concrete form.

The importance of the setting, the details of the physical location, will be apparent to anyone familiar with Honeycombe's fiction. Jersey and the northwestern tip of Scotland, Cape Wrath, figure prominently; their topography is as vital an element of the story as are the relationships of the characters. If anything, they are used even more compellingly than was the Northumbrian coast in the later *Dragon under the Hill*, which tells of a modern family assailed by forces from the Viking era.

In both novels, the protagonists are essentially well-meaning people confronted with situations beyond their understanding. But whereas the evil of *Dragon* strikes from without the family circle, exacerbating existing differences, that of *Sand* comes from within. It is a variation on the Fatal Wish, a sophisticated version of the Brothers Grimm. If we paused to work out the possible implications of our wishes, would we still ask for their fulfilment?

Unmarried lovers Annie Robbins and Hugh Dabernon, enjoying their first holiday together in the rugged isolation of Cape Wrath, are preoccupied with the present. Both by nature inclined to be solitary and introspective, they are awed by the newly realized power of their emotions. The holiday comes to a grim climax when Hugh, running in pursuit of Annie on the beach, collapses and dies. Forced to leave him in the path of the incoming tide while she seeks help, Annie finds the owners of their rented caravan only reluctantly sympathetic.

The local doctor sedates her after pronouncing Hugh dead. But something within her fights off the drug and drives her out into the night, to the caravan, where his body lies. She lays her hand on his head and murmurs his name.

183

Afterwards, walking by the sea, she sees a dark figure and flees back to the caravan. The bunk which held Hugh's body is empty.

From here on, Annie is alone with the consequences of her love. When Hugh stumbles back from the beach, she packs up their things, guides him to their car and drives south. She does not attempt to deceive herself about his condition. The journey to Jersey is a black dream. A poor driver, she comes close to killing herself at several points along the way. Getting Hugh aboard a plane at Glasgow Airport stretches her courage to the limit.

Given the tricky task of deciding just how 'alive' Hugh should be, Honeycombe makes of him a voiceless figure without breath or heartbeat, physically slow and clumsy, only his eyes expressing the emotions locked within him. Is the force which sustains his shambling progress his own or a projection of Annie's desperate longing? Certainly, her being is the magnet which draws him; even when she is out of sight, he turns unfailingly in her direction.

Jersey, once reached, proves to be the antithesis of a refuge. Only in their familiar home does the horror of her situation fully overtake her. She phones for Hugh's older brother, George, who arrives ill-tempered and drunk. When he grasps the truth, he proceeds to become even drunker. Always jealous of his younger, taller, better-educated sibling, he sees a unique opportunity for revenge. For a while, the novel teeters dangerously upon the brink of gruesome farce. George 'kidnaps' Hugh and drives off with him, but crashes. Ironically, only his victim survives.

Love, which has defied death, has no power over physical decay. Remorselessly, Hugh's flesh corrupts and falls apart. Annie, in a walking trance, is put into a home by a kindly doctor who is ignorant of Hugh's continued existence. In their locked and lifeless house, the undead man waits for his vanished lover. The day will come when they will be reunited, on another shore, beside another sea.

Unflinchingly, Honeycombe pursues their Frankensteinian relationship to its dreadful, yet affecting, conclusion. For anyone familiar with Jersey, the view across St Ouen's Bay will never look the same again.

First edition   London: Hutchinson, 1969
First US edition   New York: Weybright, 1969

88
COLIN WILSON
The Philosopher's Stone

H. P. Lovecraft, that heroic describer of the indescribable, created a pantheon of Elder Gods whose malign activities for ever threatened to overwhelm mankind. Popular during his lifetime within the limited sphere of weird pulp fiction, his posthumous success has been phenomenal. The strangest aspect of it is the way in which he has influenced authors whose abilities are often superior to his own. He has become an Elder God of Fantasy, Dean of that remarkable seat of learning, Miskatonic U.

Colin Wilson is an alumnus of Lovecraft's fictitious college. Colliding in print with the Master's friend, editor and promoter, August Derleth, he was challenged to try writing a Lovecraftian story, instead of criticizing his literary failings. The gage was not taken up immediately, but when Wilson began to write an sf novel, *The Mind Parasites* (1967), he cast it in that form. It enjoyed a favourable critical reception, and two years later he explored the same territory again, in *The Philosopher's Stone*.

Lovecraft has been accused of having an anti-scientific attitude, though it might be more accurate to say that he was antipathetic towards twentieth-century life in general. Scientists figure frequently in his fiction; more often than not, their discoveries are undesirable, but rarely attain the catastrophic proportions common to their real-life counterparts. Psychic fall-out is usually localized. Wilson, essentially pro-science, strives to rationalize their menace. Wisely, unlike certain other native writers, he does not attempt to transplant those fungoid New England landscapes in Britain's crowded acres.

The story begins in sober fashion, with thirteen-year-old Howard Lester being informally adopted by Sir Alastair Lyell, a wealthy practitioner of music and science. Attracted by the boy's enthusiasm for both subjects, he invites him to share the resources of the family mansion. For twelve years Howard lives a dream-like existence, reading, travelling, debating, learning. He gains the first faint glimmerings of an idea destined to dominate his life and, perhaps, the future of the human race. It springs from the mind's ability to control sickness and the ageing process. When his patron and mentor dies, he sinks into a long spell of depression, but gradually the irrepressible spirit of enquiry surfaces again.

Spurred on by the chance hearing of a scientific lecture on the radio, he contacts the lecturer, Sir Henry Littleway. Littleway's suggestion that the mind may be seeking to defy the tyranny of time, that it may be capable of existence in ages other than the present, fascinates him. One of the more curious conclusions at which Howard arrives, presumably shared by the author, is that marriage weakens the male sexual urge. Here, he appears to be confusing the strength of the urge with the frequency of its expression within the marital relationship. Happily, this piece of pseudo-data is not essential to the development of his formula for an expanded consciousness.

Together with Littleway, he devises an experiment to test the nature of the pre-frontal cortex. In the course of this, the tip of an electrode breaks off and is left embedded in the subject's brain. The consequences are astounding. The Neumann alloy of which the tip is composed acts as an amplifier of nerve impulses. The affected person's mental horizons expand enormously. Howard and Littleway subject themselves to the process and it proves to be repeatable. Breakthrough follows upon breakthrough. Both men acquire the ability to project their personalities into the past of the objects which surround them. Time takes on an almost physical quality, as if they were peering down an infinitely receding precipice. Howard's talents in artistic matters extend into areas previously beyond his scope. It will not surprise anyone familiar with Wilson's *The Craft of the Novel* (1975), in which he pointed out how every major novelist since Richardson had gone wrong, to find that Howard thinks Shakespeare inept.

The narrative, which up to this point has rather ploddingly sought to establish the scientific plausibility of Howard's and Littleway's activities, now takes off into the wild blue yonder. Their time-scanning is checked by an incomprehensible barrier, just as intimations of a previously unguessed-at prehistoric civilization are becoming apparent. An inimical influence is at work, affecting not only themselves but the behaviour of their scientific associates. Gradually, they realize that the Sage of Providence was drawing, unwittingly, upon 'memories' of an incredibly remote era when constructing his eldritch mythology. There were giants in those days, but they were not human.

Man was fashioned as a precision tool by which the Elder Gods could manipulate their Earthly environment. He is the Frankensteinian monster who escaped when disaster overtook his masters. Pre-lunar satellites, sinking continents, titanic sleeping entities—all figure in a vision of the past which opens up gulfs beside which the nuclear threat dwindles into impotence. Our future becomes a race against time. Can the human race be awakened into full consciousness before the buried Gods re-emerge to claim their heritage?

Wilson displays much ingenuity in circumventing that familiar obstacle in tales of Elder Gods—given such awesome powers, how could they have fallen? It makes an engrossing story, even if a touch of Lovecraft's pit-spawned paranoia would have been welcome, here and there.

First edition   London: Arthur Barker, 1969
First US edition   New York: Crown, 1971

89
M. JOHN HARRISON
The Pastel City

Should you see M. J. Harrison clinging to one of the more vertical and unfriendly-looking bits of Britain's terrain, he is probably getting to grips with the material of another novel. For him, the structure of the land isn't just what his characters walk upon. It is a part of them, a participant in the story. His fantasies are filled with images recalling those of Jacquetta Hawkes's unforgettable *A Land* (1951): 'In all these legends human beings have seen themselves melting back into rock . . . limbs and hair melting . . . and solidifying into these blocks of sandstone, limestone and granite.'

Tolkien was an early user of industrial imagery in an Heroic Fantasy setting. Whatever else *The Lord of the Rings* may be, it is at heart a protest against the encroachment of the Machine Age upon the countryside; not the countryside of tractors and combine harvesters, but a medieval ideal. Criticism of his reluctance to portray the evil of Sauron and his minions in graphic detail is misguided. The evil is embodied in the sterile, smoking ramparts of slag which define Mordor's ever-expanding boundaries, the sickly rainbowed pools of chemical poisons eating into woodlands and meadows. Children of the industrial wastelands are fascinated by the rusting, enigmatic shapes and iridescent streams among which they grow up; so much so that they are often impelled to reinterpret them later in various media. For them, Harrison's Viriconium evokes nostalgia for the future.

Into a world of dead and dying empires he introduces tegeus-Cromis, a *fin-de-siècle* hero with a Byronic touch. He is the finest swordsman in the land, who believes himself a better poet. With his heroic days put behind him, he lives like a hermit in Balmacara, a tower by the sea. Until war breaks out again.

Methven Nian, who had become ruler of Viriconium ten years or more before, was keenly aware that he had inherited a kingdom in decline. Dependence upon the machinery of past technologies, combined with the exhaustion of natural resources, threatened to bring on a Dark Age. At the borders, the savage Northmen were a growing threat. He recruited a band of specialists: Norvin Trinor the strategist, Tomb the dwarf, Labart Tane, Benedict Paucemanly the aeronaut, and tegeus-Cromis. While they led his armies, he worked to revive scientific disciplines and to conserve the remaining functioning technology. His mistake was to leave the throne to two conflicting claimants, his daughter Jane and the pretender, Canna Moidart. The war signals Canna's bid for power.

Harrison's future Earth has been likened to those of Vance, Clark Ashton Smith and Ballard, and does have elements suggestive of them all. It differs from those of Smith and Vance in having been depleted by the short-sighted activities of mankind rather than the unaided action of time. The relationship between the landscape and the psyche thus becomes a perpetual interaction, each reshaping the other. Viriconium is recognizably north-western England in a rather more advanced state of decay, the area to which the author returned after living for some years in London. Opportunities for rock-climbing being limited in the inner city, he is reputed to have worked out by scaling walls.

Canna's secret weapon is an army of homicidal automata, the *geteit chemosit*. They are the artifacts of an earlier and richer age, one which felt it could afford to invest heavily in death. As Methven Nian's daughter says: 'How could they have constructed such things . . . when they had the stars beneath their hands?'

Swords are useless against them. An energy weapon capable of stopping their advance doesn't seem to exist. The problem arises in *The Pastel City*, as it usually does in this type of story, of convincingly combining futuristic science with pre-gunpowder weaponry. Burroughs handled it in his Barsoomian stories by stipulating a code of honour which the baddies, and even John Carter, transgressed. Charles Harness had his characters protected by personal force-fields, which could be penetrated by comparatively slow-moving objects such as swordblades. Harrison deals with the situation as deftly as its basic implausibility permits. Too often, a post-Catastrophe scenario is used to indulge someone's wishful thinking about a rural England (not Britain) cleared of its surplus millions and their peevish demands for food, housing and recognition. In *The Pastel City* there are solutions, but they are dearly bought and temporary. Canna's automata may destroy her enemies but cannot be checked when their function has been fulfilled; in the end, they will destroy her. Her opponents discover a counter-force, but it can be employed only at the cost of a revolution which may obliterate their way of life.

A Storm of Wings (1979) continued the history of Viriconium and some of the first novel's characters, though after a lapse of eighty years. It was succeeded by *In Viriconium* (1982) and a collection of short stories, *Viriconium Nights* (1985). In what might be termed a series, had he not condemned the 'series mentality' some years previously, he has taken the genre into untrodden territory, perhaps as far as it can go without losing its way.

First edition   London: New English Library, 1971
First US edition   Garden City (NY): Doubleday, 1972

90
ANGELA CARTER
The Infernal Desire Machines
of Dr Hoffman

Angela Carter's public persona, impeccably middle-class tones and Redgravesque features crowned by wild grey hair might be food for male fantasies were it not for her fiction. Speculation upon her hidden depths falters before the opulently erotic detail of a series of short stories and novels, of which *The Magic Toyshop* (1967) and *Several Perceptions* (1968) won the Llewellyn Rhys and Somerset Maugham awards respectively. One short story, 'The Company of Wolves', and a novel, *The Magic Toyshop*, have been blown up into feature films. Whether the screen could contain the baroque extravagances generated by Dr Hoffman is something else, but it would be fascinating to see someone try.

Dr Hoffman, a grey widower who likes to keep Mrs Hoffman's corpse about the place, disseminates hallucinations from his seedy castle in the mountains of South America. The machinery behind his onslaught upon the everyday is powered by eroto-energy, derived from the couplings of volunteers installed in tiered beds, like battery hens. From the castle, these fantasies descend upon the City, home of the narrator-hero, Desiderio. Where they strike, the dead walk, rivers run backwards, horses gallop neighing out of the canvases of Stubbs and architecture assumes the proportions of a Druillet temple. As life's daily routines dissolve slowly into an opium dream, only Desiderio and his chief, the Minister of Determination, remain psychologically immune.

They accept an invitation to parley with the Doctor's ambassador, a meeting which ends in stalemate. Intrigued by the exotic and apparently male ambassador, Desiderio discovers that 'he' has left behind an embroidered handkerchief. It bears the name of the Doctor's daughter, Albertina. Albertina is a mistress of disguise and in a sense the greatest of her father's creations.

The Ministry of Determination's computers finger a peepshow owner as being somehow connected with the hallucinations. Desiderio, handed the assignment of finding and assassinating Dr Hoffman, begins with the peepshow's blind, alcoholic owner. The Doctor once had a partner, the mysterious Mendoza; the owner may, or may not, be him. To may or may not be is a condition common to many of Angela Carter's characters. Sampling the peepshow machines, Desiderio sees a panorama of a jungle, beyond which looms a castle, the whole scene framed by female genitalia. Later, he realizes that it was a preview of his coming journey with Albertina, who proves to be the gateway to her father's stronghold.

In the best private-eye tradition, Desiderio is made the fall guy for the murder of a young girl. He goes on the run, after being wounded in a brush with the Determination Police. Rescued by a riverine community of Indians, his half-Indian parentage helps him fit in with their way of life, to the extent of becoming betrothed to their leader's daughter. By chance, he learns that he is to be eaten at the climax of the wedding ceremony, in order to spread his virtues throughout the tribe. Escaping, he rejoins the peepshow, now on the road with a carnival. Making himself generally useful, he acquires an insight into Phenomenal Dynamics, the theoretical basis of Dr Hoffman's hallucinatory devices.

Desiderio and Albertina are constantly being faced with the prospect of having portions of themselves fed into other people's orifices, or having portions of other people introduced into theirs. He becomes friendly with the Acrobats of Desire, a team of nine Moroccans, who seal the bond by buggering him. Barely has he limped to the seclusion of a cave before the Acrobats, the entire carnival and a nearby city are annihilated by an earthquake.

Adrift again, he meets a vampire-fanged Count, the Erotic Traveller. It proves to be a reunion with Albertina, in the guise of the Count's valet, Lafleur. Her erotic employer has not yet penetrated her secret, for he favours the Moroccan approach. After being captured by Oriental pirates, whose mouths are the least eloquent of their orifices, the three are shipwrecked upon the African coast. Captured by cannibals, they once more face ingestion. The Count expires in a cooking-pot, with more than a hint that he has invented the entire episode out of a desire for self-immolation. Desiderio, in an uncharacteristically heroic gesture, kills the cannibal chief and escapes with Albertina.

Dr Hoffman's devices have by now induced the condition of Nebulous Time, in which the imagination can give birth to chimerae with all the physical characteristics of reality. A familiarity with *Gulliver's Travels* thus brings about the detention of Desiderio and Albertina by a tribe of Centaurs, who have certain traits not shared by Swift's unbearably noble Houyhnhnms. These include the inevitable orifice-orientated activities, such as defecation as an act of reverence, and the multiple rape of Albertina. Fortunately, these Centaurs do not live up to their mythical kin in every respect.

Putting all of this behind them, the couple arrive at the castle, where Desiderio at last confronts the grey Doctor. Finding that he is to be cast once more in a sacrificial role, he rebels, and unintentionally becomes the saviour and hero of the City. At the novel's end, having destroyed the master of illusions, he has nothing with which to occupy his declining years but dreams of the past.

First edition   London: Hart-Davies, 1972
First US edition, as *The War of Dreams*   New York: Harcourt Brace, 1974

91
ALAN GARNER
Red Shift

Scratch any given number of writers and you'll find an equivalent number of amateur psychoanalysts, in love with the esoteric language of the trade. Their analyses, usually of fellow-writers, have all the clinical detachment of a party political broadcast and are not unaffected by the size of the subject's sales figures. Alan Garner has forestalled such scrutiny by choosing to peg out his own dirty linen in public. Beginning with *The Weirdstone of Brisingamen* (1960), a children's fantasy, he has worked through his inner conflicts in a series of novels of increasing depth and maturity, to a painful culmination in *Red Shift*.

In so doing, he has produced some of the best fantasy fiction of our times, has been, inevitably, compared with Tolkien and has annexed Alderley Edge as a stamping-ground for his characters. He has also upset a number of people whose business it is to supervise children's reading-matter, which is no small compliment to the judges who gave him the Carnegie Medal and the *Guardian* Children's Book Award.

An address such as Toad Hall, Blacken-cum-Goosetry, might suggest a denizen of Hobbit country, but any resemblance between Garner's work and that of Tolkien is little more than blurb-writer's shorthand. A photograph taken during an interview by writer-publisher Charles Partington, while *Red Shift* was being written, shows a lean and sombre man, the antithesis of Tolkien's avuncular presence. The mythical and the mundane meet in his novels; the place is here, the time is now. Geographically, his location is uncannily apposite, for Toad Hall, a fifteenth-century timbered house, stands only a crow's flight from the Jodrell Bank radio-telescope.

In the above interview, Garner traced the gradual elimination of the fantasy element from his work: '. . . Until by *The Owl Service* it was fairly straightforward adolescent paranoia. And in the book I'm writing at the moment there is no suggestion of . . . what is commonly known as fantasy.' The book was *Red Shift* and few readers would support the author's disclaimer. The visions of Macey, which link a disintegrating Vietnam-like Roman Britain to our global village, are pure and essential fantasy. These, and the stone axehead handled by the characters in all three eras of the story, are the threads binding in time the relationships of contemporary adolescents, seventeenth-century victims of the Civil War and tribal Britons, the enduring women and the emotionally crippled men.

Tom lives with his parents in a caravan. His father is an Army veteran who prefers this cramped dwelling to Married Quarters. Privacy for Tom means donning earphones to shut out sound and listen to the music in his head. He falls in love with Jan, daughter of two psychiatric case-workers. Her parents are so involved with their patients that she communicates with them largely via their answering-machine, though she is reluctant to admit it.

More mature than Tom, her outspokeness soon brings her into conflict with his mother, whose sexual relationship with his father has degenerated into a humiliating and all-too-audible form of blackmail. Away from the imprisoning caravan, the lovers discover, in a mock-ruinous folly on the summit of Mow Cop, an axe-head hidden in the stonework. Here, the band of Britons in the service of the Ninth Legion had made their last retreat. From the beleaguered church in nearby Barthomley, where Jan and Tom will meet again, the villagers watch for enemy troops and Thomas looks to Mow Cop, drawn by a power he cannot explain, before the barbarism of the Civil War destroys the community.

For Jan and Tom in their industrialized Britain, the possibility of being called upon to die for their beliefs no longer involves an element of personal choice. He is conscious of life as a perpetual countdown to zero. Intellectually he can encompass a universe measured in billions of stars, lifetimes of laggard light; emotionally, a day's distance between him and Jan reduces him to despair. Impotent and compulsively articulate, he cannot exorcise his demon by talk. Across the centuries, his frustrated rage reaches out to Macey and becomes a bewildering vision, beyond interpretation. The end of the affair is undeclared, as the lovers recede from each other, leaving darkness between.

Red Shift stands or falls on the strength of its dialogue, which forms the major part of the narrative. Garner's device of having Romano-British tribesmen talk like American servicemen does eventually make its point, though the initial effect is jarring. The closing chapter, in which three overlapping conversations are blended in a continuous track, is brilliantly and movingly done. Subsequently, as if feeling that he had exhausted this particular vein of self-analysis, Garner began to write something closer to straight autobiography with *The Stone Book* (1976). For many, however, *Red Shift* remains as the high-point of his work.

First edition   London: Collins, 1973
First US edition   New York: Macmillan, 1973

92

L. SPRAGUE DE CAMP and
FLETCHER PRATT
The Compleat Enchanter

An ex-flyweight boxer who translated novels from the German, devised enormously elaborate naval war games and was born on an Indian reservation sounds a little too rich for credibility. Fletcher Pratt was, and did, all of these things, as Sprague de Camp affectionately recalls in *Literary Swordsmen and Sorcerers* (1976). He also, when he wasn't being an historian or a cookery expert, wrote fantasies. The best known of these are the Harold Shea stories, written in collaboration with de Camp, for *Unknown*.

The Roaring Trumpet and *The Mathematics of Magic* were published in 1940, and *The Castle of Iron* in 1941. Together they make up *The Compleat Enchanter*, which was followed in 1960 by *Wall of Serpents*, a rather less successful compilation of two later adventures. Curiously, considering that both authors were naval warfare buffs, the series is largely landbound.

The title, *The Mathematics of Magic*, provides a key to the rationale of the stories. Shea, Reed Chalmers and Walter Bayard are three psychologists attached to the privately endowed Garaden Hospital who develop a system based upon symbolic logic theoretically capable of transferring people and objects into other realities. To use it, the experimenter must condition himself into thinking in appropriate terms. If he wishes to enter a reality in which magic is the dominant force, then acceptance of the existence of magic must become part of his world-picture. Once this formula, dubbed the 'syllogismobile' by the irreverent Shea, has been worked out in the requisite detail, the trick is done, save for putting it to the test.

More mercurial than the conservative Chalmers or the indolent Bayard, Shea cannot resist jumping the gun. Having decided that Cuchulinn's Ireland would have more than its fair share of pretty girls, he prepares himself by making an intensive study of its legends. Alone in his apartment, he recites the formula. Seconds later, his highly polished riding-boots are planted in the icy mud of a bleak countryside, under a snow-laden sky. The syllogismobile has worked, up to a point. Only the world is that of the Icelandic Eddas, and the time is the eve of Ragnarök.

Cultural snobbery has ordained that the deities on Mount Olympus should attract more attention from scholars and satirists than their northern counterparts. When writers do turn to the Eddas for inspiration, the prospect of so much ice and doom too often seems to numb their sense of the (intentionally) absurd. De Camp and Pratt, undeterred, do for the Aesir what Thorne Smith did for the Greek pantheon.

Shea finds himself adrift in a land of sorcery, muscular maidens and teeth-rattling buffoonery, where he is scorned as a weakling and an ignoramus. To his further dismay, he can no longer read the English of the vital formula. His matches, torch and pistol won't work. Though he adapts to the situation fairly rapidly, to the extent of winning a grudging respect from the Aesir, his efforts only succeed in gaining him a front-line position as Ragnarök looms.

Thrown back into his native reality by a hostile sorceress, he gets together with Chalmers and Bayard to refine the formula and overcome the language problem. Middle-aged, academic Chalmers confesses to a secret desire to go adventuring; he and Shea choose the world of Spenser's *Faerie Queene*, with its knights and damosels, scholars and enchanters. Shea, still smarting from his recent lessons, resolves to go properly equipped. His choice of weapons and costume drew some friendly flak for the authors from more knowledgeable readers, who felt sure that a rented Robin Hood outfit and a fencing *épée* would be no match for plate armour and broadswords.

Once in the field, Chalmers begins to grasp the possibilities of applying his scientific training to the theory and practice of magic. There has been an unexpected distraction for Shea in the shape of redheaded Belphebe, a woods-dwelling lady who shoots a mean arrow. When they are cornered by the Blatant Beast (accidentally summoned by Chalmers while trying to conjure up a parrot), their lives can be ransomed only by satisfying its hunger for new stories. Embarrassed, in those innocent pre-Chatterley days, by Belphebe's presence, Shea cannot remember anything but *The Ballad of Eskimo Nell*. Red-faced, he ploughs through it, leaving the monster stupefied and Belphebe intrigued.

Their adventure ends in a battle with the wicked magician-knight Busyrane and his Enchanter's Guild, a wild mêlée of swords, goblins, serpents, bats and flying hands. Shea returns to the Garaden, leaving a magically rejuvenated Chalmers to get better acquainted with the beautiful Florimel.

A third jump, into Ariosto's *Orlando Furioso*, reunites Shea with his favourite redhead. Saracens, some uncommonly loutish paladins, a reluctant werewolf and a magic carpet keep the ball rolling. It may be that it wasn't possible to recapture the original sparkle of the series after this, but *The Compleat Enchanter* remains a classic of its kind.

First edition Garden City (NY): Nelson Doubleday, 1975
(a book club original edition)
There has been no UK edition of the omnibus
First UK edition of *The Incompleat Enchanter* London: Sphere, 1979
First UK edition of *The Castle of Iron* London: Remploy, 1973

93
KINGSLEY AMIS
The Alteration

Among the mainstream novelists who emerged during the post-Second World War years, Kingsley Amis was one of the first to proclaim an allegiance to sf and Fantasy. His American lectures on the subject eventually became *New Maps of Hell* (1960), a survey sufficiently idiosyncratic to raise the blood-pressure of many orthodox devotees. Since then, he has become a contributor as well as a critic, with a string of novels and short stories to his name.

The Alteration is a story set in a world where there has been no Reformation and Rome is still the spiritual ruler of Britain and Europe. The title has a double meaning; it is the other meaning which has the most immediate and personal significance for the protagonist, Hubert Anvil. Poul Anderson, when writing one of the better additions to the *Conan* canon, was dissuaded from including a castrated character on the grounds that it might disturb younger male readers. No doubt the youthful audience for Amis is made of sterner stuff. They will need to be, for the threat of castration dogs Hubert from the opening chapters. At ten years of age, he is the finest boy soprano known to the Church of Rome, and the purity of his voice must be preserved.

As he sings to an enraptured congregation at the funeral service for His Most Devout Majesty, King Stephen III of England and her Empire, the net is closing in. Two members of Rome's musical elite have journeyed to England to hear him; both are well qualified to appreciate the painful necessity of what must be done. There are dissenting voices among the English religious hierarchy, but not on humane grounds. Hubert promises to become a composer of outstanding ability, a future ornament to his homeland's musical establishment. To conform to Rome's demands would cut short his development in that direction.

Anvil Senior, a prosperous merchant and zealous supporter of the Church, agrees to sign a document permitting the operation. There arises the delicate task of explaining to his son exactly what the consequences will be. It must be said here that the chief obstacle to the suspension of disbelief in *The Alteration* is not Hubert's unfamiliar world, but Hubert. He is a singularly unconvincing ten-year-old. His double helping of talent—great singer and gifted composer—is acceptable, but he displays an understanding of human motivation and social nuances incredible in a young boy, especially one from such a sheltered background. It is as if Amis were trapped by the necessity of having a pre-pubertal protagonist and in order to convey certain information and establish reader-identification could only resort to making him implausibly sophisticated. This said, Hubert is a sympathetic character and his unequal struggle against the power of Rome is a suspenseful one.

At the request of the Pope, Anvil father and son travel to the Vatican. The incumbent is a Yorkshireman and tone-deaf, but shrewd enough to maintain an outward show of interest in the arts. Amis extracts some sly humour from the Pontiff's calculatedly homely style when entertaining his guests. This episode also broadens the physical scope of the novel, as the Anvils speed towards Rome across a Channel bridge, on a train capable of reaching almost 200 m.p.h. But even the Pope cannot make it run on time. It is interesting to compare the technology of *The Alteration* with that of Keith Roberts's *Pavane* (1968), which deals with a world in which the Spanish Armada won, as did John Brunner's *Times without Number* (1962). Amis acknowledges Roberts's fantasy by listing it among the 'underground' works proscribed by the Vatican.

Hubert, increasingly reluctant to accept his fate, becomes a focus for conflicting factions. His mother is opposed to the alteration, and the family's spiritual adviser, Father Lyall, who is her lover, refuses to countersign the form of consent. He is interrogated by the Secular Arm and comes to a brutally apposite end. The New Englander Ambassador invites Hubert to sing at his residence; when he learns of Rome's intentions, he devises a scheme to smuggle him to North America, where rebels, schismatics and scientific heresies flourish. Considering the extraordinary importance of their quarry, the security services are remarkably dull-witted; Hubert, aided by his elder brother and the Ambassador's staff, boards the transatlantic airship *Edgar Allan Poe* undetected. All seems set fair for freedom. And then occurs what can only be described as an Act of God.

Believers in the Vatican Conspiracy theory will find rich pickings in *The Alteration*. Before the novel's close, there has been, off-stage, a war with 30 million casualties and an abortive attempt to spread Plague, all in the sacred cause of population control. Dead men don't breed.

Nor do male sopranos.

New England, anyone?

First edition   London: Jonathan Cape, 1976
First US edition   New York: Viking, 1977

94
FRITZ LEIBER
Our Lady of Darkness

If plate tectonics don't do the job first, California may just split from the United States under the sheer accumulated weight of money and talent. Hard up against the Pacific, Californians have given up on wild surmising and have elected to colonize the twenty-first century instead, ahead of the rest. Fritz Leiber has been living there for quite a while.

The big city is Leiber's natural habitat. Even his scurrilous heroes, Fafhrd and the Gray Mouser, whose wanderlust leads them into far and fantastic lands, swagger and swash to best effect in the alleys of fabled Lankhmar. Outwardly a huddling-place where proximity provides security, he sees it as a focus for dark forces, a warren of innumerable concealing spaces. Walls enclose, rather than exclude, its horrors. Sometimes it is a machine clicking mindlessly through its daily programme, where the penalty for awareness can be insanity. Leiber's city is San Francisco.

Corona Heights is a chunk of darkness looming over the faded dream-scapes of Haight-Ashbury. Raw and rocky, an unurbanized anomaly, it is visible from Franz Westen's apartment through a gap between two high-rises. Having spent four years in San Francisco in drunken mourning for his dead wife, he has yet to know the city. As he emerges from his prolonged wake and the world comes into focus, the pale-brown jagged crest draws him. A writer of stories of the supernatural, his imagination seeks to fill the void left by the death of his wife by giving a fanciful life to his surroundings—the slim, soaring elegance of a television tower rising from the morning fog, or the bright pattern of books laid out upon his bed like a paper lover. Two floors below lives his much younger girlfriend, Cal. For all her nearness, she does not yet exist for him so vividly as these totemic mistresses.

Insidiously, the city begins to invade his awakening consciousness. In a Haight-Ashbury bookstore he finds one of those better-left-unread works, which he, naturally, proceeds to read. *Megapolisomancy: A New Science of Cities* is a late nineteenth-century forecast of the coming psychological pressures of metropolitan life. 'The ancient Egyptians only buried people in their pyramids,' writes the author, Thibaut. 'We are living in ours.' Surveying Corona Heights through binoculars, across two miles of rooftops, Westen thinks he sees a thin brown figure waving at him. Soon he is panting up the Heights' rocky slopes. From the top, he scans this new view of San Francisco. Finally, he focusses the glasses upon the window of his own apartment. A thin brown figure waves back at him.

Westen tries to formulate some mundane explanation for these apparitions, but events remorselessly reinforce their unholy reality. His story provokes an outburst of speculation among his friends in the apartment block, ranging from accounts of drug trips to a description of Cal, who is a musician, calming a wardful of psychiatric patients by playing the piano.

Her ability to manipulate moods through music is to prove of greater importance than she or Westen can yet imagine. His quest for the truth behind the strange theories of Thibaut entangles him in the lives of past writers, including the ubiquitous H. P. Lovecraft and Clark Ashton Smith. Leiber mixes imaginary books and once-living authors into half-real histories which cross and recross the borders of the fantastic, dragging readers and characters unresistingly behind them.

Westen returns to Corona Heights in the hope that his previous sighting was somehow in error. Before leaving his apartment, he has marked the window with a square of fluorescently coloured card, rendering it unmistakably his. Again he focusses the binoculars upon it. But this time, the long brown fingers reach across the city *into* the lens. Hurling them away in panic, he takes refuge in the nearby house of a friend.

The history of Thibaut has become more than a subject for literary speculation. Something obscurely evil has its source in *Megapolisomancy*, with Westen as its target. His widely read friends debate the subject, chiefly to grisly and comfortless effect. Tales of a dark lady who was Thibaut's constant companion only inspire disturbing dreams. It is left to a Spanish neighbour, illiterate in English, to pinpoint the diabolic hidden 'bomb' ticking away within the apartment.

Westen's final struggle with the embodied force is an authentically nightmarish episode, the more so for its having taken on, Arcimboldo-fashion, the form of his lifelong love. Only Cal, strengthened by her love for him, can endure the blood-chilling implications of its presence. Under Leiber's hand, 'burying your head in a book' has taken on peculiarly unpleasant overtones. Have a good read.

First edition   New York: Berkley, 1977
First UK edition   London: Millington, 1978

95
TIM POWERS
The Drawing of the Dark

The Anubis Gates, a later and more ambitious novel than *The Drawing of the Dark*, won for Tim Powers the Philip K. Dick Memorial Award. If that lengthy and somewhat confusing book deserved an award, then what were the judges thinking of in 1979? It must have been a rich year in which *Dark* could pass unremarked.

Powers, a Buffalo-born American now living in a fantasy called California, seems to have a weakness for Irish protagonists with the initials B.D. *Anubis* had its Brendan Doyle, *Dark* has its Brian Duffy. Unlike Doyle, Duffy's character is allowed to develop sufficiently for the reader to care about his fate, instead of being subordinated to a serpentine plot. A grizzled swordsman roving sixteenth-century Europe, he finds that greater matters than his next meal ride on his skill with a blade.

The Turks, reversing the Crusading efforts of the West, are hammering at the gates of Christendom. Duffy, having done his share of hammering the Turks, is eking out a living teaching swordsmanship in Venice. Challenged to a canal-side brawl by three young aristocrats, he bests them, without serious damage to anything other than their egos. From an upper window, he is hailed by Aurelianus, a wizard. The outcome is the offer of a job as bouncer at the Zimmerman Inn, owned by Aurelianus, where the famous Herzwesten Beer is brewed. Duffy thinks the offer odd, what with the Inn being a full month's journey away, in Vienna, but the pay is good and he knows the city. He accepts.

Matters become more than odd as he crosses the Alps, the least of them being assorted attempts to kill him. A small army of dwarves rescues him from an ambush; monstrous forms accompany him, behind and before, with apparently friendly intent. On the last stage of the trip, he joins forces with Bluto, a hunchbacked Swiss bombardier also hired by Aurelianus. Bluto has also been plagued by unaccountable attempted assassinations, but the pair reach Vienna intact.

Within the walls is a collection of characters unrecorded by official historians. Aurelianus has cast his nets in some distant and curious places. Duffy is more immediately interested in his former lover, Epiphany, now as grey as himself and widowed. Their latter-day relationship, brief and doomed, threads its way through strange and violent events. Other familiar faces are those of a band of Swiss mercenaries, the landsknecht, with whom he served in past campaigns. Presently a longship-load of superannuated Vikings is added to the garrison. They have the useful attribute of taking the supernatural for granted. Useful, because there is going to be a lot of it about. Down in the beer-cellar, something is brewing.

The Dark is a brew fermenting in an ancient vat beneath the Inn, a process which has continued for thirty-five centuries. It is a remarkable liquor, with a literally magical potency, and several of the less orthodox pilgrims to Vienna are there because it is almost time to tap the vat. Aurelianus intends to draw the Dark for one imbiber only, and that one is in hiding outside Vienna, guarded by his spells. He is the wounded Fisher King, Arthur, and Aurelianus is Merlin. Duffy, to his alarm, begins to have recurrent and, to him, meaningless visions, which prove to be foreshadowings of Arthur's departure to Avalon. He is to serve as a vehicle for the King, his consciousness submerged when events require it by the greater personality.

The crisis of the West is drawing close. If the wizard's magic fails, the sorcery behind the steel and cannon of the Turks will overwhelm Vienna and sweep across Europe. And Ireland too. Arthur must take the field against the East.

Powers has obviously done exhaustive research into the civil and military lore of the period, and for the most part wears his erudition lightly. The action set-pieces are described with a sharp awareness of the confusion attendant upon hand-to-hand combat. The fact that sixteenth-century Vienna will be, for most readers, as distant from reality as any city of the *Arabian Nights*, helps in integrating the magical elements with the historical. The joins don't show.

Duffy and Aurelianus achieve some stature as characters, the latter being of the T. H. White school of Merlins, using something suspiciously like penicillin to treat Duffy's numerous wounds. At the close, the battered Irishman is relieved to find that his involuntary symbiosis with King Arthur does not involve being carried off to misty retirement. He is himself once more, though with some added scars, both physical and mental.

Together with the surviving Vikings and a bag of gold, he sets sail from Vienna for an indefinite destination. His dream of retiring to Ireland has died with Epiphany, if he was ever temperamentally capable of realizing it. Yet he did once, unofficially, drink of the Dark, and no man can be quite the same after that.

First edition   New York: Ballantine, 1979

96
GEOFFREY HOUSEHOLD
The Sending

With Conan Doyle, it was Sherlock Holmes; with Michael Moorcock, it is Elric of Melnibone; with Geoffrey Household, *Rogue Male*. Household has been in the business for longer than many current practitioners have been alive, but to the publishing trade he is still the man who wrote that astonishing pre-Second World War thriller.

In a way, the durability of the label is justified, for he has never stopped writing it. Constantly, his hunted heroes take to the hills, or the moors, to have space about them in which to strike back. Alfgif Hollaston, landowner, ex-Indian Army colonel (post-Imperial India) is no exception. The difference is that his pursuer travels with him. It is fear.

Though it can be conjectured that *The Sending* is a product of the growing market for fantasy, it could, with little alteration, fit easily into the period which inspired *Rogue Male*. Which does not imply that it is dated. Rather, it is timeless, sparely and sharply written. The only concession made to the stock furnishings of the horror story is a grass-covered burial mound, which Hollaston, in typical Household fashion, sees as reassuring evidence of his ancestral roots. Long established in a rural society, he judges his neighbours on the basis of shared interests, not by orthodox symbols of status. High on his list is Paddy Gadsden, a saddler whose skills include an understanding of horses which has gained him a reputation even on the Continent.

Paddy dies in an inexplicable accident, killed by Hollaston's car. Hollaston, at the time, is attending a party given by the new owner of the nearby Manor House and has left his car at home. The police are satisfied that he was not directly involved, but suspect he may know the identity of the driver. Hollaston is puzzled by the presence of Paddy and his killer in a lonely country lane at night, and the motive for the killing, if it was deliberate. The author's choice of such a clumsy method of murder is never convincingly justified.

Hollaston finds that he has inherited Meg, Paddy's pet polecat, an animal held in some regard by many local people. It becomes clear that Meg functioned as Paddy's familiar, having an instinct for sensing sickness in animals and humans. The legacy is in recognition of Hollaston's affinity with the animals and of powers which he possesses but does not wholly accept. During his Indian service, he became the blood-brother of the shaman of a primitive tribe, the Birhors, and learned much of the mental transmission of messages between man and animal. He is a moderately successful landscape painter, whose particular gift is for capturing, at times, the spirit behind the physical appearance. A widower in his mid-forties, the death of his wife after two weeks of marriage has left him burdened with guilt-induced impotence.

The guilt has no basis in fact, but he refuses to seek psychiatric help. And then, out of nowhere, comes the sending, the fear which cannot be evaded.

At first, he can only run, though running gives only the illusion of relief. Too tough mentally to believe that he is going mad, he can still think of no one with the power or inclination to visit such terror upon him. Gradually, logic asserts itself and he begins to analyse his situation. In doing so, he has to acknowledge that his shamanistic talents are greater than he had suspected. Aided by Rita, an Oxford history don who rented a cottage on his land and with whom he is carrying on a resolutely platonic affair, he uncovers the true reason for Paddy's death. The foreign mourners at the saddlemaker's funeral were not there solely because of his widespread reputation as a craftsman; they and he were members of a coven. Paddy volunteered to die in order to protect the coven's Grand Master. Because the other members have a higher opinion of Hollaston's gifts than he has himself, they fear that he may be aware of the truth, and so he must be dealt with.

In a moment of inspiration, Hollaston decides to paint the shape of his fear. The effort is successful; the presence is exorcised and he is free. Then Rita appears to be affected by it. Hollaston, seeking revenge, crosses to the Continent to seek out Odolaga, the Basque master of the coven. Armed with a hunting-knife, goose feathers, a piece of whipcord and twelve ballpoint pens, he stalks his quarry through the Pyrenees. As in the climax of *Rogue Male*, innocent objects combine to form weapons. The aim is not to kill Odolaga, but to frighten him; to make him believe that his one-time Victim has powers equal to his own. Hollaston's ruse succeeds. He finds Rita in good spirits upon his return. All should be well —but he has much still to learn about himself. The meaning of 'Alfgif' is 'Gift of the Elf'.

First edition   London: Michael Joseph, 1980
First US edition   Boston: Little Brown, 1980

97
TERRY PRATCHETT
The Light Fantastic

The late Ted Carnell, while editing *Nova Publications*, published a short story about a deal with the Devil. It was a familiar subject, exploited more than once by his contributors, but never before by Terry Pratchett. Moreover, it was a genuinely funny fantasy. The author was thirteen years old.

Nova Publications has gone into the long night, but many of the writers whose careers burgeoned in their pages continue to flourish, with Terry Pratchett prominent among them. His view of the universe is as irreverent as ever and his technique is capable of sustaining the joke to novel-length, and beyond. On the jacket of *The Colour of Magic* his publishers compare him to Jerome K. Jerome, J. R. R. Tolkien, James Bridie and Douglas Adams. He will probably survive it.

The cosmology of these linked novels may be of a low order of probability, but it has a certain familiarity. With its titanic flippers churning cosmic dust and gases, A'tuin the Great Turtle ploughs through space towards some destination known only to itself. Four enormous elephants stand upon A'tuin's back, supporting, in their turn, the Disc-world with its tiny attendant sun. In comparison with our violent universe, the arrangement has the comforting charm of a clockwork toy. Down on the ground in the Disc-world, the charm is less apparent. In this improbable cosmos, magic is a potent force.

Rincewind, a graduate of the wizardly Unseen University, wears the bronze octagon awarded by that elusive institution. For him, it is the magician's equivalent of a BA (failed). Hustled out of the University after stealing a look into the forbidden Creator's Grimoire, he leaves knowing only one spell. This rune has such terrifying potentialities that he dare not voice it. Instead, using his talent for languages, he ekes out a living in polyglot Ankh-Morpork, a downmarket counterpart of Lankhmar with added violence. If Ankh-Morpork had a Yellow Pages, 'Heroes' would form a fat section.

Greed and professional curiosity involve Rincewind with a hazard never encountered by Fafhrd and the Mouser—the tourist. Twoflowers, an insurance clerk from the wealthy and near-mythical Agatean Empire, is looking for Adventure, to be recorded by his iconograph. He carries a generous weight of gold coinage and has an attractively hazy notion of its value in local terms. But, above all, he has the Luggage. The Luggage is a tourist's dream, a wooden chest with the interior capacity of a Tardis, and its own retrieval system. It also has multiple legs, a fair turn of speed and a touchy disposition. Lured by exotic magic and easy money, Rincewind becomes Twoflowers's guide.

Complications immediately ensue. The Patrician of the city lays it upon Rincewind to protect the stranger at all costs; the Agatean Empire must not be given any excuse for aggression. Barely has the wizard absorbed this before the Agatean Grand Vizier lays it upon the Patrician to dispose of Twoflowers, lest he return to the Empire bearing subversive foreign ideas. The Patrician thinks it unnecessary to inform Rincewind of this change of priorities. A word to the Assassin's Guild should take care of the matter.

Needless to say, it doesn't.

Twoflowers drags a quivering Rincewind through breathless encounters with warriors, gods and dragons, blithely unaware of personal danger. For him, this is life in Technicolor and infinitely preferable to his desk in the insurance office. Even so, he cannot overlook the opportunities presented by a population innocent of actuarial tables. He sells fire cover to the landlord of his inn, The Broken Drum. Catching on to the possibilities, the landlord touches off an inferno which devastates Ankh-Morpork. Their hectic itinerary takes them to the Disc-world's rim, over which the ocean pours endlessly into starry gulfs, casting up an eight-hued rainbow. Hard on Rincewind's heels, and highly piqued, follows Death. Wizards rate the dubious privilege of a personal appearance by Death at the appropriate moment, but Rincewind has a tendency to be elsewhere.

The second instalment of his saga, *The Light Fantastic*, contrives to be even funnier than the first. Rincewind, still burdened with the fearful rune insecurely imprisoned within his skull, is brought back to Unseen University by a crisis in Disc-world affairs. A strange red star has appeared, growing and growing until its fiery light dominates the sky, by day and by night. It has given rise to a cult of worshippers whose history promises to be both brief and violent. At the same time, the Masters of Wizardry have accepted a new leader, who is intent upon organizing them within an inch of their lives. When all of this welter of incident and invention has been brought to some kind of resolution, Twoflowers embarks for home and the office, unaware of the death threat hanging over him. If the author is still aware of it, he doesn't say so. The publishers scored one out of four with their blurb: there are long stretches in both novels which could fairly be described as a Hitch-Hiker's Guide to Heroic Fantasy. Which is no bad thing.

The Colour of Magic
First edition   Gerards Cross (UK): Colin Smythe, 1983
First US edition   New York: St Martin's, 1983

The Light Fantastic
First edition   London: Gollancz/Smythe, 1986
First US edition   New York: New American Library, 1987
(preceded by an SFBC book club edition in 1986)

98
THOMAS M. DISCH
The Businessman: A Tale of Terror

When American sf writer and editor Judith Merril came to London, she was part of a literary exodus. Michael Moorcock's revamped *New Worlds* had proved to be a lure for Americans dissatisfied with the restrictions of their homeland markets. They crossed the Atlantic, eager to join the revolution. A short walk from the power-centre in Ladbroke Grove, Judith Merril briefly established a secondary focus in Portland Road. Among the expatriates who gathered there, sometimes literally about her feet, was Thomas M. Disch.

He had never been a devotee of mainstream sf. The 'new' techniques of story-telling which so disturbed traditionalists were new only to a readership which preferred its beloved mind-blowing concepts to be presented in solid, old-fashioned prose, decorated with representational artwork. For writers such as Disch, conscious of the wider literary spectrum, the real appeal lay in applying these techniques to what they saw as the true concerns of the late twentieth century. Dragon-riding and Moon-walking did not figure prominently on their lists.

Perhaps fortunately for British institutions, he kept his sights resolutely trained upon his fellow-Americans. A string of stories in *New Worlds* established him as a sophisticated skewerer of contemporary ideals, habits and ambitions. 'Camp Concentration', 'The Asian Shore' and 'Linda, Daniel and Spike' are only a few of his memorable contributions, the latter title made even more memorable by being displayed upon a nude rear view of the indispensable Diane Lambert. Few magazines command such devotion from their staff. When he turned from sf to write a tale of possession and haunting, he did not neglect the targets punctured by his previous work.

For the several ghosts of *The Businessman*, the afterlife is as hedged about with restrictions as any aspect of their material existences. Like Scrooge's unfortunate partner, they remain shackled to the impedimenta of their old routines—iceboxes, supermarkets, automobiles, television. Beyond the grave or the jar, there is work to be done, rites of passage to be undergone, levels of competence to be achieved. On this plane, the novel must compete with the bizarreness of the afterlife as portrayed by orthodox religion. Fortunately, Disch has the advantage of a sense of humour.

Robert Glandier, *The Businessman*'s businessman, drags in his wake a chain of worldly priorities as weighty as that of Jacob Marley. He also carries a lot of weight before him. Since his marriage at thirty to the much younger Giselle Anker, he has intermittently battled against the flabbiness induced by booze and business dinners. Now, eleven years older and a widower, he has given up the fight, leaving to his tailor the task of covering up the ravages of indulgence.

As Robert takes on more and more all-too-solid flesh, the grave divorces Giselle, atom by atom, from her corporeal form. Meanwhile, her widowed mother, Joy-Ann, is trying to equate the knowledge that she is financially secure with the fact that she is dying of cancer. Glandier pays dutiful visits to his mother-in-law, who overfeeds him on buttered waffles, unaware that he murdered Giselle. She goes to visit her daughter's grave and sees a flower miraculously blossom from the soil. Kneeling to examine it, she discovers that the bloom is really a child's hand. As it clasps one of her fingers, Joy-Ann falls dead and Giselle's voice cries: 'Mummy, I'm free!'

It took only one visit each from three spirits to reform Scrooge, but Grandier's core is tougher than his exterior. Moreover, his assigned spirits have problems far removed from any faced by Christmas ghosts. Giselle has barely time to savour her release from the grave before she is drawn into her husband's brain and trapped there. She regains human, if ghostly, form only to learn that she is carrying Grandier's child. The posthumous child, when born, is resolved to protect his Daddy at all costs, sometimes in ways which Daddy does not appreciate. Grandier finds that his well-worn rut of drinking, guzzling and patronizing the special services of the Bicentennial Sauna is no longer deep enough to hide in. Disintegration begins.

The action becomes lunatically involved. Giselle and Joy-Ann recruit the help of John Berryman, an alcoholic poet whose mad charm survived his fatal fall from Minneapolis's Washington Avenue Bridge. Berryman was well known as a writer and lecturer until his death in 1972; it would be interesting to know how any surviving relatives or friends reacted to this no-holds-barred characterization. The trio's ability to inhabit and manipulate objects and animals results in surreal flight and pursuit sequences, participated in by dogs, frogs, a figure of the Virgin Mary in a supermarket trolley, a murderous heron and a headless (wooden) Negro jockey. With a little ungentlemanly help from a severed hand, virtue triumphs. In Disch's world, death can be fun, unless you're looking forward to getting away from it all.

First edition   London: Jonathan Cape, 1984
First US edition   New York: Harpers, 1984

99

PETER ACKROY' '
Hawksmoor

At the end of *Hawksmoor*, the author declares that any relation to real people, either living or dead, is entirely coincidental. As his cast includes eighteenth-century figures such as Sir Christopher Wren, his definition of 'coincidental' is obviously not the accepted one. Judged by that standard, *Hawksmoor* would be a chronicle of coincidence. That it might be more would affront the professedly rational Sir Christopher, but would be a statement of the obvious to his fellow-architect Nicholas Dyer.

Dyer is Ackroyd's version of Hawksmoor, in historical fact Wren's assistant; in the novel, Hawksmoor is the modern police detective whose life is linked to Dyer's. Dyer lives in an age of enquiry and sceptical rationalism, but is emotionally a child of the fearful years of the Plague and the Great Fire of London, an orphan wandering amid miasmic pits choked with the dead and the near-dead. Skilled in his profession, his abilities attract the notice of Wren and his advancement is rapid.

He is commissioned to design seven London churches. Familiarity with great men, however profitable, has bred contempt rather than gratitude. In the ranks of the august Royal Society, he sees a collection of poseurs and mountebanks who essay to measure the measureless, blind to the reality of the immense and awful void surrounding their midden. They walk among horror and remain ignorant of the Truth, as do the ministers of the religious Establishment. Dyer's seven churches will be secretly dedicated to more than one god and the covert dedications will be sealed with human blood.

For Nicholas Dyer, sole survivor of a plague-stricken family, was marked as a promising pupil by the mysterious Mirabilis and proved to be a scholar apt to his teachings: that Sathan, the crucified one, is the true God of this world; that Man is born to, and lives in, corruption; that the works of the ancients, who recognized these truths, underlie all that we see around us. The foundations of Dyer's churches will draw strength, like graveyard trees, from the numberless corpses which lie in their shade, the dead whose dust has permeated the City air down the centuries. It might well have confounded him to know that in a future time the mountebanks would often be cast in the role of Sathan.

Time is one more universal mystery about which Dyer is at odds with the Fellows of the Royal Society. Again, could he have known it, it might have amused him that future Fellows would concoct theories about the nature of Time as fabulous as his own. He is to learn a dreadful lesson regarding it, as is his twentieth-century counterpart, the CID detective Hawksmoor. Like reflections in a glass, the architect and detective pursue an elusive figure along a trail of bloodshed and death, in the shadow of the seven churches. Both men become increasingly isolated from their professional colleagues, increasingly regarded by them as at the very least eccentric, at the very worst, mentally unstable. Hawksmoor, investigating a succession of apparently motiveless killings, is himself a subject for investigation by others as he recedes from reality. Finally, in a kind of Limbo, the two achieve a ghastly communion with each other.

The London of *Hawksmoor*, seen through the distempered gaze of Nicholas Dyer and the bleak scrutiny of the detective, is a cheerless place. To Dyer, the bustling eighteenth-century streets are little more than a lid for a noisome cesspit of human corruption and hypocrisy. In Hawksmoor's swollen metropolis, vagrants squat and squabble in crumbling refuges, or huddle in alcoholic camaraderie about illegal fires on riverside wastelands. Pathologists, inheritors of the scientific tradition, dispassionately dissect the flesh of murder victims, their chill impersonality less comprehensible than the perverted humanity of the killer. Like a recurring chorus of the Fates, children thread their way through streets old and new, hardly aware of the significance of the rhymes they chant. In desolate rooms, worlds fall apart as madness creeps in.

The author, a poet and Cambridge graduate, dealt with the historical events preceding *Hawksmoor* in *The Great Fire of London*. He also, rather appropriately, at one time edited the *Spectator*. The city and the period are obviously of absorbing interest to him, though he sees them in a very different light to that of writer of the standard bodice-ripper. In Nicholas Dyer's London, the roots of our present society are clearly discernible; alienation is common to both, rather than being a fashionable twentieth-century catchword. It is to be hoped that Peter Ackroyd will not abandon fantasy. The genre needs writers of his insight and erudition.

First edition   London: Hamish Hamilton, 1985
First US edition   New York: Harpers, 1986

100

TOM HOLT

Expecting Someone Taller

Fantasy and comedy are cousins. Together they produced some of the happiest entertainments in a tradition going back at least to Twain's *Yankee*, through Cabell, Thorne Smith, John Collier, and became almost an independent genre during the great days of *Unknown Worlds*, fantasy fiction's equivalent of *Black Mask*.

Writers like Anthony Boucher ('The Compleat Werewolf'), L. Sprague de Camp and Fletcher Pratt (the 'Harold Shea' stories), Fritz Leiber, Henry Kuttner and even L. Ron Hubbard, before his sense of the ridiculous gave way to Holy Pomposity, cheered up our war- and post-war years with a series of spoofs and satires on what had previously been the province of more portentously morbid writers like Poe, Stoker and Lovecraft. Unwitting and deeply embarrassed werewolves, vampires unable to stand the taste of blood, heroes who abhorred violence, and hideous monsters who wanted only to open small grocery businesses in Ohio were *Unknown*'s stock in trade in the days before humour was banished from our shelves by the relentless Universal Ironies and Common Room Wit of Tolkien and his even more sober followers.

In those dark times we needed Boucher or de Camp but publishers, being the timid creatures they are, preferred to perpetuate a trend celebrating the depressive comforts of quasi-religion in the implacably second-rate prose of the Heinleins or Clarkes, mediocre prophets of an all-too-easily-imagined future. Their monstrous catalogues of reactionary conservatism, misogyny and high school philosophising became, as with Ayn Rand a decade earlier, the pseudo-radical bibles of a generation which soon readily returned to a fold it had only pretended to leave.

In fantastic comedy the Gods very rarely have a sense of humour and indeed the Wagnerian seriousness of magicians, demigods and the other supernaturals is what frequently provides a foil for writers whose sceptical heroes and heroines, like so many latter-day Alices, can't help perceiving the fundamental ridiculousness of those who blithely hold the power of life and death over the universe.

This kind of humour is the ideal antidote to all pseudo-literary Tolkenoid pomposities and makes me optimistic for a funnier, if not better, world. Not only is the best humour back in print but newer authors like M. John Harrison, Terry Pratchett and now Tom Holt are expanding on the tradition, doing rather more for fantasy than Douglas Adams has done for sf. Publishers with the voices of lions and the hearts of rabbits are at last convinced that not everyone requires the consolations of religiosity in their light reading.

Intelligent, original and solidly entertaining, Tom Holt is a very good comic fantast and *Expecting Someone Taller* is a superb début, introducing us to perhaps the nicest of reluctant heroes, Malcolm Fisher.

All his life Malcolm has been conditioned to believe himself a failure, existing only to offer contrast to his altogether more favoured sister. But when he accidentally runs over a Frost Giant, disguised as a badger, he finds himself the inheritor of the Tarnhelm, a magic cap, and also the actual Ring of the Nibelung. The Tarnhelm lets him change shape at will. The Ring quite simply makes him Master of the World. Meanwhile the surviving cast of *Götterdämmerung*, all eager to acquire these items, are waiting in the wings.

For the first time in its history the Ring has a really pleasant owner, with the result that simply by being his ordinary, decent self, Malcolm creates a Golden Age on Earth. However, he soon realises that he has a terrible responsibility to remain even-tempered at all times, because, if he doesn't, earthquakes are felt in California, typhoons threaten the Malay Archipelago, diplomatic relations break down between the US and USSR and the English cricket team looks likely to lose a crucial match. By and large Malcolm controls himself and the age of peace and plenty continues.

This situation doesn't suit the more apocalyptic and romantic sensibilities of Wotan, Alberich, the Rhinemaidens and a variety of Volsungs, Valkyries, Trolls and Norns whose various vested interests seem likely to bring about positively the last Twilight of the Gods, this time written not by Wagner but by Gilbert and Sullivan.

All this is thoroughly and satisfactorily resolved in the best traditions of comedy. Tom Holt's delightful, readable, cheerfully intelligent book offers first class comic relief to fantasy fans and to readers who simply mourn the passing of S. J. Perelman, Gerald Kersh or, dare I say?, even P. G. Wodehouse.

First edition   London: Macmillan, 1987
First US edition   New York: St Martin's, 1988

Index